THE ULTIMATE CHURCH

AND

THE PROMISE OF SALVATION

by

Jerome P. Theisen, O.S.B.

Foreword by

Kilian McDonnell, O.S.B.

ST. JOHN'S UNIVERSITY PRESS
Collegeville, Minnesota
1976

Acknowledgement is made to the following publishers for permission to quote from their published material: America Press, 106 West 56th St., New York, N.Y. 10019. The Belknap Press of Harvard University Press, 79 Garden St., Cambridge, Massachusetts. Doubleday & Co., Inc. 501 Franklin Ave., Garden City, N.Y. 11531. W. B. Eerdmans Publishing Co., 255 Jefferson, S.E., Grand Rapids, Mich. 49502. Helicon Press, Inc., 1120 N. Calvert St., Baltimore, Maryland 21202. Paulist Press, 1865 Broadway, New York, N.Y. 10023. Seabury Press, 815 2nd Ave., New York, N.Y. 10017. Sheed and Ward, 6700 Squibb Rd., Mission, Kansas 66202. Yale University Press, 92 A Yale Station, New Haven, Conn. 06520.

Dedication

For my parents William and Mae on their
65th wedding anniversary.
Long have they lived the salvific reality
of the Church of Christ.

Contents

Foreword

Vatican II represents a major ecclesiological development, and this in various ways. For some decades preceding it, Roman Catholic ecclesiology was dominated by one biblical image, that of the mystical body. Though this image is a dominant one in Pauline ecclesiology, it by no means exhausts the biblical meaning of the church. The one-sided emphasis on mystical body resulted in an ecclesiological biologism where the total life of the church was seen too exclusively in terms of the body image. *The Dogmatic Constitution on the Church* quite consciously moves away from such an ecclesiology. Noting that "in the Old Testament the revelation of the kingdom has often been conveyed in figures of speech," it proceeds to assert that "in the same way the inner nature of the Church was now to be made known through various images" (Art. 6). Having stated the principle of plurality, the *Constitution* enumerates a great variety of New Testament images of the church: sheepfold, flock, tract of land, vineyard, edifice, house, household, temple, the new Jerusalem, bride, mother. To insure that the image of the mystical body receives its rightful place, Article 7 at some length develops this biblical image. Article 9 is devoted to God's action in the formation of a community of salvation, the people of God. The emphasis upon the variety of biblical images points the way to a fuller, richer understanding of the inner life of the church. It reinforces another prime concern of Vatican II, to present the church as a mystery (Art. 5).

The accent on the variety of biblical images of the church and on its character as mystery is accompanied by an awareness that she does not exhaust the mystery of salvation. She is not the whole mystery of the kingdom but its "initial budding forth" (Art. 5). Those who have not received the gospel are related to her in various ways. "Those also can attain to everlasting salvation who through no fault of their own do not know the gospel of Christ or his church, yet sincerely seek God and, moved by grace, strive by their deeds to do His will as it is known to them through the dictates of conscience" (Art. 16). How those inculpably ignorant of the gospel are related to the mystery of Christ and to the church as the community of salvation is not clear to the fathers of Vatican II (cf. *Decree on the Missionary Activity of the Church*, Art. 7; *Pastoral Constitution on the Church in the Modern World*, Art. 22). God works by grace in "an unseen way," in "a manner known only to God." This ambiguity in no way diminishes the reality of the church as the community of salvation nor her duty to preach the gospel.

Jerome Theisen has taken up the themes of multiple images and models and the related subject of the certainty and ambiguity of the church's role as a community of salvation. The ecclesiological urgency is greater today than it was at the close of Vatican II. Millions conceive of the church only in reference to an institutional model. With the widespread disenchantment with all forms of institutions (government, university, education, military, industry) there has been an accompanying disillusionment with the church. Undoubtedly the institutional model still has aspects which must ultimately be present in any viable ecclesiology (visibility and continuity). But this model is the least convincing today and tells one the least about that which so much preoccupied Vatican II, namely, the inner life of the church. The student of ecclesiology should know what models are convincing both as faithful reflections of the biblical witness and as responding to the needs of the 1970's. Theisen presents a variety of models which might fulfill this double function of fidelity to the sources and credibility.

Has not also the question of ambiguity taken on added significance these past fifteen years? One is not only faced with the vast multitude who, through no fault of their own, have never heard the gospel. There is that other multitude of whom it is said that they have heard the gospel and belonged to the community of salvation and have rejected them both. How are such related to the church as the mystery of salvation? The question of the church and salvation is not just a theological bone on which scholars can sharpen their historical teeth. It is an important pastoral problem today.

As a professor who has taught ecclesiology for some years, I can appreciate how useful Jerome Theisen's book will be in seminaries and universities. His presentation is lucid, theologically aware, and pastorally sensitive.

Kilian McDonnell

Acknowledgments

I wish to acknowledge the theology students who in my teaching experience asked questions about the church and salvation. They were not a little responsible for instigating this research, the major portion of which was completed during a sabbatical year (1969–1970) at Yale Divinity School. I wish to acknowledge the helpful seminar discussions with Dr. George Lindbeck; also conversations with Dr. Jaroslav Pelikan and Msgr. Myles Bourke. I am appreciative of the kind service of Dr. Raymond Morris, librarian of Yale Divinity School, and his cordial staff. I wish to thank my confrere Father Meinrad Dindorf, O.S.B., for his professional aid in preparing the manuscript for publication.

A special note of thanks is due the Rev. Michael Blecker, O.S.B., president of Saint John's University, Collegeville, for giving his support to this study and enlisting that of Herbert and Margaret Richter, whose grant has made its publication possible.

Collegeville, Minnesota   Jerome P. Theisen, O.S.B.
Saint John's University
August 1976

ix

Introduction

It is no secret that today the Church of Christ is undergoing anxious self-analysis. We need only glance at current theological literature to ascertain the extent of the analysis. Theologians deal with topics such as the self-understanding of the church, its relationship to the state and the world, its mission in society, its involvement in movements of liberation, its unity, its continuity with the church of the apostles, its structures of leadership. Many Christians question the church: What is it? What is it doing? Who needs it?

We intend to analyze one aspect of the church's self-understanding: its relationship to those outside its confines, especially those being saved outside its visible limits. Thus the precise focus of our study is not an analysis of the ways in which the church acts as an agent of salvation for those within the church. It is presumed that, in dependence on Jesus, the church can and does act as an instrument of salvation for those within its confession; for it communicates the word of the gospel, the joy of the sacraments, the promise of life. The focus is rather the ecclesial mediatorship of *all* salvation. Does the church function as an agent of salvation for those who are in fact being saved anywhere in the world, even if they have not heard the word of Christ or do not believe in him? Is all salvation ecclesial? Is all salvific grace ecclesial? If someone is being saved at a distance from the church, does the church act as the mediator of his or her salvation? Is there in fact salvation outside the church? If so, how does the church function in regard to this salvation? What relationship exists between the church and these saved outside its boundaries? What is the extent of the soteriological role of the church? Does the axiom *extra ecclesiam nulla salus* (outside the church no salvation) demand church involvement in all salvation wherever it occurs in the world?

An historical approach to these questions must deal quite properly with this ancient axiom *extra ecclesiam nulla salus*. Since the days of Origen and Cyprian this axiom has elbowed its way into countless theological writings and magisterial decrees. It has been used as a wall, dividing those within from those without the church. It has been employed as a club to beat into salvational non-existence those who found themselves outside the camp of the church. It has been promoted as a means of exhortation, both to confirm those within and to attract those without the church.

The axiom has long been esteemed in official circles, even to the point of being regarded as infallible in character. We may quote in this regard the well-known 1949 letter which the Holy Office in Rome directed to the then archbishop of Boston, Richard Cushing: "Among those things, however, which the church has always preached and will never cease to preach that infallible axiom too is contained by which we are taught that 'outside the Church there is no salvation'."[1] It is paradoxical that this statement appears in a letter which rejects a literal and rigid interpretation of the adage, an interpretation espoused by Leonard Feeney and his followers.

The adage as formulated by Cyprian is erroneous, and if taken literally today is heretical. What is involved here is a classical example of a formula, badly conceived in the beginning, misunderstood through the ages, and today heretical in its obvious and literal sense. Little wonder that theologians have expended much energy in clarifying and/or explaining away this axiom and that much ill will is still generated by its use.

In the same letter of the Holy Office the axiom is interpreted in such a way that the church is extolled as the medium of salvation: "The Savior did not only command that all the gentiles enter the church, but he also established that the church is the medium of salvation without which no one can enter the kingdom of heavenly glory."[2] This position is qualified, however, by the statement that an implicit desire for the church is sufficient for salvation, a desire

---

[1] "Inter ea autem, quae semper Ecclesia praedicavit et praedicare numquam desinet illud quoque infallibile effatum continetur, quo edocemur 'extra Ecclesiam nullam esse salutem'." *Enchiridion Symbolorum Definitionum et Declarationum de Rebus Fidei et Morum.* Ed. by H. Denzinger and A. Schönmetzer, S.J. 33rd ed. (Barcelona: Herder, 1965), no. 3866. (Hereafter cited as DS.)

[2] "Neque enim in praecepto tantummodo dedit Salvator, ut omnes gentes intrarent Ecclesiam, sed statuit quoque Ecclesiam medium esse salutis, sine quo nemo intrare valeat regnum gloriae caelestis." DS 3868. Cf. this statement in Pius XII's *Humani Generis*: "Some reduce to a meaningless formula the necessity of belonging to the true church in order to gain eternal salvation." *Acta Apostolicae Sedis* 42 (1950), p. 571. The same idea was contained in a catechism published about the same time: "Why did Jesus Christ found the Church? Jesus Christ founded the Church to bring all men to eternal salvation. (a) The Church instituted by Christ is the only way to eternal salvation. Christ gave the Church the means whereby man can be sanctified and saved." *A Catechism of Christian Doctrine*, Revised Edition of the Baltimore Catechism (Paterson, N.J.: St. Anthony Guild Press, 1949) p. 105.

that is contained in the disposition of soul to conform to the will of God.

Most modern Roman Catholic theologians, it is true, do not question the mediatorial role of the church in all work of salvation. But they are careful not to embrace a literal interpretation of the axiom *extra ecclesiam nulla salus,* for they realize that theologians and the official magisterium of the past few centuries acknowledged salvation outside the visible confines of the Roman Catholic Church. In their disquisitions about the ways in which those outside the church can receive the offer of saving grace, modern theologians exercise extreme subtlety and caution. They do not wish to leave the impression that Catholics exclude whole sections of mankind from the way of salvation. But they feel obliged to accept the axiom as defined and traditional doctrine. Thus presupposing the axiom and the concept of the church as the mediator of all graces, they proceed to explain how all peoples are tendered the offer of salvation through the church. A few examples will illustrate this procedure.

Chapter 7 of Henri De Lubac's influential work on the church bears this significant title: "Salvation Through the Church." He holds that, while God himself is the source of all grace and salvation, this same grace and salvation is mediated to people through the church:

And thus it is that God, desiring that all men should be saved, but not allowing in the concrete that all should be visibly in the church, wills nevertheless that all those who respond to his call should in the final account be saved through his church. *Sola Ecclesiae gratia, qua redimimur.*[3]

De Lubac enumerates the usual ways in which an outsider may be saved and joined to the church in some fashion. But, though he cites the weight of tradition, he does not elaborate on the *precise* manner in which the church functions as the universal medium of salvation.

More recently the same position is represented by Edward Schillebeeckx. Speaking of anonymous Christianity and the need for its sacramental visibility he says:

Because the world-wide activity of Christ's grace is carried out in and through the Church, since his 'going away' is related to the Church's post-paschal reality as the Body of our Lord, in virtue of the Spirit of God, this very grace is essentially 'Church founding.'[4]

[3] *Catholicisme; les aspects sociaux du dogme* (Paris: Les Éditions du Cerf, 1938), p. 174.

[4] "The Church and Mankind," in *The Church and Mankind. Concilium,* Vol. 1 (New York: Paulist Press, 1965), p.88. Cf. also pp. 78, 91.

The salvific grace of Christ can become effective worldwide only in and through the church; there is no "direct" redemptive line between the glorified Christ and the anonymous Christian who is being saved. Schillebeeckx offers an explanation of this economy of grace when he observes that the church is precisely the post-paschal locus of the risen and glorified Christ, the place of encounter with Christ and his Spirit. The invisible and exalted Christ is represented nevertheless by his Spirit and the church:

In his Body, the Church, wherein the Holy Spirit dwells, he intends to remain as the source of all grace. Hence, this Body, the Church, becomes the condition or the embodiment of our restored relationship with Christ and our entrance into the kingdom of God. Christ, absent from the universal human community, is made present again through the resurrection in the Church, his Body on earth.[5]

Thus the church becomes a real mediator of the grace of Christ, a link with the historical Jesus and with the Christ in glory. Without the church there would be no contact with Christ, who is essential for salvation. Schillebeeckx points up the fact, attested frequently in the history of Israel and the early church, that some person or some collectivity is representative of the whole and is essential for the salvation or destruction of the whole.[6] So too the church as a collectivity, as the body of Christ, becomes the representative of the whole of mankind in matters of salvation.[7]

The theology of ecclesial salvation is traditionally set in terms of medium, necessity, and instrument. The church is regarded as the medium of salvation, the means to achieve the goal of salvation. The church is viewed as necessary for salvation. And this necessity is not just one of regulation or precept which admits of exceptions (*necessitas praecepti*); but it is a necessity of means which is re-

---

[5] *Ibid.*, p. 80.

[6] *Ibid.*, p. 72.

[7] Cf. J. Beumer, "Extra ecclesiam nulla salus," in *Lexikon für Theologie und Kirche*. 2d ed. Vol. 3 (Freiburg: Herder, 1959), col. 1320. J. Alfaro, "Christus, Sacramentum Dei Patris: Ecclesia, Sacramentum Christi Gloriosi," in *Acta Congressus Internationalis De Theologia Concilii Vaticani II* (Rome: Typis Polyglottis Vaticanis, 1968) pp. 4–9. W. Beinert, *Um das dritte Kirchenattribut; die Katholizität der Kirche im Verständnis der evangelisch-lutherischen und römisch-katholischen Theologie der Gegenwart*. Vol. 2 (Essen: Ludgerus-Verlag, 1964), p. 551. Richard P. McBrien, critical of this prevailing concept of the church, sees the need for the church not as an ordinary means of salvation but as an instrument of the Kingdom of God: "Non-Christians, too, 'need' the Church. Indeed, the whole world 'needs' the Church, for the human community cannot long survive without fidelity to what is essentially human and criticism of what is fundamentally inhuman or antihuman." *Do We Need the Church?* (New York: Harper and Row, 1969), p. 228.

quired for the attainment of the goal of salvation (*necessitas medii*). It is understood, of course, that the church is only *instrumentally* the medium of salvation, for its causality (efficient, final, or exemplary) is dependent upon the one mediator, Jesus Christ.

Scholastic theology devised this terminology to elaborate an interpretation of the axiom and of the need for the church. It used the concept of medium, one might suggest, as a way of interpreting the activity of the church in the process of salvation wherever it occurs. The concept of medium might even have been regarded as an attenuation of the extremely rigid position which simply excluded those outside the boundaries of the visible church. But we might pose some questions to the scholastic theologian: Must this terminology be abandoned? Is it too strong and too inflexible? Must it be qualified? Must it cede to terminology more in accord with other theologies? Does this scholastic theology and its accompanying terminology overstress the agency of the church? An affirmative answer will generally be given to these questions in the course of our investigation, for both the terms of the discussion and the theological framework of the questions have changed considerably in the last few decades.

Moreover, the theologies of salvation, especially those relating to non-Christians, have proceeded beyond the bare formula and have made it increasingly difficult to repeat the axiom without the introduction of qualifications which seem to contradict its very wording. For instance, the theologian Joseph Fenton in explaining the axiom is led to make this statement: "A man who intends or wills to enter the Church is really not a member of it in any way whatsoever. If he were already a member, his desire would be absurd."[8] The person with such an intention can be saved, and he or she is saved without being a member of the church (to use Fenton's terminology). But what then becomes of the axiom? There is indeed salvation outside church membership. Some might respond that the church is the medium of salvation. But is this sufficient to save the axiom? Is it not better to abandon the axiom and to seek new ways

---

[8] *The Catholic Church and Salvation in the Light of Recent Pronouncements by the Holy See* (Westminster, Maryland: The Newman Press, 1958), p. 113. Cf. p. 10: "The unbaptized martyr for Our Lord passed from this life 'within' the *ecclesia fidelium*, despite the fact that he died without having attained the status of *fidelis*." Also, p. 92: "The person who is not a member of the true Church, but who is 'within' it only by the force of an implicit desire or intention to enter it, has no such advantage." The linguistic and theological problem of the axiom was pointed up some decades ago by Anselm Stolz, O.S.B., "Extra Ecclesiam nulla salus," in *Der katholische Gedanke* 10 (1937), pp. 101–112.

of articulating the manner in which the church relates to people around the world, especially those being saved?

This study is directed primarily to the history and current understandings of the axiom, but secondarily to the ways in which theologians express the relationship of the church to non-Christians who are being saved.

Responses to the question of church and salvation vary according to one's notion of the church and one's view of its relationship to people. A broad, inclusive notion of the church would seem to provide easy answers to our questions; conversely, a narrow, exclusive concept of the church apparently multiplies difficulties. A moderately inclusive view would seem to carry with it both the advantages and disadvantages of the two polar views. How shall we define the Church of Christ? Due to its multi-dimensional character, the church does not admit of easy definition. It would be convenient indeed to call forth from the decrees of Vatican II a succinct definition of the church, but we look in vain for one that is comprehensive. The *Dogmatic Constitution on the Church* must be supplemented by other decrees of the council, all of which feature various aspects of the church in the world of today. The resulting view of the church, while wide-ranging and magnificent, cannot be regarded as altogether balanced and harmonious.

Since it is not possible to review here the whole range of definitions of the church, we will limit ourselves to broad, representative descriptions. Our purpose is merely to provide a working description of the church, one that will serve our discussion of the relationship between the Church of Christ and the salvation of the non-Christian.

The Roman Catholic Church understands itself as the people of God, summoned by the Father, animated by the Holy Spirit, and assembled through common belief in the lordship of Jesus Christ. As an assembly in the world, embracing both local gatherings and the union of world-wide communities, it is rooted in the visible society of men and women, sharing in their historical growth and development. It is the visible embodiment of the love of God in Christ, manifesting and communicating to the world the life and word of Christ, its Savior and Teacher. Visible, sinful, and always in need of renewal, it is nevertheless mysteriously joined to Christ as his body and loving bride. It is the kingdom of Christ and the house of God in the Spirit.

Built up initially around the apostles and Peter it continues to manifest an apostolic and Petrine structure. Through its entire existence, and officially through its college of bishops, it continues to celebrate the word and the sacraments, to bear witness to the event of Christ, and to encourage godly living. But its activity is not directed solely to believers; missionary by nature, it produces a work of Christian witness for the whole of mankind. In imitation of Jesus it strives to grow in love, self-sacrifice, and humility. True to its pilgrim nature it grows in love and faith, and it hopes for the eschatological realities when Christ will hand over the kingdom to the Father and God will be all in all.

Christians other than Roman Catholic acknowledge many of these features of the Roman Church. That the ecclesial characteristics which they share with the Roman Catholic Church establish them as Christian communities and churches, and not just as individual Christians with isolated relationships with the Catholic Church, is an explicit teaching of Vatican II. The council's *Dogmatic Constitution on the Church* declares that the Church of Christ subsists in the Roman Catholic Church (Art. 8). It thereby moves away from the simple equation of the mystical body of Christ and the Roman Catholic Church, an equation espoused by Pope Pius XII in his encyclical *Mystici Corporis* (1943). Vatican II acknowledges real ecclesial realities (e.g., baptism, sacred scripture) in the Christian churches separated from the Roman Catholic Church. These realities permit churches of both East and West to share, at least in various degrees of perfection, in the one Church of Christ. The Roman Catholic Church has always referred to the Orthodox communities as churches, but it has refrained from using the word "church" in a technical and theological sense to describe the Protestant churches of the West. Vatican II, while following the traditional practice of not designating the separated Christian churches of the West as "churches" in the technical sense, agrees to describe them as "churches and ecclesial communities." It does not wish to sort out the various ecclesial realities to determine which ones finally coalesce to constitute an authentic church. But Vatican II does not bar further theological development in the recognition of the "church" character of these Christian communities of the West. By selecting the phrases *ecclesiae et communitates* or *communitates ecclesiales* the council indicates that "among the separated communities of the West there are also those which should be regarded as Churches, but left open, or referred to theologians, the question which communities were intended by this in concrete terms."[9]

---

[9] J. Feiner, "Decree on Ecumenism. Commentary on the Decree," in *Commentary on the Documents of Vatican II*. Ed. by Herbert Vorgrimler. Vol. 2 (New York: Herder and Herder, 1968), pp. 77–78.

For our purposes it is sufficient to recognize that ecclesial realities do exist in the Christian communities separated from the Roman Catholic Church, that these ecclesial realities are means of salvation, and that they manifest an incorporation into the body of Christ. While according to the teaching of Vatican II these ecclesial realities are found fully and perfectly in the Roman Catholic Church, they are present in other Christian traditions, especially in the Orthodox churches. Thus to go beyond Vatican II and to account for the Christian realities of non-Roman churches, we may — in keeping with the aim of this study and not without theological support — recognize the manifestation of the Church of Christ in the multitude of Christian churches and designate them here as church or Church of Christ.

Our question concerns Christianity as a whole (the ecclesial realities wherever they are found) and its salvational relationship to people who do not claim the name of Christ. In what way is the Christian ecclesial community, understood in the broadest sense as those who profess the name of Jesus, related salvifically to the people of the world at large?

Some Christian theologians prefer to expand the boundaries of the church to include the whole of mankind which is objectively redeemed in Christ and concretely offered the grace of salvation. According to this view, the people of God would be as extensive as mankind itself. We will address ourselves to this wide notion of the church in Chapter 4. But for now we may state that this is not our understanding of the church. If the church were as broad as mankind, there would be little reason to ask the questions posed above, for then the only point at issue would be the church's varying degrees of visibility and all salvation would be quite simply ecclesial.

Since we are concerned about the *salvation* of non-Christians, we must at least outline the notion of salvation which we are assuming in this study. The Christian concept of salvation, of course, is exceedingly complex. It lies at the core of the Christian experience. It is found on every page of the scriptures. It is propounded unceasingly by Christian writers.

Without attempting to exhaust the dimensions of salvation, it will be helpful to list without comment various ways in which it is traditionally expressed. Salvation is called the forgiveness of sins, participation in the divine life, union with the person of Christ, freedom, righteousness, peace, entry into the kingdom, active imitation of Jesus, knowledge of the truth, security of hope, love of God, confident faith, resurrection in Jesus, eternal life and vision of God, enlightenment, transformation of the total person and his cosmos, the kindness of the Father, the assistance of God, the word of God, the healing of the mind, the presence of God himself. The notion of grace is not exactly identified with salvation, but the process of salvation certainly includes the many aspects of divine healing, assisting, re-creating, and presence. We must distinguish, of course, between the very process of salvation and the ultimate term of the process. The ultimate term of the process is the exalted and risen life of union with God, the person's full participation in the eschatological kingdom of God (however this must be understood in terms of the transformed person and universe). The process of salvation is already an actuality, for at the present time it is possible for the person to be forgiven his or her sins, to be renewed in the Spirit, to enjoy the presence of Christ. This relationship to the Father in Christ, which may be termed in traditional theological language as a proper relationship to God, is compatible with the continual need for forgiveness and renewal. When we speak of the relationship between the Church of Christ and the salvation of the non-Christian, we refer to the situation of the person at a distance from the church who is indeed in the process of salvation. We assume that it is possible for him or her to receive the grace of Christ, to be forgiven his or her sins, and to be properly related to God. Our question here, while not dealing directly with the end phase of salvation, concerns the role of the church in this process of salvation. What is its ecclesial dimension? How is this person related to the church? How is the church active in the process of his or her salvation?

In this study we must presuppose both the over-arching reign of God our Savior "who desires all men to be saved and to come to the knowledge of the truth" (1 Tm 2, 4) and the role of Jesus Christ, the one mediator between God and man (cf. 1 Tm 2, 5), in whose name alone there is salvation (cf. Acts 4, 12). To be sure, both of these subjects merit renewed analysis today.

In this study we must also leave unexamined the many personal ways in which God deals with men and women at a distance from the church. We cannot, for instance, discuss the mediational character of non-Christian religions and of loving human acts. We acknowledge the positive values of non-Christian religions and the salvific dimensions of acts of human concern.

Our study is divided into six chapters. In the first chapter we will provide a background for an understanding of the contemporary question by sketching a history of the axiom *extra ecclesiam nulla salus*, for historically the questions were examined under the rubric of this axiom. In the second chapter we will examine the documents of Vatican II as embodying the most recent declarations of the Roman Catholic magisterium on the subject of church and salvation. In the third chapter we will trace the thought of four contemporary Roman Catholic theologians who not only manifest a development in their own theological writings but who also are responsible, along with other theologians and events, for a development of doctrine on this issue. In the fourth chapter we will examine a number of popular models of the church to determine their value or ambiguities when used as frameworks of understanding the question of the relationship between the church and the salvation of those living at a distance from the church. In the fifth we will note the limited role of the church in the process of salvation. In the sixth, finally, we will propose some tasks of the church in its service to mankind.

Chapter 1

Outside the Church No Salvation,
A History of the Axiom

The current development of ecclesiological doctrine bearing upon the relationship between the Church of Christ and the salvation of people outside the church cannot be appreciated unless it is seen in the light of its historical genesis. Unfortunately there is no exhaustive monograph tracing the historical development of this relationship. In this chapter we propose to offer a historical survey of the axiom, confident that even a brief exposure to the line of development will lend depth to an evaluation of the problem in contemporary theology. We will attempt to determine also to what extent the papal and conciliar decrees of the past define the question and direct the range of solutions for the future.

It is presumed throughout the history of this question that Christ is the center and source of salvation, redemption, justification, and reconciliation. The New Testament clearly indicates that "there is salvation in no one else, for there is no other name under heaven given among men by which we must be saved" (Acts 4, 12). It also insists on the necessity of faith and baptism: "I solemnly assure you, no one can enter into God's kingdom without being begotten of water and Spirit" (Jn 3, 5; cf. Heb 11, 6; Acts 2, 37–41; Mk 16, 15–16). This passage concerns adults and their need for baptism to enter the kingdom of God. But does Jesus exclude the unbaptized from salvation? Father Raymond Brown, exegete and Johannine scholar, makes this comment:

There is no evidence that the author was concerned with denying the kingdom of God to those who through no fault of their own are unbaptized. His immediate concern was one of contrasting flesh and Spirit, and of insisting that life from above is not the same as

1

ordinary life and cannot be received without the work of the Spirit.[1]

The importance of the salvific role of the church, while not stated directly, is implied in the movements of faith and baptism which permit access to the church. One of the most significant references to the relationship between salvation and the waters of baptism is 1 Peter 3, 18–22:

For Christ also died for sins once for all, the righteous for the unrighteous, that he might bring us to God, being put to death in the flesh but made alive in the spirit; in which he went and preached to the spirits in prison, who formerly did not obey, when God's patience waited in the days of Noah, during the building of the ark, in which a few, that is, eight persons, were saved through water. Baptism, which corresponds to this, now saves you, not as a removal of dirt from the body but as an appeal to God for a clear conscience, through the resurrection of Jesus Christ, who has gone into heaven and is at the right hand of God, with angels, authorities, and powers subject to him.

Through an unequal comparison the author of 1 Peter indicates that Christians pass through the saving waters of baptism and gather in a community, just as in the days of Noah only a few persons were saved by gathering in the ark. Christian authors of later times frequently take up the image of the ark as a type of the church and most understand it in the sense that within the church there is salvation and outside of it there is perdition.

The place of the church is also implied in many other scriptural images which bespeak an intimate union between Christ and the church, e.g., the body of Christ, the vine and the branches.

The New Testament images imply salvation within the church. Do they also indicate that there is no salvation outside the church? It seems unwarranted to draw this conclusion. Scripture is clear that God wills the salvation of all men (cf. Jonah; 1 Tm 2; Acts 10, 15. 34–35) and that all are endowed with a moral conscience and are exercised by the presence of God (Rm 1; Acts 17, 22–31). It would seem better to conclude — and we choose not to pursue a biblical theology of the issue — that the scriptures do not consider our precise question, namely, that any salvation that there is in the world comes through the church, that the church is necessary for the salvation of every person who is in fact being saved.

[1] R. E. Brown, S.S., "One Baptism for the Remission of Sins — New Testament Roots," in *Lutherans and Catholics in Dialogue*. Vol. 2, *One Baptism for the Remission of Sins*. Ed. by Paul C. Empie and William W. Baum (Washington, D.C.: National Catholic Welfare Conference, 1967), pp. 15–16.

The axiom *extra ecclesiam nulla salus* is customarily tied to the name of Saint Cyprian, but in fact versions of the adage antedate his writings. Saint Ignatius of Antioch (d.c. 110), for example, approximates the saying when he prescribes doctrinal unity and union with the church and the bishop as the requirements of attachment to God and Jesus Christ:

Every man who belongs to God and Jesus Christ stands by his bishop. As for the rest, if they repent and come back into the unity of the church, they too shall belong to God, and so bring their lives into conformity with Jesus Christ. But make no mistake, my brothers; the adherents of a schismatic can never inherit the kingdom of God. Those who wander in outlandish by-ways of doctrine must forfeit all part in the Lord's passion.[2]

Ignatius directs this exhortation to schismatics, those who have severed the bonds of union with the bishop. They have no part in the saving effects of Christ's passion. Thus Ignatius has a particular situation in mind: schism. The lot of those outside the church is not the focus of his attention. He maintains that there is salvation in the church, not in the schismatic groups who have cut their ties with the bishop.[3]

A counter-trend is represented by the thought of Saint Justin Martyr (d.c. 165) who holds that the fulness of the divine Logos resides in Jesus Christ but that all rational beings share in the Logos:

We have been taught that Christ was First-begotten of God and we have indicated above that He is the Word of whom all mankind partakes. Those who lived by reason [logos] are Christians, even though they have been considered atheists: such as, among the Greeks, Socrates, Heraclitus, and others like them; and among the foreigners, Abraham, Elias, Ananias, Azarias, Misael, and many others whose deeds or names we now forbear to enumerate, for we think it would be too long. So, also, they who lived before Christ and did not live by reason were useless men, enemies of Christ, and murderers of those who did live by reason. But those who have

---

[2] *The Epistle to the Philadelphians*, 3, 2–3. *Early Christian Writings. The Apostolic Fathers.* Transl. by Maxwell Staniforth (Baltimore: Penguin Books, 1968), p. 112.

[3] Cf. V. Corwin, *St. Ignatius and Christianity in Antioch* (New Haven: Yale University Press, 1960), p. 204: "But whatever the influences may have been that bore on Ignatius' thought about the church, there is no gainsaying the fact that he saw it as the scene and the mediator of salvation. Within the church, instituted and empowered by God, those being redeemed were given grace, so that in the end they could 'attain unto God'." Also T. F. Torrance, *The Doctrine of Grace in the Apostolic Fathers* (Edinburgh: Oliver and Boyd, 1948), p. 73: "But in Ignatius we have a doctrine of union with Christ through the Church."

lived reasonably, and still do, are Christians, and are fearless and untroubled.[4]

Justin, writing primarily as an apologist of Christianity for the benefit of non-Christians, does not provide a well-developed doctrine of the church. His Logos doctrine, however, allows him to detect Christian values in good, noble and "reasonable" people who lived upright lives before and after Christ. For Justin there exists a Logos Christianity beyond the borders of explicit Christianity. The power of the Logos and of his Spirit are evident outside the church.[5]

The traditional teaching becomes more definite in a work which Saint Irenaeus (d. 202), bishop of Lyons, wrote against the false gnosis of his day. He champions the authentic tradition of the Christian and Roman Church, the only place where he finds quite briefly the right doctrine and the Holy Spirit.

All those who do not hasten to the Church do not partake of the Holy Spirit, but by an evil thought and bad action they defraud themselves of life. For where the Church is, there too is the Spirit of God; and where the Spirit of God is, there is the Church and every grace.[6]

It is presumed here that the Holy Spirit and all grace are found only in the church. Thus the rigid interpretation of salvation in the church and the lack thereof outside the church is already sketched out in this passage. It will be repeated by later fathers and theologians, often with gradual modification.

Clement of Alexandria (d.c. 211) is another pre-Cyprian witness to the connection between the church and salvation. He simply terms the church itself salvation: "To follow Christ is salvation. . . . Thus believing alone and being reborn is perfection in life, since God is never weak. For just as his will is a work and this is called the world, so also his decision is the salvation of men and this is called the church."[7] Like Justin he appreciates the partial truths found among the philosophers, but he insists on the fulness of wisdom and knowledge in Christ.

Tertullian (d. after 220), the North African trailblazer of Latin

<hr>

[4] *Apology I*, Chap. 46. *Writings of Saint Justin Martyr*. Transl. by T. B. Falls (New York: Christian Heritage, Inc., 1948), pp. 83f. J. Migne, *Patrologiae cursus completus. Series Graeca* (Paris 1857 ff), 6, 397. (Hereafter cited as PG.) Cf. *Apology II*, Chap. 10, *ibid.*, p. 129 (PG 6,460). Also Chap. 13, *ibid.*, pp. 133f (PG 6,466).

[5] L. W. Barnard, *Justin Martyr. His Life and Thought* (Cambridge: Cambridge University Press, 1967), esp. p. 149.

[6] *Against Heresies*, Bk. 3, Chap. 24, 1 (PG 7,966).

[7] *The Tutor*, Bk. 1, Chap. 6 (PG 8,281).

theology who ended his life as a Montanist, wrote a homily on the mystery of baptism. In keeping with traditional teaching he assumed the necessity of baptism. But he puzzled over the fact that none of the apostles, save Paul, is known to have received baptism. He concluded that a bypassing of baptism in their case was warranted in view of their being chosen disciples, their companionship with Jesus, and their faith. "Since they were attendant upon him who promised salvation to every one that believed: 'Thy faith,' he used to say, 'hath saved thee,' [Mt 9, 22] and, 'Thy sins are being forgiven thee,' [Mt 9, 2] when the man believed but yet was not baptized."[8] Tertullian suggested, furthermore, that before Christ's passion, death, and resurrection, faith was sufficient; afterwards the command of baptism was added to that of faith. Tertullian also acknowledged another substitute for water baptism, a baptism of blood: "We have indeed a second washing, it too a single one, that of blood, of which our Lord said, 'I have a baptism to be baptized with,' [Lk 12, 50] when he had already been baptized. . . . This is the baptism which makes actual a washing which has not been received, and gives back again one that has been lost."[9]

It is significant that while Tertullian cites the precept of baptism he allows two substitutes for water baptism — faith and martyrdom. It is also significant that he represents the position, later pursued with vigor by Cyprian, that heretical baptism is invalid; heretics do not possess the one baptism.[10] Finally, it is significant to note that Tertullian views the flood of Genesis as a type of baptism and the ark as a figure of the church.[11] Noah's ark becomes a frequent image of the church, and it brings up rather concrete images about who is aboard the ship of salvation and who not.

In the early third century there was a clash between Hippolytus, the anti-pope who was eventually reconciled to the church and died a martyr in Sardinia (c. 235), and Callistus, who led the Church of Rome as pope from about 217 to 222. Hippolytus, a rigorist in church discipline, pictures the church as the new Eden and as the society of saints. For this reason, among others, he accuses Callistus of receiving sinners, e.g., repentant *lapsi*, into the church: "But he [Callistus] also said that the ark of Noah was made into an image of the Church, wherein were dogs and wolves and crows and all clean

---

[8] *Homily on Baptism*, 12. *Tertullian's Homily on Baptism*. The Text edited with an Introduction, Translation and Commentary by Ernest Evans (London: SPCK, 1964), p. 29.

[9] *Ibid.*, 16 (Evans, p. 35).

[10] *Ibid.*, 15 (Evans, p. 33).

[11] *Ibid.*, 8 (Evans, p. 19).

and unclean [animals]. Thus, he affirms, ought the Church to do likewise." [12] Here Callistus, an assumed laxist, is understood to take up the ark image to manifest a specific point — his leniency with regard to the quality of residents in the ark.

From one standpoint Origen (d.c. 253), one of the most original theologians of the early church, continues the Logos thought of Justin. All rational beings in the world share in the reasoning power of the Son of God, the very Logos of the Father. In this sense the power of the Logos is more extensive than that of the Holy Spirit, for the Holy Spirit only dwells in the saints:

I am of the opinion, then, that the activity of the Father and the Son is to be seen both in saints and in sinners, in rational men and in dumb animals, yes, and even in lifeless things and in absolutely everything that exists; but the activity of the Holy Spirit does not extend at all either to lifeless things, or to things that have life but yet are dumb, nor is it to be found in those who, though rational, still lie in wickedness and are not wholly converted to better things. Only in those who are already turning to better things and walking in the ways of Jesus Christ, that is, who are engaged in good deeds and who abide in God, is the work of the Holy Spirit, I think, to be found. [13]

Origen is very explicit about salvation in the church: "Let no one fool himself; outside of this house, i.e., outside of the church, no one is saved; for if someone goes outside, he becomes responsible for his own death." [14] This passage occurs in an elucidation of the harlot episode of the book of Joshua where the spies tell Rahab: "If any one goes out of the doors of your house into the street, his blood shall be upon his head, and we shall be guiltless" (Jos 2, 19). The harlot's house is marked with a scarlet cord which, according to Origen, symbolizes the blood of Christ; the house itself which contains the family of the saved is a sign of the church. "By that sign let all those find salvation who are found in the house of her who was once a harlot, after their cleansing in water and the Holy Spirit and in the blood of our Lord and Savior Jesus Christ." [15]

If it is true that salvation is ensured only for those within the church, a further question which must be put to Origen is the extent of the church. In one passage he seems to widen the notion of

---

[12] *Philosophumena*, or *The Refutation of All Heresies*, Bk. 9, 12. Transl. by F. Legge (London: SPCK, 1921), p. 131.

[13] *On First Principles*, Bk. 1, Chap. 3, 5. Transl. by G. W. Butterworth (New York: Harper and Row, 1966), p. 34.

[14] *Homilies on Joshua*, 3, 5 (PG 12, 841f). Cf. *Homilies on Jeremiah*, 5, 16 (PG 13, 520f).

[15] *Ibid.*

church to include the whole of creation. In this passage he comments on these words of Paul: "When all things are subjected to him, then the Son himself will also be subjected to him who put all things under him, that God may be everything to every one" (1 Cor 15, 28). He notes, according to the same apostle, that we are the body of Christ:

The body of Christ, therefore, is the whole of mankind, nay rather perhaps the whole of creation, and each one of us is a member and part. If one of us who are called his members becomes sick and travails under some illness of sin, that is, if he is marked by the stain of some sin and is not subject to God, rightly he [Christ] is not yet said to be subject whose members are those who are not subject to God. But when he shall keep all those who are called his body and members in a state of health so that they labor under no disease of disobedience — all the members being healthy and subject to God — rightly it says that he is subject to him [God] when we his [Christ's] members obey God in all things.[16]

Origen's universalism, which is evident in this passage, tones down considerably the ultimate seriousness of the stance taken in his *Homilies on Joshua*. The presumed universality of the body of Christ as well as of the final health of everyone eliminates a narrow understanding of the church and salvation. The sick members of his body are nonetheless members destined for ultimate reformation and salvation. Origen's view thus differs sharply from the rigid position assumed by Cyprian, his North African contemporary.

We turn now to Saint Cyprian (d. 258), bishop of Carthage, who more than any other church father bears responsibility for the formulation and the rigid interpretation of the axiom. It is clear from the foregoing, however, that he is not the originator of the concept. It is interesting to note that he too, like Origen, cites the house of Rahab as a type of the church:

This mystery declares that those who will be victorious and escape the destruction of the world must gather in only one house, that is, in the church. But whoever goes out from the gathering, that is, whoever withdraws and departs from the church, though he has attained grace in the church, will be guilty, that is, the fact that he will perish will be imputed to himself.[17]

The person who leaves the house of the church perishes because only in the church are gathered the elect and the saved.

Cyprian centers his ecclesiology around the concepts of indivisi-

---

[16] *Homily 2 on Psalm 36* (PG 12, 1330).

[17] *Letter* 69, 4. *Corpus Scriptorum Ecclesiasticorum Latinorum* (Vienna: C. Gerold's Son, 1866ff), 3,753. (Hereafter cited as CSEL.)

bility and unity. The church is one and indivisible. This is true both of the local church presided over by one bishop and of the church universal presided over by the *collegium* of bishops:

God is one, and Christ is one, and the church is one, and the chair established on Peter by the voice of the Lord is one. One cannot set up an altar other than the one altar, and one cannot create a new priesthood other than the one priesthood. Whoever gathers elsewhere scatters.[18]

The lapsed and schismatics withdraw and place themselves outside the unity of the church. Historical circumstances constrained Cyprian to formulate this theological attitude toward the lapsed and the schismatics. The lapsed abounded in the persecution of Decius (250–251). Schisms too occurred during Cyprian's episcopate: the Schism of Novatian in Rome and the Schism of Felicissimus in Cyprian's episcopal city. Cyprian's stance with regard to the lapsed and schismatics was decisive and clear; he did not hesitate to exclude them from the one church.

The schismatics do not form a new division of the one Church of Christ, nor do they constitute an altogether new church; for the church remains one and indivisible. At times Cyprian's lament over schismatic activity seems to imply a many-sided split of the church, but actually his intention is to insist on the oneness of the church even as he decries the harm of tearing off individuals from the church. Opposing the uncanonical appointment of Novatian in Rome Cyprian writes:

Sadness of heart touched me when I learned that you there, contrary to the ordinance of God, contrary to the law of the gospel, contrary to the unity of the catholic institution, have agreed to the creation of another bishop, that is, to the establishment of another church — something that is not right and not allowed.[19]

Whoever is separated from the church and joined with an adulteress is separated from the promises of the church, nor will he who has abandoned the church of Christ arrive at the rewards of Christ. He is a foreigner; he is profane; he is an enemy. Now he cannot have God as a father who does not have the church as a mother. If whoever was outside the ark of Noah was able to escape, he too who is outside the church will escape.[20]

The person who is joined to an adulterous sect is removed from the promises of the church and the rewards of Christ, for he cannot

---

[18] *Letter* 43, 5 (CSEL 3, 594).

[19] *Letter* 46, 1 (CSEL 3, 604). Cf. *Letter* 51, 1–2 (CSEL 3, 614–616).

[20] *The Unity of the Catholic Church*, 6. *Corpus Christianorum. Series Latina* (Turnhout: Brepols, 1953ff), 3,253. (Hereafter cited as CC.)

receive the rewards of Christ unless he is in the church: "How can he who is not with the spouse of Christ and in his church be with Christ?"[21] The church is a mother who nourishes her children but she cannot nourish them if they do not remain with her. The church is an ark outside of which are the floodwaters of perdition. These images of the church are not original with Cyprian but he gladly assumes them to express the strict necessity of the church for salvation.

Union with the church includes union with the bishops of the church, specifically with the local bishop. Since the church is founded on the bishops, salvation is contingent upon maintaining union with them. Schismatics are outside the church and outside the way of salvation because they have severed their union with the bishops. Holy virgins who live in concubinage and obstinately refuse to correct the situation are not re-admitted to the church. "Let them not think that life or salvation abides for them if they refuse to obey the bishops and priests."[22]

The picture of the faithful gathered in harmony around their bishop is beautifully expressed in another letter:

There [Jn 6, 68–70] speaks Peter, upon whom the church was built, teaching in the name of the church and showing that, although the stubborn and proud multitude of those unwilling to obey withdraws, yet the church does not withdraw from Christ, and the people united to the bishop and the flock clinging to their shepherd are the church. Wherefrom you ought to know that the bishop is in the church and the church in the bishop; and if one is not with the bishop, he is not in the church. And those who, not having peace with the priests of God, creep up stealthily and believe they are in secret communion with certain ones flatter themselves to no avail. For the one catholic church is not rent or divided, but it is surely joined and united by the bond of bishops [*sacerdotes*] who are in harmony with each other.[23]

Perhaps Cyprian's conception of the union of bishops among themselves and of the union of the faithful with their bishops is excessively juridical. If this is so — and some scholars point to his legal terminology[24] — we may conclude that his juridical mentality

---

[21] *Letter* 52, 1 (CSEL 3, 617).

[22] *Letter* 4, 4 (CSEL 3, 476).

[23] *Letter* 66, 8 (CSEL 3, 732–733). M. Bévenot, S.J., says, "*sacerdos* stands primarily for 'bishop' in Cyprian." *St. Cyprian, The Lapsed. The Unity of the Catholic Church.* Transl. and annotated by Maurice Bévenot, S.J. (Westminister, Maryland: The Newman Press, 1957), p. 80, note 20.

[24] C. Daly, "Absolution and Satisfaction in St. Cyprian's Theology of Penance," in *Studia Patristica.* Vol. 2 (Berlin: Akademie Verlag, 1957), pp. 202–207.

is one reason, among others, for his rather rigid notion of the church.

Cyprian insists on the necessity of baptism for entrance into the church, but he also recognizes martyrdom as a substitute for water baptism: "Then they [catechumens with the proper faith] are not deprived of the sacrament of baptism, inasmuch as they are baptized with the most glorious and greatest baptism of blood, concerning which the Lord also said that he had another baptism to be baptized with."[25] In the same context Cyprian refers to the robber on the cross who received the Lord's promise of paradise even without baptism.

Cyprian draws a number of unsatisfactory conclusions from his concept of the church. One is that martyrdom for those outside the church is of no avail:

Even if such men are killed in confession of the name, that stain is not washed away, not even by blood; the inexpiable and serious fault of discord is not purged, not even by martyrdom. He cannot be a martyr who is not in the church.[26]

Another unwarranted conclusion is that the Spirit is not imparted outside the church. And without the presence of the Spirit there is no power of baptism, no forgiveness of sins, and no sanctification:

If one could baptize, he could also give the Holy Spirit. But if he cannot give the Holy Spirit because, established outside, he is not with the Holy Spirit, he cannot baptize the one who approaches since baptism is also one, and the Holy Spirit is one, and one is the church which Christ our Lord founded in its origin and plan of unity upon Peter.[27]

Because of this, since the church alone has the life-giving water and the power of baptizing and of cleansing men, let him who says that someone can be baptized and sanctified with Novatian first show and teach that Novatian is in the church or presides over the church.[28]

Thus Cyprian concludes that "there is no salvation outside the church."[29] Disunity severs the lifeline that joins a person to the saving God. "He who does not maintain this unity, does not retain the law of God, does not hold the faith of the Father and the Son, does not hold life and salvation."[30]

These passages should suffice to indicate the rigidity of Cyprian's

[25] *Letter* 73, 22 (CSEL 3, 795–796).
[26] *The Unity of the Catholic Church*, 14 (CC 3, 259). Cf. *Letter* 73, 21 (CSEL 3, 794); 55, 17 (CSEL 3, 636); 55, 29 (CSEL 3, 647).
[27] *Letter* 70, 3 (CSEL 3, 769).
[28] *Letter* 69, 3 (CSEL 3, 752). Cf. *Letter* 66, 2 (CSEL 3, 728); 69, 10 (CSEL 3, 758).
[29] *Letter* 73, 21 (CSEL 3, 795).
[30] *The Unity of the Catholic Church*, 6 (CC 3, 254). Cf. *Letter* 4, 4 (CSEL 3, 477).

not a partaker of divine love. Thus they who are outside the church do not have the Holy Spirit.[44]

Augustine distinguishes neatly between the sacrament as an external rite and the spiritual content of the sacrament. The sacrament is administered and received in the fullest sense when the invisible element is conjoined to the visible. But he elaborates a sacramental theology which allows for the reception of one before the other. He cites the situation of the thief on the cross who received the grace of forgiveness without the sacrament of baptism. He also refers repeatedly to the centurion Cornelius who was enriched with the Holy Spirit even before baptism.[45] However, the Spirit does not come in these situations if the person contemns the sacrament. In general, it seems that Augustine acknowledges the possibility of receiving the Spirit before baptism when the two (visible sacrament and invisible grace) are rather closely conjoined. Thus his view is not precisely identical with some modern suggestions that the grace of salvation at a distance from the church has its sacramental visibility and efficacy in the Church of Christ.

Augustine acknowledges two substitutes for baptism of water: martyrdom and faith. In his work *On Baptism* he reflects on Jesus' promise to the robber, "Today you will be with me in paradise" (Lk 23, 43). He concludes: "I find that not only suffering for the name of Christ but also faith and conversion of heart are able to make up for the lack of baptism if by chance for want of time the lack cannot be remedied by the celebration of the mystery of baptism."[46] The faith he has in mind is not implicit or anonymous; it is explicitly directed to Christ, conversion of heart and baptism. Thus the salvation that accrues to this faith is related to the church and the sacrament of baptism.

Though Augustine modifies Cyprian's position to some extent, he still demands union with the church for salvation:

Outside the Catholic Church he [the Donatist bishop Emeritus] is capable of everything except salvation. He can have honor, he can have the sacraments, he can sing alleluia, he can answer amen, he

---

[44] *On the Correction of the Donatists*, or *Letter* 185, 50 (CSEL 57, 44).

[45] *On Baptism*, Bk. 4, Chap. 24 (CSEL 51, 259); *Against the Letter of Parmenian*, Bk. 2, Chap. 15, 34 (CSEL 51, 88); *Sermon* 99, 11–12 (PL 35, 601f); *Sermon* 266, 4–7 (PL 35, 1226–1229); *Questions in the Heptateuch*, Bk. 3, Chap. 84 (CSEL 28, Pars II, 306).

[46] *On Baptism*, Bk. 4, Chap. 22 (CSEL 51, 257). In his *Retractations* (Bk. 2, Chap. 44) Augustine finds the example of the thief inappropriate because "it is uncertain whether he had been baptized" (CSEL 36, 153). Cf. *Nature and Origin of the Soul*, Bk. 1, Chap. 9 (CSEL 60, 311); *The City of God*, Bk. 13, Chap. 7 (CSEL 40, Pars I, 622).

can retain the gospel, he can have faith in and preach in the name of the Father and the Son and the Holy Spirit; but he can never find salvation except in the Catholic Church.[47]

The heretics and schismatics can celebrate the sacraments but their rites are ineffectual for salvation since they are performed outside the church.

In short, Augustine transmits to the middle ages a rather exclusivist understanding of the adage *extra ecclesiam nulla salus*. While he refines Cyprian's position, especially with regard to the validity of baptism outside the church, he still insists on the necessity of the church for salvation. Union with the church is conceived rather rigidly; it is required for the reception of the Holy Spirit and eternal life.

A century after Augustine, Fulgentius of Ruspe (d.533) reiterated the adage in a sharp and exclusivist formulation:

Hold most firmly and do not doubt that anyone baptised outside the Catholic Church cannot come to share eternal life if before the end of this life he does not return and become incorporated into the Catholic Church. For the apostle says, 'If I have all faith and know all mysteries, but do not have charity, I am nothing' [I Cor 13, 2]. And we read that also in the days of the flood no one could be saved outside the ark.[48]

Hold most firmly and do not doubt that not only all pagans but also all Jews, heretics, and schismatics who terminate the present life outside the Catholic Church will go into eternal fire 'which was prepared for the devil and his angels' [Mt 25, 41].[49]

We may close our survey of the patristic period with a passage from a commentary of Pope Saint Gregory (d.604) on the book of Job, for it exemplifies the continued use of the ark typology. The passage is also significant because it found its way into medieval canon law. Gregory says:

It is [the church] alone which guards those placed within it with the strong bonds of love. Thus even the floodwaters bear the ark up to the heights but destroy all those which they found outside the ark. It is [the church] alone in which we truly contemplate the divine mysteries.[50]

The ancient fathers, attached as they were to the church as the

---

[47] *Sermon to the People of the Church of Caesarea*, 6 (CSEL 53, 175).

[48] *On Faith, to Peter*, Chap. 37 (PL 65, 703f).

[49] *Ibid*., Chap. 38 (PL 65, 704). Cf. 39 (PL 65, 704).

[50] Bk. 35, Chap. 8 (PL 76, 756f). Cf. *Decretum*, Pars II, c.24, q.1., c.22. E. Friedberg, *Corpus Iuris Canonici*. Vol. 1 (Leipzig: Ex officina Bernhardi Tauchnitz, 1879), col. 974.

realm of salvation, customarily interpreted the ecclesial passages of the New Testament in a rigid sense. Their conviction of the necessity of the church was so marked that they generally excluded from salvation everybody who was not within its fold.

These passages from the fathers manifest not only the attitude of the ancient church but also that of the medieval church. The medieval church continued to regard salvation as a patrimony of the church; it regarded itself as the locus of the forgiveness of sins, the Holy Spirit, and the life of Christ. It was taken for granted too that bishops and priests were the custodians of this life, that the Christian life depended upon them as upon a fount of knowledge and grace. Thus the people came to look to them more and more for the means of grace and of union with the Spirit; separation from them meant exclusion from the salvific lifeline to God.

We proceed now to the high middle ages in which the theory and the practice of *extra ecclesiam nulla salus* reached their apogee of importance. That the axiom should receive added weight during these centuries is understandable when one considers the prominent position of the church in medieval society. It is also understandable, in view of the exaltation of the papacy during this time, that the axiom should become intimately bound up with the Roman pontiff.

It continues to be axiomatic that there is no salvation outside the church, but the concept of the church is altered appreciably during this period. At the height of the period the tension between the *sacerdotium* and the *imperium* mounts in favor of the *sacerdotium*. While both realms are generally acknowledged as God-given, the spiritual and priestly realm is exalted above the temporal and regal. The spiritual realm itself achieves its point of culmination and focus in the person of the Roman pontiff who assumes a fulness of power over kingdoms and peoples. He takes on the aspect of a vicar of God and becomes not infrequently the ultimate authority in both spheres. The medieval church of salvation is decidedly a Roman church presided over by the pope and his cardinals.

Another dimension of the medieval church is its corporate and juridical character. The church is viewed as a *congregatio fidelium*, a gathering of the faithful who are both a *societas perfecta* and a structured organization. The corporation with its officers and representative powers becomes a model for the self-understanding and action of the church. The corporate character of the church implies — according to the theory gradually evolved by the canonists of the time — that power and authority reside with the people and that officers exercise this authority in their name. In case of necessity, in fact, the people themselves can exercise the authority. Such representative power is developed especially in the action of a council, which is viewed at first as constituting with the pope the highest instance of authority in the church, and which is seen later, with the gradual rise of conciliar thought, as superior to the pope.

The corporate image of the church is applied both to the church at large and to the church in the city of Rome. The faithful of the church can be regarded as its members and the officeholders its head; or again the college of cardinals can be viewed as the body and the pope its head. It is Brian Tierney's thesis that the juridical notion of the church, developed by medieval canonists, led both to the extreme papalist position and to the later conciliar theories of the church.[51]

This overview of the medieval concept of the church will serve as an introduction to a number of texts that refer explicitly to the idea of church and salvation. We may cite, first of all, Pope Innocent III's letter (December 18, 1208) to the archbishop of Tarragona. It includes a profession of faith demanded of the Waldensian Durandus de Osca on his return to the Roman Church. The profession, which is offered as a model for other returnees, contains a version of the axiom: "We heartily believe and orally confess the one church, not of heretics, but the holy, Roman, Catholic, apostolic [church], outside of which, we believe, no one is saved."[52] The axiom is familiar. But we note especially the reference to the *Roman* Catholic Church outside of which there is no salvation. The Roman Church receives decided emphasis in this document.

The Fourth Lateran Council (1215) is the first ecumenical council to cite the axiom. It makes a passing reference to it in its definition of faith against the Albigensians and the Catharists:

There is one universal church of the faithful outside of which absolutely no one is saved; in this [church] the same Jesus Christ is himself the priest and sacrifice; his body and blood are truly contained in the sacrament of the altar under the species of bread and wine. The bread is transubstantiated into his body and the wine into his blood by the divine power so that in bringing about the mystery of unity we may receive from him and he from us.[53]

The formulation of the axiom is traditional, probably stemming directly from Cyprian, but the ecclesiology of the passage may be

[51] B. Tierney, *Foundations of the Conciliar Theory. The Contributions of Medieval Canonists from Gratian to the Great Schism* (Cambridge: Cambridge Univeristy Press, 1955).

[52] DS 792.

[53] DS 802. Chap. 1, On the Catholic Faith.

termed sacramental and eucharistic. The reference to no salvation outside the church appears in a dependent clause, while the main burden of the text pertains to the mystery of unity which the faithful of the church have in the one sacrament of the Eucharist. Thus, although the axiom is included here in a decree of a general council of the church and even in a profession of faith, it does not form the subject of specific conciliar consideration. The council merely records the traditional (assuredly accepted) axiom and does not make it the subject of a definition. In other words, the axiom is not promulgated by solemn definition in such a way that the subsequent development of Christian doctrine could proceed only within the limits of the proposition that there is strictly no salvation outside the church.

It is significant that Saint Thomas Aquinas (d.1274), in a commentary on this creed, shifts the focus of the statement from the church to that of faith. After citing the words "there is one, universal church of the faithful outside of which absolutely no one is saved," he continues:

But the unity of the church exists primarily because of the unity of faith; for the church is nothing else than the aggregate of the faithful. And because without faith it is impossible to please God, for this reason there is no room for salvation outside the church. Now the salvation of the faithful is consummated through the sacraments of the church, in which [sacraments] the power of the passion of Christ is effective.[54]

In effect, Thomas is saying that outside of faith there is no salvation, though the kind of faith he envisions is the faith of the church, the faith of those who are gathered together in a church (*congregatio fidelium*).[55]

But the *congregatio fidelium* has a Petrine structure which Thomas acknowledges. This highly significant statement occurs in his work called *Against the Errors of the Greeks:* "It is shown also that it is necessary for salvation to be subject to the Roman pontiff."[56] At first blush it seems that Aquinas advocates a rigid salvational form of attachment to the church — subjection to the bishop of Rome. However, an accurate interpretation of *Against the Errors of the Greeks* is not easily managed. It was occasioned by a writing called *A Booklet on the Faith of the Holy Trinity* which Pope

[54] *Expositio Primae Decretalis ad Archidiaconum Tudertinum.* Ed. by Raymond A. Verardo, O.P., *Opuscula Theologica.* Vol. 1 (Turin: Marietti, 1954), p. 425.

[55] Cf. *Summa Theologiae* (Turin: Marietti, 1952f), Pars III, q.8, a.4, ad 2.

[56] Part 2, Chap. 36. Ed. by Raymond A. Verardo, O.P., *Opuscula Theologica.* Vol. 1 (Turin: Marietti, 1954), p. 344.

Urban IV (1261–1264) delivered to Thomas for comment and evaluation. The booklet was probably written by Nicholas of Durazzo,
bishop of Cotrone, and designed as a compilation of texts from
Greek church fathers and councils to prove the doctrinal and disci-
plinary deviations of the Greeks.[57] In point of fact the compilation is
replete with unauthentic passages and sketchy paraphrases of patristic texts.

In *Against the Errors of the Greeks*, then, Aquinas presents a
résumé of the compilation and cites many of its unhistorical passages. When he says, "It is shown [*ostenditur*] also that it is necessary for salvation to be subject to the Roman pontiff," Aquinas is not
quoting the compilation verbatim but is crystallizing the thrust of
the passages that refer to the bishop of Rome. By way of example he
quotes two spurious texts, one ascribed to Cyril of Alexandria, the
other to Maximus the Confessor.[58] Was Thomas merely summarizing the work which Urban IV passed on to him? Did Thomas put
credence in the ancient texts? Was he inclined to accept the position that subjection to the Roman pontiff is necessary for salvation?
It would seem that Thomas, living in a milieu in which the bishop
of Rome held the first chair in Christendom, presupposes that the
fulness of the Christian life demands obedience to the pope and
that deliberate exclusion of the papal position in the church results
in infidelity. The word *ostenditur* would seem to indicate that he is
merely drawing together the argument of the compilation. But
since the passage occurs in the second part of his summary (where
he wishes to show from the historical authorities "how the truth of
the Catholic faith is both taught and defended") and not in the first
part of the work (where he wishes "to expose those matters which
seem doubtful" in the sources) one is inclined to suppose that
Thomas accords some credence to the citations and to the necessity
of obedience to the Roman pontiff.[59] However, there is evidence
that Thomas relinquishes credence in these texts after the death of
Urban IV, for he does not cite the compilation in later writings.[60]

---

[57] Cf. the introductory notes of Raymond A. Verardo in the Marietti edition, especially p. 273.

[58] Cf. notes 1 and 2, p. 344, of the Marietti edition.

[59] Prooemium, p. 315.

[60] So P. Glorieux, "Autour du *Contra errores graecorum.* Suggestions
chronologiques," in *Autour D'Aristote. Recueil d'Etudes de Philosophie Ancienne et
Médiévale offert à Monseigneur A. Mansion* (Louvain: Publications Universitaires de Louvain, 1955), pp. 497–512. Also, M. B. Crowe, "St. Thomas and the
Greeks: Reflections on an Argument in Hans Küng's *Infallible?" The Irish
Theological Quarterly* 39 (1972), p. 268: "1) St. Thomas's suspicions about the texts
in the *Libellus* went further than his expressed disquiet with the translation; this is

Thus in his later *Summa Theologiae* Thomas reiterates the church dimension of salvation without specific reference to subjection to the pope. Addressing himself to the question of the necessity of the Eucharist for salvation, he says:

In this sacrament two matters are considered, namely, the sacrament itself and the content [*res*] of the sacrament. We have said, however, that the content of the sacrament is the unity of the mystical body, without which there can be no salvation. For no one has access to salvation outside the church, just as there was none in the flood outside the ark of Noah — which signifies the church, as is found in 1 Peter 3, 20-21.[61]

Both doctrine and imagery derive from tradition, but they are introduced with a shift of emphasis. The church, outside which there is no salvation, is here termed the mystical body. While this designation does not imply an invisible church, it does stress the more spiritual bonds of union in Christ's church. The essential characteristic of union with Christ and his church is the sacramental *res* or content that can be had even without the actual reception of the sacraments of baptism or Eucharist.

Finally, Thomas' references to salvation in the church and to subjection to the Roman pontiff must be qualified by his views of faith and revelation. He grants that some persons may be in a position where they do not recognize explicitly all the truths of the Church of Christ, where they would have only an implicit faith in the Savior. Addressing himself to the question of the salvation of gentiles, he says:

If, however, some were saved without the reception of revelation, they were not saved without faith in a mediator. For though they did not have explicit faith, they still had implicit faith in divine providence and they believed that God is the deliverer of men according to ways pleasing to himself and according to what he revealed to those knowing the truth.[62]

---

seen from the fact that he made little or no subsequent use of those texts; and 2) the doctrine of the primacy found in other works of Aquinas does not depend upon the *Contra Errores Graecorum* and should be considered on its merits."

[61] Pars III, q.73, a.3. Cf. *In Symbolum Apostolorum, scilicet "credo in Deum" Expositio*, art. 9; *Opuscula Theologica*. Ed. by Raymond M. Spiazzi, O.P. Vol. 2 (Turin: Marietti, 1954), p. 212: "Unde nullus debet contemnere, nec pati ab ista Ecclesia abiici et expelli; quia non est nisi una Ecclesia in qua homines salventur, sicut extra arcam Noe nullus salvari potuit."

[62] *Summa Theologiae*, Pars II-II, q.2, a.7, ad 3. In the earlier *De Veritate* (1256–59) Thomas speaks in terms of explicit faith: "If someone grows up in such circumstances [in the forest or among brute animals] and follows the lead of natural reason in the desire for good and the flight from evil, it must be held most certainly that God

Thus, though explicit faith of adults requires acceptance of the Trinity and subjection to the pope, it is possible for a person to achieve salvation with only an implicit faith in these truths of the Christian religion.

In another context he notes that upon reaching the age of discretion a child can deliberate about himself:

And if indeed he directs himself to the proper end, he will achieve the remission of original sin through grace. If however he does not direct himself to the proper end, according to his capacity of discretion at that age, he will sin mortally since he does not act according to the power within him.[63]

A person can direct his life toward God in more or less explicit faith and this is sufficient to achieve the forgiveness of sins and divine life. But it is, nevertheless, a life of faith and of attachment to Christ.

Thus on the one hand Thomas is committed to the traditioned doctrine of no salvation outside the church and of obedience to the pope within the church; but on the other hand he maintains that in certain circumstances more or less implicit faith is sufficient for salvation.

We come now to the weightiest document of the long history of the axiom. It is Pope Boniface VIII's bull *Unam Sanctam* of November 18, 1302. The document marks the time when papal power as opposed to the *imperium* is already past its zenith; but paradoxically the tenor and style of the bull exalt vehemently, almost desperately, the Roman see. The conflict between Boniface VIII and Philip IV (the Fair) of France occasioned the polemical document; even more important was the French bishops' wavering allegiance between the pope and the king. Understandably then, the pope insisted on the oneness of the church and its power.

For our purposes the beginning and the end of the papal declaration are important. The bull begins with this paragraph:

Faith urges and constrains us to believe in and to embrace the one, holy, catholic, apostolic church, and we firmly believe and absolutely confess this [church] outside of which there is neither salva-

---

would reveal to him the matters that must be believed; he would do this either by internal inspiration or by a certain evangelist of faith whom he would send him, as he sent Peter to Cornelius (Acts10)." *De Veritate*, q.14, a.11, ad 1. *S. Thomae Aquinatis Opera Omnia*, Vol. 9 (Parma: Peter Fiaccadori, 1859), p. 246. Cf. also: " . . . although the sacrament of baptism was not always necessary for salvation, faith, of which baptism is the sacrament, was always necessary." *Summa Theologiae*, Pars III, q.68, a. 1, ad 1.

[63] *Summa Theologiae*, Pars I-II, q.89, a.6.

tion nor forgiveness of sins. . . . This church represents the one mystical body; the head of its body is Christ, and God [the head] of Christ. In this [church] 'there is one Lord, one faith, and one baptism' (Eph 4, 5). To be sure, at the time of the flood there was one ark of Noah, a type of the one church; and this ark finished to one cubit from the top had one pilot and captain, that is, Noah. We read that outside the ark all living creatures were destroyed.[64]

This opening paragraph contains teaching that we have observed in previous documents: the unity and unicity of the church, the forgiveness of sins and salvation only in the church, the ark as a type of the church. Following ancient tradition the necessity of the church is here closely associated with baptism (which may also be prefigured by the floodwaters). We note too that the ark of the church bears only one steersman, an allusion which had obvious implications for the troubles of that day. There is only one head of the church, Christ himself; and his vicar is also only one, Peter and his successors in the Roman see.

The document concludes on a peremptory pitch: "We declare, state, and define that it is absolutely necessary for salvation that every human creature be subject to the Roman pontiff."[65] An interpretation of this sentence, which is commonly regarded as dogmatic and binding,[66] must take into consideration the prevailing juridical and corporate notion of the church. It must also take into account the canonical exaltation of the power of the papacy over the spiritual and temporal realms.

In the same year that *Unam Sanctam* was promulgated, Giles of Rome issued and dedicated to Boniface VIII a work entitled *On Ecclesiastical Power*. The following quotation allows one to catch the flavor of the work:

If the official position of the supreme pontiff is most holy and spiritual and such spirituality consists in a prominence of power, it is well said that the supreme pontiff, living most spiritually according to his official state and according to the prominence of power, judges all things, that is, he has dominion over all things and he himself cannot be judged by anyone, that is, no one can be superior or even equal to him.[67]

[64] DS 870.

[65] DS 875.

[66] Cf., for instance, M.-D. Chenu, O.P., "Dogme et Théologie dans la bulle *Unam Sanctam,*" in *La Parole de Dieu*. Vol. I, *La Foi dans l'Intelligence* (Paris: Les Éditions du Cerf, 1964), pp. 361–369. Also M.-D. Chenu, O.P., "Unam Sanctam," in *Lexikon für Theologie und Kirche*, Vol. 10 (Freiburg: Herder, 1965), col. 462.

[67] Bk. 1, Chap. 2. Ed. by R. Scholz (Weimar: H. Böhlaus, 1929. Reprint: Scientia Aalen, 1961), p. 9.

Giles espouses an extreme form of papal supremacy. Ultimately the sacred and secular authority can be exercised only through ecclesiastical power which culminates in the pope. Boniface's position represented in *Unam Sanctam* is not as extreme as that of Giles, but it reflects the mentality of Giles and of other papalists.[68]

Another literary source of *Unam Sanctam* is the above-examined work of Thomas, *Against the Errors of the Greeks*. Clearly the author of the bull selected two important phrases from the work ("to be subject to the Roman pontiff" and "on the necessity for salvation") and inserted them into the final paragraph of the bull. Obviously the phrases suited the purpose of the bull, but their inclusion did not authenticate the patristic texts upon which they were based, nor did they record the more mature position of Thomas.

The doctrinal import of the document is the unity of the church and the unicity of its power; it has one temporal head, the pope of Rome, to whom all the faithful owe allegiance. It is taken for granted — according to traditional teaching — that there is only one ark of salvation, the Catholic Church which has only one leader, Peter and his successors. There is no question of any other church. It is highly unlikely that this bull is deciding the question about the manner in which people outside the visible church achieve or do not achieve eternal salvation. This is not precisely the disputed question.

The problem of the papacy loomed larger than ever during the fourteenth and fifteenth centuries. Theologians of a papalist bent continued to exalt the papacy as the center of the church and the way of salvation. But the conciliarist notion developed apace, espe-

---

[68] Cf. Thomas Boase, *Boniface VIII* (London: Constable and Co., 1933), p. 319. Also Thomas Gilby, *Principality and Polity. Aquinas and the Rise of State Theory in the West* (London: Longmans, Green and Co., 1958), pp. 37f: "Humanly speaking the Canonists almost, but not quite, succeeded in committing the Church to a temporal theocracy. . . . Official claims were more circumspect than those of the publicists of the Canonical vogue. Boniface VIII may personally have agreed with these young Turks, nevertheless his Bulls *Ausculta Fili* and *Unam Sanctam* advanced no novel and explicit claim to direct dominion over the world. . . ." Cf. this passage in Boniface's letter attached to the bull *Ausculta Fili*, in which letter he refers to the pope as the vicar of Christ, the successor of Peter, and the judge of the living and the dead: "Sic veri Noe es [Philip] arcam ingressus, extra quam nemo salvatur, catholicam scilicet Ecclesiam, unam columbam immaculatam, unici Christi sponsam, in qua Christi vicarius Petrique successor primatum noscitur obtinere: qui sibi collatis clavibus regni coelorum, judex a Deo vivorum, et mortuorum constitutus agnoscitur; ad quem, sedentem in judicii solio, dissipare pertinet suo intuitu omne malum." Cited by L. Tosti, *History of Pope Boniface VIII and His Times*. Transl. by E. J. Donnelly (New York: Samuel R. Leland, Inc., 1910), p. 534.

cially in the wake of the Western schism of the papacy beginning in 1379. If the church is a *congregatio fidelium* — juridically conceived in terms of a corporation — its bishops, cardinals, and popes can be viewed more and more as representatives of the authority that resides in the whole people.

The mediatorial role of the *sacerdotium* diminished in importance in the minds of many believers. This was due both to the corporation notion of the church and to the moral and intellectual state of a large segment of the clergy. Their style of living was often a hindrance to piety. It was easy to form the impression that the institutional church represented by its priests, bishops, cardinals, and popes, could be bypassed in favor of the bible and direct contact with Christ and God. Salvation could be achieved in the church simply because the church is the gathering of the faithful, the gathering of those who believe.

Another development was that represented by John Wyclif and Jan Hus. For them the real church is the gathering of the predestined. Understandably, therefore, salvation is achieved in the church but only because the church is composed of those whom God has predestined. Jan Hus, for instance, says: "The unity of the Catholic Church consists in the bond of predestination, since here individual members are united by predestination, and in the goal of blessedness, since all her sons are ultimately united in blessedness."[69] The present visible church contains some who are not predestined; thus they are in the church but not really of the church. As the reprobate they are like chaff, present in the church for a time, but ultimately separated from the predestined. Conversely, the predestined may fall away from the visible church for a time, but they will not remain away permanently.

It follows that one cannot be sure of the predestination of popes and bishops. If their manner of life is upright, one may suppose that they are predestined; if their style of life is evil, one may presume not. Wyclif denied the validity of the sacraments administered by evil-living clerics. Hus acknowledged the validity of their sacraments but denied the validity of their jurisdiction. "No one represents Christ or Peter unless he follows him in his moral action, since this is exactly the condition on which he has received this representative jurisdictional power."[70] Hus reasons that the pope may be the head of a part of the church, the Church of Rome, but

[69] *The Church*, Chap. 1, in H. A. Oberman, *Forerunners of the Reformation. The Shape of Late Medieval Thought Illustrated by Key Documents*. Translations by P. L. Nyhus (New York: Holt, Rinehart and Winston, 1966). p. 218.

[70] Cited by H. Oberman, *ibid.*, p. 209.

not the head of the whole, universal church; Christ alone is the head of the body of the church, the body of the predestined. Thus it is not necessary "for every Christian to have recourse to the pope and as a necessity for salvation to recognize him as head of the Church and most holy father."[71] The factors that are important for salvation are predestination and the headship of Christ, not the popes and the councils. In this way Hus bypasses both the popes and the councils and appeals directly to Christ.[72]

The Council of Constance (1414–1418) condemned a series of propositions either excerpted from the works of Wyclif and Hus or designed to encapsulate their thinking. Wyclif's proposition 41 pertains to our subject:

It is not necessary for salvation to believe that the Roman Church is superior to other churches. [Censure:] This is erroneous if by Roman Church one understands the universal church or the general council or insofar as one would deny the primacy of the highest pontiff over other particular churches.[73]

The problem here, of course, is an understanding of the Roman Church. Wyclif denies the *de jure divino* character of the papacy and rejects its headship over the universal church. Proposition 29 of Hus also refers to the historical origin of the pope:

The apostles and the faithful priests of the Lord labored to regulate the church in those things which are necessary for salvation; they did this before the office of the pope was introduced, and thus they would do until the day of judgment if the pope were to fade out of the picture — something which is highly possible.[74]

Both series of propositions indicate the council's wish to condemn the idea that the church must be limited to the gathering of the predestined.

Some years later the subject of the church and salvation appeared in the Council of Basel-Florence. In one of its decrees (February 4,

---

[71] *The Church*, Chap. 7. *Ibid.*, p. 235.

[72] A similar idea is found in Dietrich of Niem's *Ways of Uniting and Reforming the Church* (1410): "The pope cannot and ought not to be called the head of this Church, but only the vicar of Christ, his vicegerent on earth, yet only while the key does not err. In this Church and in its faith every man can be saved, even if in the whole world a pope cannot be found, the reason being that upon this Church alone has the faith of Christ been handed down. For suppose there were no pope, but only one faithful person: even then the power of binding and loosing would be available. In this Church are the seven sacraments and our entire salvation." Cited in *Advocates of Reform: from Wyclif to Erasmus*. Ed. by M. Spinka (Philadelphia: Westminster Press, 1953), p. 151.

[73] DS 1191.

[74] DS 1229.

1442), actually a bull prepared by Pope Eugene IV for the re-union of the Copts with the Roman Church,[75] the traditional teaching is cited as one of the beliefs of the church:

[The Roman Church] firmly believes, professes, and proclaims that no one living outside the Catholic Church, not only pagans but also Jews, heretics and schismatics, can become sharers of eternal life; but they will go into eternal fire, 'which has been prepared for the devil and his angels' (Mt 25, 41), unless they are joined to the church before the end of their life. The unity of the ecclesiastical body is of such value that only for those who remain in it are the ecclesiastical sacraments profitable for salvation, and only for these do fasts, almsgiving and other duties of piety and exercises of Christian warfare bear the fruit of eternal rewards. 'No one can be saved, no matter how many alms he gave, no matter if he poured out his blood for the name of Christ, no one can be saved unless he remains in the bosom and unity of the Catholic Church.'[76]

The words are familiar. They are taken from the writings of Fulgentius of Ruspe, whom we cited above. It is rather significant that the pope and the council choose to enunciate the traditional doctrine according to the harshest, even erroneous, formulation. Under the circumstances — a proposal for re-union — one can understand the insistence on the necessity of a bond of union with the Roman Catholic Church.

What dogmatic value should we ascribe to the decree? The doctrine itself is traditional. The whole paragraph is either a direct quote from Fulgentius or a paraphrase of ancient teaching to the effect that works of piety are of no value outside the church. It must be admitted that the solemnity of the document is great, for it is a decree of an ecumenical council and designed to formulate the faith of the Catholic Church. But the question of purpose remains. Did the council focus its attention on this question of the relationship between church and salvation, on the precise situation of those who live and are saved at a distance from the church? Did it wish to define this problem? It would seem not. No one at the time questioned the traditional doctrine, thus it did not become the direct object of consideration and definition.[77]

---

[75] *Epistolae Pontificiae ad Concilium Florentinum Spectantes*. Ed. by George Hofmann, S. J. (Rome: Pontificium Institutum Orientalium Studiorum, 1946). Epistola no. 258, especially p. 51.

[76] DS 1351.

[77] As an example of a theologian's defense of the necessity of attachment to the Roman pontiff, see Andreas de Escobar, O.S.B., *Tractatus Polemico-Theologicus de Graecis Errantibus*, no. 60. Ed. by Emmanuel Candal, S.J. (Rome: Pontificium Institutum Orientalium Studiorum, 1952), pp. 46–47: "QUADRAGESIMA SEPTIMA CON-

Moving on to the era of the Protestant Reformation, we discover somewhat surprisingly but understandably that the major reformers did not differ from the medieval church in declaring that there is no salvation outside the church. They offered different views of the church, it is true, but they retained the thrust of the axiom. Luther says:

Whoever would find Christ must first find the church . . . outside the Christian church there is no truth, no Christ, and no salvation.[78]

I believe that no one can be saved who is not part of this community and does not live in harmony with it in one faith, word, sacrament, hope and love; and no Jew, heretic, pagan, or sinner will be saved with it unless he is reconciled and united with it and conformed to it in all things.[79]

According to Luther the church is the community of believers in Jesus Christ. It is the gathering of those who are moved by the Holy Spirit and the word of the gospel and who seek forgiveness of their sins and attachment to the Lord Jesus. It is the community of those who celebrate the sacrament of baptism and of the Lord's Supper and who proclaim the message of salvation in Jesus Christ. It is a holy church both because of the presence of the Holy Spirit and because of the sacred word of the gospel; but it is not without sin, for the believers are still in the flesh and are subject to sins and failures. The church is apostolic because it continues in the faith of the apostles; it is catholic because it is directed to all peoples. It is manifest and visible in its word and sacraments, its ministers and offices, its public prayer and even or especially in the persecutions that it bears. But it is also hidden and invisible in its faith and Spirit. Ultimately only God draws its boundaries and traces out the true limits of the church, both in its inner and in its outer realities.

CLUSIO aliquorum Grecorum est, quod non est de necessitate salutis obedire Romano pontifici vel ei subesse; quia, ut dictum est supra, equales sunt ei omnes patriarche et episcopi in potestate. Sed quod ista conclusio sit falsa, et quod sit de necessitate salutis obedire Romani pontificis mandatis, et ei subesse tamquam Christi vicario in terris et pastori christianorum supremo. . . . Concluditur ergo, secundum doctores Grecos, quod de necessitate salutis est in ecclesia Romana manere, et pape Romano obedire, et fidem eiusdem Romane ecclesie ac eius mores et regulas ac precepta servare." Cf. also Fantinus Vallaresso, *Libellus de ordine generalium conciliorum et unione Florentina*. Ed. by Bernard Schultze, S.J. (Rome: Pontificium Institutum Orientalium Studiorum, 1944), Chapters 50–52, pp. 92–94.

[78] *Kirchenpostille 1522, D. Martin Luthers Werke. Kristische Gesamtausgabe* (Weimar, 1883ff), Vol. 10, I, 1, p. 140. (Hereafter cited as WA.)

[79] *Eine kurze Form der zehn Gebote, eine kurze Form des Glaubens, eine kurze Form des Vaterunsers*, 1520, WA Vol. 7, p. 219.

Outside this church there is no salvation. "Where Christ is not preached, there is no Holy Spirit to create, call, and gather the Christian church, and outside it no one can come to the Lord Christ."[80] It is clear that Luther does not alter the traditional teaching of the necessity of the church for salvation. He develops his own notion of the church and it is outside this church that there is no salvation.

John Calvin, too, who bases his notion of church on the election of God, holds that there is no salvation outside the church. He propounds this doctrine in the context of an exposition of the visible and external character of the church:

But as it is now our purpose to discourse of the visible Church, let us learn, from her single title of Mother, how useful, nay, how necessary the knowledge of her is, since there is no other means of entering into life unless she conceive us in the womb and give us birth, unless she nourish us at her breasts, and, in short, keep us under her charge and government, until, divested of mortal flesh, we become like the angels (Mt 22, 30). For our weakness does not permit us to leave the school until we have spent our whole lives as scholars. Moreover, beyond the pale of the Church no forgiveness of sins, no salvation, can be hoped for, as Isaiah and Joel testify (Is 37, 23; Joel 11, 23).[81]

Calvin repeats the same teaching when speaking of the external marks of the church: "The knowledge of his body, inasmuch as he knew it to be more necessary for our salvation, he has made known to us by surer marks."[82]

The Zwinglian tradition may be found in a confession of faith written by Zwingli's successor in Zurich, Heinrich Bullinger, and published in 1566 as *The Second Helvetic Confession*. In Chapter 17 we find this statement:

But as for communicating with the true Church of Christ, we so highly esteem it that we say plainly that none can live before God who do not communicate with the true Church of God, but separate themselves from the same. For as without the ark of Noah there was no escaping when the world perished in the flood; even so do we believe that without Christ, who in the Church offers himself to be

[80] *The Large Catechism, the Creed,* in *The Book of Concord.* Transl. and ed. Theodore G. Tappert (Philadelphia: Fortress Press, 1959), p. 416. Also: "Outside the Christian church (that is, where the Gospel is not) there is no forgiveness, and hence no holiness." *Ibid.,* p. 418. Cf. *Vom Abendmahl Christi. Bekenntnis,* 1528, WA Vol. 26, p. 507.

[81] *Institutes of the Christian Religion.* Bk. 4, Chap. 1, Section 4. Transl. by H. Beveridge (Grand Rapids, Mich.: W. B. Eerdmans, 1966), Vol 2, p. 283.

[82] *Ibid.,* p. 289.

enjoyed of the elect, there can be no certain salvation; and therefore we teach that such as would be saved must in no wise separate themselves from the true Church of Christ.[83]

That the issue was not really a cause of division between the churches is indicated by its absence from the decrees of the Council of Trent (1545–1563). The nearest reference is the council's insistence on the necessity of baptism for salvation.[84] Its *in re* or *in voto* terminology[85] is a prime source of the subsequent theological explanations of actual or desired attachment to the visible church.

The common Catholic teaching of the period — and indeed for a few centuries — may be found in the Roman Catechism, the catechism decreed by the Council of Trent and issued in 1566:

Among these [Old Testament figures of the church] the ark of Noah has an illustrious meaning. It was constructed by divine command for the very purpose of eliminating any doubt that it signifies the church. God so established this church that all those who enter it by baptism would be safe from all danger of eternal death; but all those who abide outside of it are overwhelmed by their own faults, as happened to those who were not received into the ark.[86]

An influential theologian of this period, Cardinal Robert Bellarmine (1542–1621), cites the axiom and explains it in a manner that will be common in Roman Catholic circles up until Vatican II: "The saying 'outside the church no one is saved' must be understood of those who are not of the church: neither in actuality [*re ipsa*] nor in desire [*desiderio*]; this is the way theologians commonly speak of baptism."[87] After Bellarmine's time theologians generally answered the question of salvation outside the church in terms of a desire for baptism and entry into the church.

We will not pursue here the development which led the major Protestant churches to come to the position where they acknowledged the possibility and actuality of salvation outside the church. But it might be helpful to cite by way of illustration Karl Barth, a prominent theologian close to our own times. His concept of the church as the community of professed believers in Jesus, as the

---

[83] *Creeds of the Churches*. Ed. by John H. Leith (Garden City, New York: Doubleday & Co., 1963), p. 147.

[84] Cf. DS 1618.

[85] DS 1524.

[86] *Catechismus ex decreto SS. Concilii Tridentini ad Parochos*. Pii V. Pont. Max. jussu editus (Typis Seminarii Patavini Gregoriana Edidit, 1930), Pars I, Caput X, Quaestio 19, p. 88.

[87] *De Controversiis Christianae Fidei Adversus hujus Temporis Haereticos. Opera Omnia*. Tom. II (Milan: Natale Battezzati, 1858), p. 76.

creation of Jesus in the Holy Spirit, as the revealer of reconciliation, as an event in the world of history and of today, does not prevent him from acknowledging the grace of God and salvation outside the community of believers:

Yet it is not outside adherence to the Church, but outside the adherence of all men to Him [Christ] as known and confessed and proclaimed by the Church, that there is no salvation. We must also be careful not to maintain that participation in the salvation of the world grounded in Jesus Christ is bound absolutely to the mediation of the Church and therefore to its proclamation. We have to reckon with the hidden ways of God in which He may put into effect the power of the atonement made in Jesus Christ (Jn 10, 16) even *extra ecclesiam*, i.e., other than through its ministry in the world. He may have provided and may still provide in some other way for those who are never reached, let alone called to Him, by the Church.[88]

Catholic theologians repeated the axiom in the centuries following the Reformation, but they manifested particular concern for the many peoples whom the age of world discovery revealed to them. They suggested various ways in which peoples outside the visible church could nevertheless be united to the church and thereby achieve salvation, e.g., by proposing that many belong to the soul of the church and not to its body; by supposing that adults must really be regarded as infants, morally speaking; by postulating an explicit or implicit desire for the church (*votum ecclesiae*).

During this same period the Jansenist interpretation of the maxim provoked an important statement from the Roman pontiff. In the constitution *Unigenitus Dei Filius* of 1713, Clement XI listed a series of errors ascribed to Paschal Quesnel. Among them is proposition 30: "No grace is granted outside the church."[89] The obverse of this proposition is that grace is indeed granted outside the church. Unresolved, of course, is the question of the source and direction of this grace — whether it stems from the instrumentality of the church, whether it joins a person to the church, or whether it leads to salvation without the church. But the teaching must be underscored, for it is another instance of the increased concern on the part of the church for the status of those outside the church and for a serious acceptance of the universal salvific will of God, a will that implies all-pervading grace.

The Roman Church of the nineteenth century was constrained to

---

[88] *Church Dogmatics.* Vol. IV, *The Doctrine of Reconciliation*, Part One. Transl. by G. W. Bromiley (Edinburgh: T. & T. Clark, 1956), p. 688.

[89] "Extra Ecclesiam nulla conceditur gratia." DS 2429.

devote explicit attention to the question of church and salvation. Various trends deriving from the Enlightenment, Deism, Rationalism, Romanticism, and political movements blurred the lines of difference between various religious beliefs and advocated a choice of paths leading to salvation (however salvation was envisioned). In Roman circles this attitude was dubbed "tolerance" and "indifferentism." A number of popes, including Leo XII, Gregory XVI and Pius IX, condemned indifferentism for its teaching that any religion is a valid means of salvation.[90] The popes presumed the traditional axiom as the basis of their condemnation; implied is the proposition that the Roman Catholic Church is the only medium of salvation. Pius IX, however, surpassed previous popes in his "tolerance" of those who live in invincible ignorance of the true character of the Catholic Church. He rejected a rigid interpretation of the axiom, one that would condemn outright those who live beyond the pale of the Catholic Church. We quote at length from his encyclical *Quanto conficiamur moerore* of August 10, 1863:

Again we need to recall and reprehend a most serious error in which some Catholics are unfortunately involved. They are of the opinion that men living in errors and at a distance from the true faith and Catholic unity can attain eternal life. This opinion is completely contrary to Catholic doctrine.

It is known to us and to you [bishops of Italy] that those who are in invincible ignorance of our most holy religion but who carefully observe the natural law and its precepts which God has written in the hearts of all men, who are ready to obey God and to lead an honest and upright life, can through the power of the divine light and grace attain eternal life; for God, who clearly sees, examines, and knows the minds, spirits, thoughts, and ways of all men, in his exalted goodness and mercy would not in the least allow anyone who is not guilty of voluntary fault to be punished eternally.

But the Catholic dogma [*catholicum dogma*] is also well known, namely, that outside the Catholic Church no one can be saved; and those who are contumacious against the authority and definitions of the same church and who are pertinaciously cut off from the unity of that church and from the successor of Peter, the Roman pontiff (to whom the Savior has committed the care of the vineyard), cannot obtain external salvation.[91]

One feels here the tension between the traditional axiom and the need to acknowledge the all-embracing goodness of God toward those who through no fault of their own do not belong to the church.

[90] Cf. DS 2720; 2730–31; 2785; 2917.
[91] DS 2865–2867.

Pius IX does not espouse a literal understanding of the axiom, but at the same time he is constrained to invoke the teaching as "Catholic dogma" (*catholicum dogma*). To our knowledge, this is the first time that the axiom is so qualified in an official Roman document.[92] Our investigation up to this point has led us to disavow the strictly "defined" character of the axiom. Moreover, the maxim does not become automatically defined by its inclusion in a papal allocution or encyclical. By the nineteenth century theology employed the word "dogma" in the rather technical sense of revealed and defined teaching. It seems that Pius IX overstates the history of the axiom in calling it a dogma; there is a possibility, of course, that he is using the word "dogma" in the more general sense of "teaching."

It is significant to note that some Catholic theologians of the time understood the axiom to mean only that those *culpably* outside the Roman Catholic Church cannot attain to salvation. Others understood it to mean that the church is the ordinary means of salvation, thus allowing for extraordinary ways in which divine grace is administered to people outside the church. Still others explained that those in grace inculpably outside the church are joined to its soul but not its body.[93] These opinions, especially the one concerning the extraordinary means of salvation, are extremely important as a backdrop to the contemporary theological scene.

The first ecumenical council to deal directly with the issue of the axiom was Vatican I. Its preparatory schema on the church contained two chapters on the subject of the necessity of the church for salvation. As is well known, diverse political and theological circumstances prevented the promulgation of these chapters, but their importance as indications of the theological climate of the day warrants citing them:

The church is a society that is utterly necessary for the attainment of salvation [title of chapter 6]. Hence, let everyone understand how necessary the Church of Christ is as a society for the attainment of salvation. For she is as necessary as is the union and fellowship with Christ, the head, and with his mystical body. Apart from her there is no other community that he nourishes and cares for as his church. . . . We therefore teach that the church is not an optional society, as if it were a matter of indifference for salvation whether

---

[92] In the allocution of December 9, 1854, he uses the words *ex fide* and points more specifically to the Roman Apostolic Church: "Tenendum quippe ex fide est, extra Apostolicam Romanam Ecclesiam salvum fieri neminem posse. . . ." DS p. 571.

[93] John King, O.M.I., *The Necessity of the Church for Salvation in Selected Theological Writings of the Past Century* (Washington, D.C.: Catholic University of America Press, 1960), pp. 3–29.

one knows it or not, whether one enters or abandons it. On the contrary, she is utterly necessary, and indeed not only by a necessity of the Lord's precept, by which the Savior prescribed that all peoples must enter it, but also by a necessity of means; for in the designated order of saving providence, the communication of the Holy Spirit and a sharing in truth and life are not obtained except in and through the church, of which Christ is the head.[94]

The schema continues in the same vein but then qualifies the axiom:

Outside the church no one can be saved [title of chapter 7]. Furthermore, it is a dogma of faith that outside the church no one can be saved. And yet those who are invincibly ignorant of Christ and his church must not for this reason be condemned to eternal punishments, for they are not bound by any fault in this matter in the eyes of the Lord, who wishes all men to be saved and to come to a knowledge of the truth and who does not deny grace to him who does what is within his power to attain justification and eternal life. But no one will achieve this [life] who dies in a condition of culpable separation from the unity of faith or church union. Anyone who is not in this ark will perish in the power of the flood. Therefore we reject and abhor the doctrine of religious indifferentism, which is both a godless doctrine and contrary to reason.[94]

In the scrutiny of this draft some council fathers wished to clarify and improve it by adding a statement to the effect that everyone who is saved belongs to the church either *in re* or *in voto*. But the drafting committee, noting a widespread displeasure with this Bellarmine-inspired terminology, explained that the matter was implied in the text, namely, that anyone inculpably dying outside the church "cannot be altogether or absolutely outside the church."[95] The fathers generally agreed in substance, though not in terminology, that some kind of attachment to the church is necessary for salvation.

For the post-Vatican I development we may turn to the research of John J. King and F. X. Lawlor.[96] Lawlor's article indicates that the papal documents continue to depict the church as the fount of saving grace for all mankind. King's study is more comprehensive.

---

[94] Cf. *Schema constitutionis dogmaticae de Ecclesia Christi Patrum examini propositum. Acta et Decreta Sacrorum Conciliorum Recentiorum. Collectio Lacensis*, Vol. VII (Freiburg: Herder, 1890), col. 569.

[95] J. Mansi, *Sacrorum Conciliorum nova et amplissima collectio* (Florence, Paris, Leipzig: Expensis Antonii Zatta Veneti, 1759ff), Vol. 51, col. 570.

[96] John King, O.M.I., *op. cit.* F. X. Lawlor, S.J., "The Mediation of the Church in some Pontifical Documents," *Theological Studies* 12 (1951), pp. 481–504.

Taking the 1949 letter of the Holy Office as a standard of judgment, he examines in sequential fashion the significant theological and magisterial writings from about 1840 to 1957. His conclusion is that the church is indeed necessary for salvation, that "the Roman Catholic Church must exercise a causal influence in every case where an individual attains salvation,"[97] and that the *in re, in voto* explanation is practically the only one which "can explain how the church actually procures salvation for the millions . . . who are to all outward appearances alien to her."[98]

For our purposes, however, the discordant voices are most revealing. Not all Catholic theologians felt obliged to repeat the teaching of Pius IX. Cardinal Newman, for example, did not require the intervention of the church in every instance of salvation. According to Newman there is a legitimate theological minimizing of Pope Pius IX's negative enunciations. As an example of such minimizing he cites this formulation of the axiom: "Out of the Church, and out of the faith, is no salvation." Then he explains:

The main sense is, that there is no other communion or so-called Church, but the Catholic, in which are stored the promises, the sacraments, and other means of salvation; the other and derived sense is, that no one can be saved who is not *in* that one and only Church. But it does not follow, because there is no Church but one, which has the Evangelical gifts and privileges to bestow, that therefore no one can be saved without the intervention of that one Church.[99]

Karl Adam propounds the view that God's grace can touch people without the mediation of the church.[100] These and similar views, which King characterizes only as inadequate or inexact,[101] are amazing in view of the generally presumed dogmatic character of the axiom, which in fact came to be interpreted more and more in terms of the necessity of the mediation of the church.

At the close of the period the papal documents continue to repeat the axiom and to extol the church as the locus of the granting of all saving graces. The encyclical *Humani Generis* (1950), for instance, reproved those "who reduce to a meaningless formula the necessity

[97] *Op. cit.*, p. xiv.

[98] *Ibid.*, p. 356.

[99] "A Letter Addressed to His Grace the Duke of Norfolk (Dec. 27, 1874) on occasion of Mr. Gladstone's Recent Expostulation," in *Certain Difficulties Felt by Anglicans in Catholic Teaching*. Vol. II (London: Longmans, Green and Co., 1896), p. 335.

[100] Cf. J. King, *op. cit.*, pp. 160–168; 347.

[101] *Ibid.*, pp. 359–360.

of belonging to the true church in order to achieve eternal salvation."[102] We need not compile a list of the many theological works and catechisms that reflect this papal teaching.

This survey leads us to conclude that although the axiom has never been the subject of a *de fide* magisterial declaration in the Roman Catholic Church, it is repeated as traditional doctrine from the earliest centuries to the present time. The axiom was naturally subject to diverse interpretations, from the heterodox and rigid to the authentic and moderate. In more recent centuries the tension between the axiom and the need to recognize salvation at a distance from the church has become acute. This led generally to a mitigated interpretation of the adage, especially in terms of ecclesial mediation; it was and is commonly assumed among Roman Catholic theologians that salvation is mediated through the church, even for those who are being saved at a distance from explicit belief in the church. This teaching that the church is the medium of all salvation continues in the theologies of the 1950's and 1960's; but an opposite trend is also apparent. The subsequent chapters will examine both of these trends in Roman Catholic circles.

[102] *Acta Apostolicae Sedis* 43 (1950), p. 571. Cf. *Acta Apostolicae Sedis* 35 (1943), pp. 206–207.

Chapter 2

Vatican II and Outside the Church No Salvation

1. Necessity of the Church for Salvation

That the subject of the necessity of the church for salvation should receive explicit attention in the decrees of Vatican II is not surprising, given the fact that Vatican I prepared but did not promulgate a schema on the question, that Vatican II was announced as a continuation of Vatican I, and that theological writers of the last one hundred years were wont to deal extensively with the matter. The fathers of Vatican II in general assume the traditional teaching but are careful to avoid the rather offensive and easily misunderstood axiom: *extra ecclesiam nulla salus*.[1] As an introduction to the examination of the documents of Vatican II it will be instructive to cite from a speech of one of the council's presidents, Cardinal Julius Doepfner. Given in Munich in January, 1964, it corresponds to the time of the council and represents rather well the prevailing attitude of the council fathers in regard to this axiom and its doctrinal content. Referring specifically to the maxim Doepfner says:

Precisely here it will become evident that it is possible to express the truth without abandoning essentials and without injuring those who think differently, and it is possible to make the meaning clear to them. The church cannot expunge the maxim if she is not to surrender her very self. The church is bound to the will of the Lord who chose to continue his work through a visible institution. But we recognize today that the word and salvation of the Lord is effective among men in many ways and stages, also outside the Catholic Church.[2]

[1] In Art. 26 of the *Dogmatic Constitution on the Church*, however, the fathers cite Aquinas in a passage which approximates the axiom. Cf. below p. 45.

[2] "Die Reform der Kirche," in *Zweites Vatikanisches Konzil. 3. Sitzungsperiode.*

The cardinal's statement betrays some ambiguity in that he upholds the maxim and still allows for salvational activity outside the Catholic Church. This is the apparent contradition that the council must face: the traditional axiom; and salvation outside the church.

Chapter 2 of the *Dogmatic Constitution on the Church* contains the council's most direct statement on the subject:

This sacred Synod turns its attention first to the Catholic faithful. Basing itself upon sacred Scripture and tradition, it teaches that the Church, now sojourning on earth as an exile, is necessary for salvation. For Christ, made present to us in His Body, which is the Church, is the one Mediator and the unique Way of salvation. In explicit terms He Himself affirmed the necessity of faith and baptism (cf. Mk 16, 16; Jn 3, 5) and thereby affirmed also the necessity of the Church, for through baptism as through a door men enter the Church. Whosoever, therefore, knowing that the Catholic Church was made necessary by God through Jesus Christ, would refuse to enter her or to remain in her could not be saved (Art. 14).[3]

To understand the content and significance of this paragraph, included as it is in the chapter on the people of God, it will be helpful if not necessary to weigh the preliminary drafts of the *Dogmatic Constitution on the Church*, for they provide clarifying insights into the succinct wording of the decree. As will be apparent, the preparatory schemata indicate a progressive refinement in formulation and a gradual shift in position with regard to the necessity of the church for salvation.

The first draft of the *Dogmatic Constitution on the Church*, prepared by the pre-conciliar Theological Commission headed by Cardinal Alfred Ottaviani and distributed to the fathers on November 23, 1962, formulates the traditional teaching of many theologians and of the magisterium of the Roman Catholic Church. It is interesting to note, however, that the axiom *extra ecclesiam nulla salus* is not explicitly cited in the draft. In omitting this traditional formula the Theological Commission must be credited with some sensitivity to the demands of ecumenism. But while omitting the formula, the Theological Commission expresses its content. It phrases the traditional teaching in a way that leaves no doubt about the necessity of the church for salvation.

Chapter 2 of this first draft bears the caption *De Membris*

Dokumente. Texte. Kommentar. Ed. by A. Beckel, H. Reiring, and O.B. Roegele (Osnabrück: Verlag A. Fromm, 1965), p. 28.

[3] Translations of Vatican II documents are taken from *The Documents of Vatican II.* Ed. by W. Abbott, S.J., and J. Gallagher (New York: America Press, 1966). Cf. *Decree on the Church's Missionary Activity*, Art. 7.

Ecclesiae Militantis Eiusdemque Necessitate ad Salutem. The very title inculcates one of the main thrusts of the chapter: the necessity of the church for salvation. Article 8, the lead article of the chapter, pertains to our subject:

[The Necessity of the Church for Salvation] The sacred council teaches, as the holy church of God has always taught, that the church is necessary for salvation and that he who knows the Catholic Church to be established by God through Jesus Christ but refuses to enter it or to remain in it cannot be saved. Just as no one can be saved unless he actually receives baptism (through which a person becomes a member of the church if he does not place an obstacle in the way of incorporation) or at least has a desire for baptism, so also no one can obtain salvation unless he is [*existat*] a member of the church or is oriented toward her by desire. However, that a person is really a member of the church or is oriented toward her by desire is not sufficient for salvation; it is further required that he die in the state of grace, joined to God in faith, hope, and charity.[4]

Anyone acquainted with manual theology of the period immediately preceding the council will recognize here a précis of the customary teaching of Catholic theologians.[5] The only omission here is the axiom itself which the commission must have deemed offensive to non-Catholics and not necessarily required in a pastorally oriented document. But the doctrine itself — the necessity of the church for salvation and attachment to it in terms of desire — receives clear and insistent formulation. Moreover, to substantiate the affirmation that the proposed teaching is traditional the draft includes a note citing various fathers of the church from Ignatius of Antioch to Fulgentius, and magisterial documents from the Athanasian Creed to the 1949 letter of the Holy Office to the archbishop of Boston.

If there is still doubt about the mind of the pre-conciliar Theological Commission regarding this question, we need only turn to a preparatory report which it presented to the Central Commission in May, 1962. *L'Osservatore Romano* contains a notice of this report:

In examining the doctrine of the nature of the church one easily

---

[4] *Schema Constitutionis Dogmaticae De Ecclesia. Acta Synodalia Sacrosancti Concilii Oecumenici Vaticani Secundi.* Volumen I: Periodus Prima. Pars IV. Congregationes Generales XXXI-XXXVI (Typis Polyglottis Vaticanis, 1971), p. 18. (Hereafter the documents are cited as *Acta.*)

[5] Note 1 of the draft actually refers to S. Tromp, S.J., *De Spiritu Christi Anima* (Rome: Gregorian University, 1960). Cf. also, for example, P. Parente, *Theologia Fundamentalis.* 4th ed. (Turin: Marietti, 1955), pp. 185–189.

understands the doctrine of its mission and irreplaceable function: no one can be saved without belonging to the church, either in actuality or at least in implicit wish, that is, in desire. On various occasions the supreme pontiffs affirmed this truth. For example, in the apostolic letter *Quotiescumque nobis* addressed to Cardinal Tien-Chen-Sin, archbishop of Peking, June 29, 1961, John XXIII wrote: 'Venerable brothers, in your teaching you will not fail to mention these great and salutary truths to the flock committed to your care: one does not render rightful and pleasing worship to God and it is impossible to be joined to him except through Jesus Christ; it is impossible to be united to Christ except in and through the church, which is his mystical body; finally, it is impossible to belong to the church except through the bishops, who are successors of the apostles and united to the supreme pastor, the successor of Peter.'

The expression *in voto*, that is, with desire, has a rather broad meaning: not only those achieve salvation who know the church and who desire to enter it and become part of it, but in fact cannot because there is no one to administer baptism to them; but those also can be saved who, though they do not know Jesus and his church, moved by actual grace direct an act of sincere and perfect love toward God. Implicit in such an act is the desire to belong to the true church if they knew it.[6]

The commission cites the stern position enunciated in Pope John XXIII's letter, but it immediately qualifies the harsh doctrine by using the *in voto* terminology found in both theological and magisterial statements of modern times. The thrust of this pre-conciliar report, therefore, does not go beyond the position taken by the Holy Office in 1949.

The first draft of the *Dogmatic Constitution on the Church* was examined by the council fathers from December 1 to 7, 1962, and it met with serious criticism for its triumphalism, its lack of inner unity, and its incompleteness.[7]

The second draft of the *Dogmatic Constitution on the Church* was prepared by an expanded Theological Commission and issued in 1963, in the interval between the first and the second sessions of the council.[8] The section dealing with the necessity of the church for salvation is distinctly re-worked:

The holy council teaches with sacred scripture and tradition that the church is an institution necessary for salvation and that

---

[6] May 10, 1962, no. 106 (30.980), p. 2. Cf. *Acta Apostolicae Sedis* 53 (1961), p. 467.

[7] Cf., for example, the comments of Bishop Emile de Smedt. *Acta*, Vol. I, Pars IV, pp. 142–144.

[8] *Acta*, Vol. II, Pars I, pp. 215–281.

therefore those men, who while knowing the Catholic Church to be established by God through Jesus Christ as necessary and who nevertheless refuse to enter her or to remain in her, cannot be saved. For that which revelation affirms about the necessity of baptism (cf. Mk 16,16; Jn 3, 5) is without doubt and by the same reason valid concerning the church, which men enter through baptism as through a door. . . . He, however, who does not live in faith, hope, and charity, but while sinning remains in the bosom of the church — indeed in its body not in its heart — is not saved, though he belongs to the church.[9]

This second draft strives to be more scriptural. Where the first draft is satisfied with the phrase "as the only church of God has always taught," the second draft bases its teaching on the words of scripture: "the holy council teaches with sacred scripture and tradition." Moreover, while both drafts link up the necessity of the church with the necessity of baptism, the second refers explicitly to the scriptural revelation of the necessity of baptism and thereby strives to provide greater support for the teaching of the necessity of the church for salvation. Most significant, however, is the abandonment of the traditional terminology of attachment to the church through desire for baptism and the church. This "baptismal" terminology of explicit and implicit desire is no longer deemed appropriate to express the necessity of the church and the salvation of people outside the church.

A number of council fathers submitted written emendations relative to this second draft. A suggestion of Maurice Baudoux, bishop of Saint Boniface, is significant. He proposes an alternate reading of the whole paragraph. It will be sufficient to cite one sentence from his proposed reading: "Thus from apostolic tradition [the church] is always proposed as a medium necessary for salvation, and actually is."[10] Apparently Baudoux is not willing to admit, as the second draft seems to imply, that scripture affirms or teaches directly the necessity of the institutional church for salvation. His concern must have been acknowledged by the drafting commission because the third draft states the issue more discreetly and indirectly in these words: ". . . basing itself on scripture and tradition." The *relatio* (that is, the public introduction and explanation) for Article 14, it is true, explains that the phrase "basing itself on scripture and tradition" was introduced "lest the magisterium be placed on one and the same level with sacred scripture and tradition."[11] But the

[9] *Ibid.*, p. 220.

[10] "Exinde, a traditione apostolica semper ut medium ad salutem necessarium proponitur, et est." *Acta*, Vol. II, Pars I, p. 295.

[11] *Acta*, Vol. III, Pars I, p. 202.

bishop's desire for a specification of the kind of tradition — apostolic tradition — was not accepted. Perhaps the drafting committee avoided the identification of the tradition because it glimpsed shades of the Council of Trent and its difficulties with the attempt to determine the nature and extent of apostolic tradition.[12]

The third draft of the *Dogmatic Constitution on the Church*, dated July 3, 1964, was presented for discussion at the third session of the council. Except for a few minor changes suggested by the council fathers this third draft of the paragraph in question became the actual form of the promulgated decree; thus we will not reproduce it here.[13]

Comparing the second and third drafts (Article 8 of the second draft has now become Article 14) we notice that the latter has been re-worded in phraseology but not in substance, at least not in the matter of church and salvation. Fortunately the mediatorship of Christ is introduced into the schema; the first and second drafts of this paragraph were content to speak of the necessity of the church without explicit reference to Christ.[14]

Now that we have sketched the genesis of the paragraph, we may proceed to an elaboration of its content. The council intends to ground its teaching about the necessity of the church for salvation on scripture and tradition. But its appeal to scripture and tradition is exceedingly brief. It restricts itself to two scriptural arguments, omitting entirely references to the history of the doctrine. One argument deals with the unique mediatorship of Christ himself: "For Christ, made present to us in His Body, which is the Church, is the one Mediator and the unique Way of salvation." Wishing to avoid any derogation of the person of Christ, the council declares in no uncertain terms that Christ is the unique mediator and way of salvation. But if this is true, why is the church necessary? The first reason enunciated in the paragraph is that the church is the body of Christ. If Christ is necessary for salvation, so is his one body, the church, for the two are intimately united. At this juncture the council judiciously refrains from repeating the traditional teaching that the church is the continuation of Christ, a teaching that was certainly familiar to most of the fathers of the council. In fact, in one of

[12] Bishop Smit recommended that the words "cum Sacra Scriptura et Traditione" be omitted altogether. Bishop Weber desired the insertion of a reference to 1 Pt 3, 20f and to the church as the ark of salvation. Neither recommendation was accepted. *Acta*, Vol. II, Pars I, p. 295.

[13] Cf. the pertinent paragraph of the third draft, called *Textus emendatus. Acta*, Vol. III, Pars I, pp. 188f.

[14] One change in the final draft was the addition of the word "faith" to indicate that Christ explicitly affirmed the necessity of baptism *and faith*.

tery, a sense common in the patristic era.[21] The salvific plan of God was known as the *mysterion* (a Greek word which translates into Latin as *sacramentum*). It could refer not only to the economy of salvation but also to the scriptures which speak of the mystery, or again to Jesus as the incarnate mystery, or finally to the church itself as a mystery.[22] The council adopts the latter sense of the word *sacramentum*, a sense that has gained merited attention from theologians in recent years.[23] Traditionally the seven sacraments of the Roman Catholic Church were viewed as efficacious signs of God's grace, as ecclesial acts which involve and effect an encounter with the risen Lord. This concept of efficaciousness and encounter is not excluded here from the sacramental dimension of the church. There is a similarity in efficacy and sign value between the individual sacraments and the great sacrament of the church. Both the church and the sacraments effect what they signify. Actually the church is the primordial sacrament of which the seven sacraments are concrete actualizations and expressions. Whenever the faithful gather for the celebration of the sacraments, the church realizes itself in a solemn and visible fashion. But even apart from a sacramental assembly the church remains the permanent sacrament of salvation.

In this first article of the constitution the church is termed a sacrament or sign and instrument (*veluti sacramentum seu signum et instrumentum*) of intimate union with God and of unity of the whole human race. The church is not just a mirror of this unity but an actual instrument for the achievement of such unity and union. Such presumably is the intentional thrust of the statement: the church is efficaciously involved in the procurement of the unity of mankind and of intimate union with God.[24] This interpretation is

---

[21] For a discussion of the council's debate over the insertion of this word into the 1963 draft see M. Bernards, "Zur Lehre von der Kirche als Sakrament. Beobachtungen aus der Theologie des 19. und 20. Jahrhunderts," *Münchener Theologische Zeitschrift* 20 (1969), pp. 29–34.

[22] Cf. C. Vagaggini, O.S.B., *The Theological Dimensions of the Liturgy* (Collegeville, Minn.: The Liturgical Press, 1959), pp. 8–12. An instance of this wider notion of *sacramentum* is offered in Article 9, where the church is called "the visible sacrament of saving unity" for everyone. A footnote refers to Saint Cyprian, *Letter* 69, 6 (PL 3, 1142B).

[23] Cf. besides Bernards, cited in note 21, E. Schillebeeckx, O.P., *Christ the Sacrament of the Encounter with God* (New York: Sheed and Ward, 1963); O. Semmelroth, S.J., *Church and Sacrament* (Notre Dame, Ind.: Fides, 1965).

[24] Cardinal Joseph Ritter commented at one point that the schema is deficient: "It is nearly silent about the way in which the church is a sign and an instrument of union." *Acta*, Vol. II, Pars II, p. 18.

confirmed by a passage in the *Pastoral Constitution on the Church in the Modern World:*

For every benefit which the People of God during its earthly pilgrimage can offer to the human family stems from the fact that the Church is 'the universal sacrament of salvation,' simultaneously manifesting and exercising the mystery of God's love for man (Art. 45).

Just how the church effects this unity is detailed, at least to some extent, in other documents of the council, especially in its many references to the tasks of the church in the world today. Of course, all this can be accomplished only in Christ (*in Christo*), only through the church's union with the one mediator. Another reference to the church as sacrament, one that appeared initially in the 1964 draft of the decree,[25] underscores even more explicitly its all-embracing efficacy. It occurs in Chapter 7, which points up the eschatological and pilgrim character of the church:

Rising from the dead (cf. Rm 6, 9), He sent His life-giving Spirit upon His disciples and through this Spirit has established His body, the Church, as the universal sacrament of salvation. Sitting at the right hand of the Father, He is continually active in the world, leading men to the Church, and through her joining them more closely to Himself and making them partakers of His glorious life by nourishing them with His own body and blood (Art. 48).

It is difficult to imagine a bolder expression of the exalted status and mission of the church and its sacramental value for the world. Having graced the church with this magnificent title, however, the council forthwith assigns it a position of service in respect to Christ. The church is a minister through whom Christ shares his life and joins people more closely to himself. What is most striking about the passage is the statement that Christ continually works in the world in order to lead men *to the church (continuo operatur in mundo ut homines ad Ecclesiam perducat)*.[26] In accord with the council's insistence on the efficacious sacramentality of the church one might have expected here the reverse kind of statement, namely, that Christ acts through the church in order to bring per-

[25] Already in 1963, in an emendation which Bishop Baudoux recommended for the then Article 8 (later 14), the church is described as the "vivum salutis instrumentum et universale sacramentum, [which] divinam misericordiam actu et efficaciter, humanis condicionibus modo accommodato, applicat." *Acta*, Vol. II, Pars I, pp. 294f. We notice especially the suggestion that the church actively and efficaciously applies the divine mercy.

[26] The direct activity of Christ is less evident in the draft reading: "Sedens ad dexteram Patris continuo operatur in mundo ut homines arctius cum Ecclesia coniungat." *Acta*, Vol. III, Pars V, p. 50.

sons into contact with himself and his life. But as it stands one could conclude from this statement that the church's task of gracing the whole world does not exclude other ways in which the risen and ever-present Christ deals with mankind. The fathers of the council provide no details about the manner in which Christ leads people to the church, for they concern themselves almost exclusively with the manner in which the church brings Christ and his message to the world.

The title of the church as sacrament of salvation or universal sacrament of salvation appears in other documents of the council but its meaning is determined basically by the all-important *Dogmatic Constitution on the Church*. For instance, the *Decree on the Missionary Activity of the Church* begins with a reference to Article 48 (just examined). "The Church," the decree affirms, "has been divinely sent to all nations that she might be 'the universal sacrament of salvation'" (Art. 1). Here the term is used to inculcate the universal orientation of the missionary activity of the church; by Christ's command and by its very dynamism the church is directed to all peoples. "As the salt of the earth and light of the world (cf. Mt 5, 13-14), the Church is summoned with special urgency to save and renew every creature. In this way all things can be restored in Christ, and in Him mankind can compose one family and one people" (Art. 1). As is evident from this passage, the saving activity of the Church is inextricably bound up with its mission.[27]

[27] Cf. Art. 5. That the council regards the church as the means of salvation is confirmed by the Protestant J. Aagaard, who writes this commentary on the decree: "The church in mission is therefore still in a real sense the sacrament of salvation (1 and 5). In mission mankind is not just told that it is already saved, but salvation achieves its effect everywhere (3), the church in mission is the means of salvation (6) for without unity there is no salvation (4 and 15)." "Some Main Trends in the Renewal of Roman Catholic Missiology," in *Challenge . . . and Response. A Protestant Perspective of the Vatican Council*. Ed. by W. A. Quanbeck in consultation with F. Kantzenbach and V. Vajta (Minneapolis: Augsburg Publishing House, 1966), p. 131. Cf. *Pastoral Constitution on the Church in the Modern World*, Art. 42. Also Suso Brechter, O.S.B.: "The axiom means that anyone who is saved finds salvation through Christ and the Church. Vatican II used the clear and positive formula: 'Ecclesia universale salutis sacramentum' (*Dogmatic Constitution on the Church*, Art. 48). The old, frequently misunderstood and misused axiom must therefore be clarified and modified: Sine Ecclesia nulla salus, or: Extra Christum nulla salus." "Dekret über die Missionstätigkeit der Kirche, Einleitung und Kommentar," in *Lexikon für Theologie und Kirche. Das Zweite Vatikanische Konzil*. Vol. III (Freiburg: Herder, 1968), p. 41. Cf. also Paul VI's November 6, 1964, address to the assembled fathers: "In us, the successor of blessed Peter, and in you, the successors of the apostles, the words of the divine mandate reecho: 'Go into the whole world and preach the Gospel to every creature.' The salvation of the world depends on the fulfillment of this mandate." *Third Session. Council Speeches of Vatican II*. Ed. by W. K. Leahy and A. T. Massimini (Glen Rock, N.J.: Paulist Press, 1966), p. 263.

A passage in the *Pastoral Constitution on the Church in the Modern World* adds an interesting dimension to the church as the sign of salvation:

Although by the power of the Holy Spirit the Church has remained the faithful spouse of her Lord and has never ceased to be the sign of salvation on earth, still she is very well aware that among her members, both clerical and lay, some have been unfaithful to the Spirit of God during the course of many centuries (Art. 43).

Apparently sinful individuals in the church do not obstruct the sign value of the church. One could, of course, explain that the church, not as burdened with sinners but as driven by the Spirit, is a sign of salvation. However, the more obvious sense of the passage is simply that the sign of salvation abides in a church which includes sinners in its midst.

The concept of the instrumentality of the church is not restricted to passages in which occur the actual words *sacramentum* or *instrumentum*. It appears as well in other places where the church is extolled as the bearer of grace and truth. Article 8 of the *Dogmatic Constitution on the Church*, without employing the word *instrumentum*, promotes the instrumentality of the church:

Christ, the one Mediator, established and ceaselessly sustains here on earth His holy Church, the community of faith, hope, and charity, as a visible structure. Through her He communicates truth and grace to all.

Though it cannot be directly concluded from this passage that the church is the only instrument of such communication, it is clear that the glorified and invisible Christ can and does work through the visible organization of the church to transmit grace and truth to all peoples. That the church is indeed such an instrument of Christ is at least suggested by an addition to this passage which was proposed by the German-speaking council fathers and the conference of Scandanavian bishops: "The church exists, therefore, in indissoluble unity, both as the fruit of the redemption of Christ and as the medium by which Christ carries on his redemption."[28] But the implication of universal instrumentality is stronger in the rest of the paragraph where the fathers of the council liken the social and Spirit-guided church to the mystery of the incarnation. The point of the comparison is not that the church prolongs the incarnation (an

---

[28] "Post 'sustentatur,' proponunt addendum: 'Ecclesia igitur indissolubili unitate simul et fructus redemptionis Christi exsistit et medium, quo Christus redemptionem suam exsequitur'" (Patres Concil. linguae germanicae et Confer. Episc. Scandin.). *Acta*, Vol. II, Pars I, p. 292.

excessive identification which the fathers in general were inclined to avoid in an effort to counter some recent romantic teaching on the subject[29]), but that there exists a likeness between the Logos and human makeup of Christ, and the Spirit-vivified and social structure of the church. Article 8 continues:

Just as the assumed nature inseparably united to the divine Word serves Him as a living instrument of salvation, so, in a similar way, does the communal structure of the Church serve Christ's Spirit, who vivifies it by way of building up the body (cf. Eph 4, 16).

The implication seems to be this: just as Christ is the one mediator, the universal instrument of salvation, so he bequeaths to the church his essential make-up and instrumentality and thereby assigns it a salvific task relating to the whole world.[30]

In another article of the same constitution the council returns to the notion of an instrumental church vivified and impelled by the Spirit of Christ:

For the Church is compelled by the Holy Spirit to do her part towards the full realization of the will of God, who has established Christ as the source of salvation for the whole world (Art. 17).

The church cooperates in the Trinitarian work of salvation, a work that proceeds from the decree of the Father, the saving event of Christ, and the urgency of the Spirit. The church is privileged to cooperate, but only to cooperate and not to become itself the absolute source of salvation. Whether there are other cooperators is beyond the scope of this passage.

Another brief allusion to the instrumentality of the church is included in the preface of Chapter 8, which delineates the ecclesial role of Mary:

Therefore, as it clarifies Catholic teaching concerning the Church, in which the divine Redeemer works salvation, this sacred Synod intends to describe with diligence the role of the Blessed Virgin in the mystery of the Incarnate Word and the Mystical Body (Art. 54).

---

[29] Bishop Weber proposed to add to the 1963 draft that the church is not only likened to the incarnation but is also its continuation. *Acta*, Vol. II, Pars I, p. 292. But the proposal was not accepted. Cf. also Bishop Seitz's emendation which refers to the church as "an efficacious instrument of grace" (*instrumentum efficax gratiae*). *Ibid.*, p. 294.

[30] An addition which Bishop Carli proposed for the 1963 draft approximates this implication. He would have the article read that the church is "the unique guardian of redemption and the divinely constituted minister" (*unica Redemptionis custos atque administra divinitus constituta*). *Ibid.*, p. 293. No additional information is given by these words of the next paragraph of Art. 8: "Just as Christ carried out the work of redemption in poverty and under oppression, so the Church is called to follow the same path in communicating to men the fruits of salvation."

The church, including Mary as the most excellent of the redeemed, is the locus of salvation in Christ.

Passing allusions to the salvific instrumentality of the church continue to emerge from documents other than the basic *Dogmatic Constitution on the Church*. These references are important insofar as they illustrate and expand on the theme of the church as an instrument of grace and salvation. One significant passage appears in the *Decree on Ecumenism*, Article 3. Addressing themselves to the lack of unity among the separated churches and communities, while granting the presence of ecclesial and salvific realities among them, the fathers of the council express forcefully the role and position of the Roman Catholic Church:

For it is through Christ's Catholic Church alone, which is the all-embracing means of salvation, that the fullness of the means of salvation can be obtained. It was to the apostolic college alone, of which Peter is the head, that we believe our Lord entrusted all the blessings of the New Covenant, in order to establish on earth the one Body of Christ into which all those should be fully incorporated who already belong in any way to God's People.[31]

The expression "all-embracing means of salvation" (*generale auxilium salutis*, literally, "the general aid for salvation") derives from the influential letter of the Holy Office to archbishop Richard Cushing of Boston (August 8, 1949). There as here the word "all-embracing" means total; it refers both to the church as a whole (not just the individual sacraments) and to the whole of mankind, the scope of the church's salvific task. The inclusion here of the 1949 expression indicates that the council seeks to draw up a statement about the universal sacramentality of the church in the direction outlined by that decisive letter designed to compose the Feeney affair. The development and advancement of Vatican II over the 1949 letter is found in the formulation "the fullness of the means of salvation." Unlike the letter, the *Dogmatic Constitution on the Church* recognizes the ecclesial realities and the effective means of salvation in other Christian churches and communities, while reserving for the Catholic Church the fullness of these means. At this point the fathers of the council direct their attention to institutions — the separated churches and communities and the Catholic Church — not to individuals taken singly in the way they capitalize on the means of salvation. It is not implied that the means are always utilized properly in the Roman Catholic Church or that some particular means could not be actualized better in a separated church or community. Nor does it suggest that the Catholic Church has arrived at a state of perfection while the other Christian churches

31 Cf. also, Art. 4.

have not. It is clear from many texts of the council that the pilgrim people of God, including people who are not fully incorporated into the one body of Christ, are continually renewing themselves through the grace of Christ until they reach the definitive eschatological events.

One comment about the unity of thought in this sentence. On the one hand the Catholic Church is portrayed as the "all-embracing means of salvation"; on the other it is identified as the "fullness of the means of salvation," which implies that partial means exist elsewhere (a fact which is expressly affirmed earlier in the article). The more traditional teaching regarding the Catholic Church as the total and all-embracing means of salvation is juxtaposed to the more recent theological view of the church as the fullness of the means of salvation. As a result the transition from one view to the other in one sentence is rather rough and discomfiting. Here is another instance of the generally accepted view that the documents of Vatican II are not of one pattern, that the new and the old are often juxtaposed.

We turn now to the *Decree on the Apostolate of the Laity* for a final reference to the instrumental role of the church in the work of salvation:

The mission of the Church concerns the salvation of men, which is to be achieved by belief in Christ and by His grace. Hence the apostolate of the Church and of all her members is primarily designed to manifest Christ's message by words and deeds and to communicate His grace to the world (Art. 6; cf. Art. 2).

The passage requires little commentary. It is clear that the whole church is apostolic and missionary in structure and that in this decree the fathers of the council spell out the apostolic task of its members. As members of the Church of Christ they are not just permitted but empowered and obliged to act as instruments of salvation.[32]

[32] Other references to salvation in and through the church include the following: *Decree on the Missionary Activity of the Church*, Art. 6; *Pastoral Constitution on the Church in the Modern World*, Arts. 3, 89; *Decree on the Eastern Catholic Churches*, Art. 26; *Decree on the Instruments of Social Communication*, Art. 3. Cf. also John XXIII's apostolic constitution *Humanae Salutis* (December 25, 1961), convoking the council for sometime in 1962; there he calls the spouse of Christ "the master of truth and minister of salvation." Also Bishop Geise: "As the sacrament of the close unity of the entire human race, and as the universal instrument of salvation in Christ, the Church proclaims the Gospel to all men, so that through its preaching they may be brought to faith, and that through baptism and sharing in the mystery of the eucharist they may be incorporated *fully* into the body of Christ. The purpose of this missionary activity is that the Church be made present everywhere as a community of salvation." *Third Session. Council Speeches of Vatican II*, p. 275.

Thus the council teaches that while the church is a total and all-embracing means of salvation and communicates the salvific fruit of redemption, it is also the sign of salvation for any manifestation of grace in the world and allows for the working of God in Christ outside its visible boundaries, a working that leads people to the church.

3. *Grace Outside the Church*

The Roman Catholic Church has traditionally and officially acknowledged the presence of grace outside its visible limits.[33] Thus when the fathers of Vatican II expressly recognize the existence of this grace, they draw upon a settled doctrinal position. They confess the grace of other Christian churches and communities, grace in the form of "many elements of sanctification and of truth,"[34] or more specifically, "the written word of God, the life of grace, faith, hope, and charity, along with other interior gifts of the Holy Spirit and visible elements."[35] "These elements, however, as gifts properly belonging to the Church of Christ, possess an inner dynamism toward Catholic unity."[36] These salvific graces form the basis of Christian unity and are oriented by their very existence to the union of the churches and communities, a union with and in the Catholic Church.

The ecclesial grace of separated churches and communities is easier to detect and acknowledge than the offer of grace to people who do not accept Christ or his church, or who perhaps have not heard of either. Vatican II teaches that for this direct offer of grace too the church is a sign, an instrument, and a sacrament.[37] We have

---

[33] Cf. the error of the Jansenists (DS 2305) and of Quesnel (DS 2426).

[34] *Dogmatic Constitution on the Church*, Art. 8. Bishop Carli would have revised the text to read "some elements" (*quaedam*) rather than "many" (*plura*). *Acta*, Vol. II, Pars I, p. 293. Bishop Simons, who after the council would write a book challenging the historical and New Testament origins of the papacy, *Infallibility and the Evidence* (Springfield, Ill.: Templegate, 1968), proposes to add that outside the church there are not only many elements of sanctification but also "persons sanctified by the grace of Christ." *Ibid*. The grace of Christ sanctifies people outside the visible boundaries of the church, and the result is that they are impelled toward "visible and complete catholic unity."

[35] *Decree on Ecumenism*, Art. 3.

[36] *Dogmatic Constitution on the Church*, Art. 8. Note 6 in the corresponding Art. 9 of the 1962 draft (*Acta*, Vol. I, Pars IV, p. 20) and note 22 in Art. 7 of the 1963 draft (*Acta*, Vol. II, Pars I, p. 225) refer to the canonical ruling that "in virtue of baptism every baptized person is subject to the laws of the church."

[37] Cf. F. Rickens, S.J.: "All these visible realities impart a like sacramental character also to the grace given outside of Christendom. This grace too is for this reason grace of the one all-embracing sacrament of salvation. For the one visible church is

already noted some council statements which seem to indicate the direct salvific action of God outside the church, but it is important to examine them and others more closely.

One such passage is the beginning of Chapter 2 of the *Dogmatic Constitution on the Church*:

At all times and among every people, God has given welcome to whosoever fears Him and does what is right (cf. Acts 10, 35). It has pleased God, however, to make men holy and save them not merely as individuals without any mutual bonds, but by making them into a single people, a people which acknowledges Him in truth and serves Him in holiness (Art. 9).

The scriptural reference is to Peter's amazement and joy at the way God brought about the conversion of the centurion Cornelius: "Truly I perceive that God shows no partiality, but in every nation any one who fears him and does what is right is acceptable to him" (Acts 10, 34f). The offer of salvation is not confined to the time after Christ, nor only to the people who have received the good news in Christ. Saving grace is a reality wherever people exist or have existed or will exist. In what sense is the present and welcoming God a grace that is ecclesial? One could say that it is ecclesial in the sense that it is granted *in view of* the church. Because the heavenly Father wishes to form a church, a community of salvation, he is present to every person and accepts whoever works justice and is religiously devoted to him. God offers the grace of life in order to form an ecclesial community.[38] So reads the passage just quoted. So also earlier in the *Constitution*:

Already from the beginning of the world the foreshadowing of the Church took place. . . . At the end of time she will achieve her glorious fulfillment. Then, as may be read in the holy Fathers, all just men from the time of Adam, 'from Abel, the just one, to the last of the elect', will be gathered together with the Father in the universal Church (Art. 2).

Another section of the *Dogmatic Constitution on the Church* holds the greatest promise for enlightenment on our subject. It is Article 16, the third of three articles designed to clarify the various ways in which people in the world belong or are related to the catholic unity of the people of God.[39] Again, there is no doubt here

the symbolic, representative, historical realization of the all-embracing, objective salvation." "Ecclesia . . . universale salutis sacramentum. Theologische Erwägungen zur Lehre der Dogmatischen Konstitution *De Ecclesia* über die Kirchenzugehörigkeit," *Scholastik* 40 (1964), p. 382; cf. pp. 369, 377f.

[38] *The Pastoral Constitution on the Church in the Modern World*, Art. 32.

[39] Cf. the end of Art. 13: "All men are called to be part of this catholic unity of the

about the ecclesial character of all grace. This is clear from the very way in which the question is posed to the council fathers. It is a question of how people of varying historical and salvational situations are related to the people of God. The first sentence of the article is decisive in this regard: "Finally, those who have not yet received the gospel are related in various ways to the People of God." God calls people, not to an isolated and individualistic relationship with himself, but to a community of the saved, to the people of God.[40]

The council situates first of all the community of Israel, the people of the covenants that always remain dear to God. There follows a paragraph on those who acknowledge a creator; foremost among these are the Moslems who believe in the God of Abraham and who are dedicated to the one God. This is the context in which we find an important statement about the presence of the Savior God to all peoples:

Nor is God Himself far distant from those who in shadows and images seek the unknown God, for it is He who gives to all men life and breath and every other gift (cf. Acts 17, 25-28), and who as Savior wills that all men be saved (cf. 1 Tim 2, 4) (Art. 16).

God is accorded the beautiful name of Savior since, as is evident from the classical text in 1 Timothy, he wills all men and women to be saved. He is present to them all, tendering them the gift of salvation. Grace is the saving presence of God himself, close to those who seek him even in shadows and images. If they seek him, he can be found together with life and salvation:

Those also can attain to everlasting salvation who through no fault of their own do not know the gospel of Christ or His Church, yet sincerely seek God and, moved by grace, strive by their deeds to do His will as it is known to them through the dictates of conscience (Art. 16).

People of God, a unity which is harbinger of the universal peace it promotes. And there belong to it or are related to it in various ways, the Catholic faithful as well as all who believe in Christ, and indeed the whole of mankind. For all men are called to salvation by the grace of God."

[40] The 1963 draft of the statement met with adverse criticism for its individualism. Cf. *Acta*, Vol. III, Pars I, p. 206. The same *relatio* espouses a definite communitarian concept of grace: "Christ redeemed all men objectively, and he calls and directs all men to the church. But all grace bears some communitarian character and is oriented toward the church." *Ibid.*, p. 206. The individualism was remedied by the more communitarian wording of the present decree. The call to a community is even clearer in Art. 2 of the *Decree on the Church's Missionary Acitivity*: "But it has not pleased God to call men to share His life merely as individuals without any mutual bonds. Rather, He wills to mold them into a people in which His sons, once scattered abroad, can be gathered together (cf. Jn 11, 52)."

We need not concern ourselves about this teaching which has been official for more than a century, nor about the theology which the council preferred to presuppose rather than to analyze (against the wishes of some fathers who requested an elaboration of the issue).[41] But we may note a slight change, both in terminology and doctrine. As we noted above, it has been customary to speak of the possibility of salvation for men and women of good conscience in terms of an implicit desire for the church (*votum implicitum ecclesiae*). That such teaching represented by the term *votum implicitum* stands behind the paragraph, however, is clear from an official footnote referring to the 1949 letter of the Holy Office in which this phraseology is employed. The suppression of *votum implicitum* is probably due to disenchantment with the term, especially since it was used indiscriminately to describe the situation of both separated Christians and the "unevangelized" in their diverse relations to the Roman Catholic Church. The suppression also indicates an advancement in the manner of conceiving the relationship of those outside to the community of the church.

Of crucial importance is the specific reference to the influence of grace (*sub gratiae influxu*) which aids people to carry out the will of God as they perceive it in the dictates of their consciences. What this grace is we are left to surmise for ourselves, but we can suggest that it is the presence of God himself together with other gifts such as qualities of mind and will, religion, parents, neighbors, etc. Some fathers of the council propose to state explicitly here what benefits and realities the so-called "unbelievers" lack as a consequence of their distance from Christianity and to affirm emphatically that they are deprived of the ordinary and normal means of sanctification. Similarly a relatively large number of bishops (152) wished to brand the state of these "unbelievers," living as they are in the messianic age, as abnormal. But the doctrinal commission thought that these requests were adequately met by the strong insistence on missionary activity expressed in the last sentence of Article 16 and in the whole of Article 17.[42] It is interesting to compare the outlook of the 152 bishops concerning the abnormal state of those living without explicit belief in Christ with the position of some theologians today (and then) who view Christianity as the extraordinary means of salvation, and who consider salvational modes outside Christianity as normal and ordinary.[43]

[41] *Acta*, Vol. III, Pars I, p. 206.

[42] *Ibid*.

[43] Cf. H. R. Schlette, *Towards a Theology of Religions* (New York: Herder and Herder, 1966).

The same comments apply to the next sentence in which the words *divina providentia, auxilia ad salutem necessaria* and *divina gratia* are employed: "Nor does divine Providence deny the help necessary for salvation to those who, without blame on their part, have not yet arrived at an explicit knowledge of God, but who strive to live a good life, thanks to His grace." Some clue to the understanding of this grace is provided in the next sentence: "Whatever goodness or truth is found among them is looked upon by the Church as a preparation for the gospel. She regards such qualities as given by Him who enlightens all men so that they may finally have life." This grace, present to those who have not yet achieved an explicit knowledge of God, includes whatever qualities of truth and goodness are found among them. They themselves do not perceive the ultimate source of these qualities, but the church can identify the font as him who enlightens every man. According to the prologue of John's gospel it is the Word who enlightens every man coming into the world (Jn 1, 9). It is important to note that these qualities of truth and goodness are not purely "natural" in origin or purpose; they are taken up into the history of salvation, constitute a *praeparatio evangelica*, and are granted in view of divine life.

The final paragraph of Article 16 points up a real salvific and missionary activity of the church, namely, rescuing people from error and hopelessness:

But rather often men, deceived by the Evil One, have become caught up in futile reasoning and have exchanged the truth of God for a lie, serving the creature rather than the Creator (cf. Rm 1, 21. 25). Or some there are who, living and dying in a world without God, are subject to utter hopelessness. Consequently, to promote the glory of God and procure the salvation of all such men, and mindful of the command of the Lord, 'Preach the gospel to every creature' (Mk 16, 16), the Church painstakingly fosters her missionary work.

This paragraph represents a rather thorough restructuring of the 1963 draft. According to this earlier draft "the church is ceaselessly impelled to lead all the non-baptized to the body of Christ so that thus the way of salvation may be broadened for them." [44] The contention of the 1963 draft is that the way of salvation is wider and safer in the church. But it implies thereby that salvation is also possible outside the visible unity of the church.

That this grace outside the church is directed to the gospel and the church is evident from the whole article and the *relatio*.

[44] *Acta*, Vol. II, Pars I, p. 222.

B. Christopher Butler scores the unclarity of the article: "It is true that, in the crucial paragraph in Chapter II which explicitly adverts to non-Catholics, the language is vague and curiously un-theological."[45] We concur with his judgment on the vagueness of the language but not on its untheological character, for the article manifests some traditional theological positions.

The same theme receives a slightly different expression in the *Decree on the Church's Missionary Activity*:

This universal design of God for the salvation of the human race is not carried out exclusively in the soul of a man, with a kind of secrecy. Nor is it achieved merely through those multiple en-deavors, including religious ones, by which men search for God, groping for Him that they may by chance find Him (though He is not far from any one of us) (cf. Acts. 17, 27). For these attempts need to be enlightened and purified, even though, through the kindly workings of Divine Providence, they may sometimes serve as a guidance course toward the true God, or as a preparation for the gos-pel (Art. 3).

We notice especially the words "exclusively" and "merely." They imply that God does work out his design secretly within the soul and that a person can perceive it through various actions, typ-ically religious and non-religious actions.

Before turning to the *Decree on Ecumenism* we may cite again in this context, as we did above in dealing with the church as the universal sacrament of salvation, a pertinent sentence from Article 48: "Sitting at the right hand of the Father, He is continually active in the world, leading men to the Church, and through her joining them more closely to Himself and making them partakers of His glorious life by nourishing them with His own body and blood." The direct sense of the words is that Christ actively leads people to the church and then through the church unites them more directly to himself.

At this point we may cite other council statements acknowledg-ing the presence of salvation and truth outside the boundaries of the Roman Catholic Church. We wish to draw attention to these affirmations without delving into the disputed and unresolved question of the precise relationship between the Roman Catholic Church and other Christian churches and ecclesial communities.

The clearest expression of this fact is found in the council's *De-cree on Ecumenism*:

[45] *De Ecclesia. The Constitution on the Church of Vatican Council II.* Ed. by E. H. Peters, C.S.P., foreword by Basil C. Butler, O.S.B., with a commentary by G. Baum, O.S.A. (Glen Rock, N.J.: Paulist Press, 1965), p. 10.

Moreover some, even very many, of the most significant elements or endowments which together go to build up and give life to the Church herself can exist outside the visible boundaries of the Catholic Church: the written word of God; the life of grace; faith, hope, and charity, along with other interior gifts of the Holy Spirit and visible elements. All of these, which come from Christ and lead back to Him, belong by right to the One Church of Christ (Art. 3).

An acknowledgement of these realities appeared in the first draft and reappeared in all subsequent drafts of the decree. The first draft, it is true, included a negative statement of this truth, namely, that "separated Christians are deprived of many means of salvation." [46] This implies of course (and the draft mentions them explicitly) that they also possess many means of salvation.

These realities of sanctification, which derive from Christ and the Spirit, are found beyond the visible limits of the Roman Catholic Church and really (Pope Paul adds "by right") belong to the one Church of Christ. These realities, present within Christian communities other than the Roman Catholic Church, are able to vivify and build up the Church of Christ. What we wish to stress here is that among the Christian churches, the Catholic Church does not have a monopoly on ecclesial realities and that the means of salvation are found in other Christian communities.[47] This fact is elucidated in the next two paragraphs of Article 3:

The brethren divided from us also carry out many of the sacred actions of the Christian religion. Undoubtedly, in ways that vary according to the condition of each Church or Community, these actions can truly engender a life of grace, and can be rightly described as capable of providing access to the community of salvation.

It follows that these separated Churches and Communities, though we believe they suffer from defects already mentioned, have by no means been deprived of significance and importance in the mystery of salvation. For the Spirit of Christ has not refrained from using them as means of salvation which derive their efficacy from the very fullness of grace and truth entrusted to the Catholic Church.

The word "Catholic" in the last paragraph was inserted by Pope Paul and it seems to be demanded by the tenor of the final sentence. The council affirms that the fullness of truth and of grace (including the means of grace) resides in the Catholic Church and

---

[46] *Acta*, Vol. I, Pars IV, p. 82. *Schema Decreti De Oecumenismo. Acta*, Vol II, Pars V, pp. 413f. *Acta*, Vol. III, Pars II, pp. 298f.

[47] Cf. Art. 4 for other statements about the riches of Christ found among the separated brothers.

that the efficacy of the means of grace that obtains in other Christian communities ultimately stems from the Catholic Church. With this statement the council assumes an aspect of the traditional stance of the Catholic Church, namely, that it regards itself as the original means of salvation. Still, if other Christian communities can boast of various means of salvation, it is not clear why these means become efficacious only through the Catholic Church.

Perhaps some clue is given in the following sentence of Article 3: "It was to the apostolic college alone, of which Peter is the head, that we believe our Lord entrusted all the blessings of the New Covenant. . . ." The argument would be this: since the Catholic Church maintains continuity with the church of Peter and the apostles, it alone received the blessings of the new covenant and if they are found elsewhere it is because they derived from the Catholic Church. Accordingly the Catholic Church functioned as a benefactor at the time other communities were separated from it, and it continues to function in this capacity today.

The Holy Spirit precedes the heralds of the gospel. The council fathers acknowledge this sequence of grace: "Sometimes He visibly anticipates the apostles' action, just as he unceasingly accompanies and directs it in different ways."[48] Another valuable reference to the activity of the Holy Spirit in the world is found in the *Pastoral Constitution on the Church in the Modern World*:

All this holds true not only for Christians, but for all men of good will in whose hearts grace works in an unseen way. For, since Christ died for all men, and since the ultimate vocation of man is in fact one, and divine, we ought to believe that the Holy Spirit in a manner known only to God offers to every man the possibility of being associated with the paschal mystery (Art. 22).

In another place, in fact immediately after quoting from Article 14 of the *Dogmatic Constitution on the Church* concerning the necessity of the church, the *Decree on the Church's Missionary Activity* adds this paragraph:

Therefore, though God in ways known to Himself can lead those inculpably ignorant of the gospel to that faith without which it is impossible to please Him (Heb 11, 6), yet a necessity lies upon the Church (cf. 1 Cor 9, 16), and at the same time a sacred duty, to preach the gospel. Hence missionary activity today as always retains its power and necessity (Art. 7).

God can lead men and women to a saving faith even though they

---

[48] *Decree on the Church's Missionary Activity*, Art. 4. The scriptural references are Acts 10, 44–47; 11, 15; 15, 8.

have no contact with the gospel or the church. In two juxtaposed paragraphs the conciliar fathers can proclaim: 1) the necessity of the church, 2) the necessity of mission, and 3) the action of God leading people to faith and baptism.[49] The continuing mission of the church (the thrust of the whole decree) retains its urgency despite the likelihood of saving faith outside the preaching of the gospel. At the same time the church still functions as the authenticating sign of God's presence, word, and sacrament.

A similar juxtaposition of thought is discernible in Article 9 of the same decree on the missions. The council fathers teach that the missionary activity of the church manifests and fulfills the will of God in the history of the world. They state: "In the course of this history God plainly works out the history of salvation by means of missions." After a reference to the work of the church in bringing about the presence of Christ by means of the sacraments, the decree continues:

But whatever truth and grace are to be found among the nations, as a sort of secret presence to God, this activity frees from all taint of evil and restores to Christ its maker, who overthrows the devil's domain and wards off the manifold malice of vice. And so, whatever good is found to be sown in the hearts and minds of men, or in the rites and cultures peculiar to various peoples, is not lost. More than that, it is healed, ennobled, and perfected for the glory of God, the shame of the demon, and the bliss of men (Art. 9).

There is a secret presence of God to the nations which is realized in the gifts of truth and grace. The church can purify, authenticate, and perfect them but only because they are already present in the hearts and minds of people. Through the ages individuals expressed their commitment to a Beyond in manifold religious systems. The fathers of the council acknowledge this commitment in their *Declaration on the Relationship of the Church to Non-Christian Religions*:

The Catholic Church rejects nothing which is true and holy in these religions. She looks with sincere respect upon those ways of conduct and of life, those rules and teachings which, though differing in many particulars from what she holds and sets forth, nevertheless often reflect a ray of that Truth which enlightens all men (Art. 2).

These religious thoughts and patterns cannot be dismissed as merely "natural," for they frequently stem from Christ himself who

---

[49] Cf. Suso Brechter's elucidation of this article in terms of the axiom *extra ecclesiam nulla salus* and the universal instrumentality of the church (above, note 27).

is the light of the world. Christ is active throughout the world, implanting his word and light of truth.

These passages from various documents of Vatican II allow us to draw some conclusions about its general trend and position on the subject of the church and salvation, specifically, the issue of the universal sacramentality of the church. Following the lead of ancient tradition and of some contemporary ecclesiologists, the council applies the concept of sacramentality to the church as a whole. As the sacrament of salvation the church is a clear sign to the nations, manifesting the loving will of the heavenly Father in the person of Jesus Christ. It is the pillar of truth and the visible embodiment of the hopes and aspirations of men and women, bringing to mind the forgiveness and reconciliation which is present now but which will be perfected in the eschatological moment of Christ's return.[50]

As universal sacrament the church is not an empty address to the nations. It is a powerful sign, effecting the reconciliation of people through the preaching of the gospel, the celebration of the sacraments, the acts of loving service, and all its ecclesial functions. The

---

[50] That this position is discernible in the decrees of the council is confirmed by several commentators. Besides those previously mentioned, cf. C. Moeller: "The richness of chapters 5 and 6 is obvious. I believe this is the first time a Conciliar constitution on the Church has brought out so clearly the *finality of the Church*; the holiness of its members, the sanctification of the People of God and, through it, in it, the sanctification of humanity, the transfiguration of the universe." "History of *Lumen Gentium's* Structure and Ideas," in *Vatican II. An Interfaith Appraisal.* Ed. by J. H. Miller, C.S.C. (Notre Dame, Ind.: University of Notre Dame Press, 1966), p. 138. Also E. Schillebeeckx, O.P., who interprets the council's use of the phrase *sacramentum mundi* in terms of the church as the full manifestation and epiphany of universal salvation: "De Ecclesia ut sacramento mundi," in *Acta Congressus Internationalis De Theologia Concilii Vaticani II* (Rome: Typis Polyglottis Vaticanis, 1968), pp. 48–53. G. Baum, O.S.A., offers a similar interpretation of the axiom; he says that Vatican II retains "the statement that outside the Church there is no salvation, but the conciliar documents also make it quite clear that this sentence is no longer taught *eodem sensu eademque sententia*. According to the repeated teaching of Vatican Council II there is plentiful salvation outside the Church. God is redemptively at work in the whole of humanity. What remains true about the ancient statement is that the redemptive action of God among men prefigures, prepares or manifests the Church. Wherever grace is given, it is given in view of the Church — and in this sense there is no salvation apart from the Church." "The Magisterium in A Changing Church," in *Man as Man and Believer. Concilium*, Vol. 21 (New York: Paulist Press, 1967), p. 69. E. Loffeld, C.S.Sp., however, interprets Vatican II in stronger terms; he speaks of an influence of the church in the salvific effect of non-Christian religions; in fact, "pagans" who begin to live by the Spirit of love are already church in an initial manner. "De functione salvifica religionum praechristianarum in contactu praeparando pleno cum Christo eiusque Ecclesia," in *Acta Congressus*, pp. 383–388.

church is effective, however, only through the presence of Christ who both sends his Spirit and is made present through its sacred actions.

The council prefers not to cite the axiom (outside the church no salvation) in theological contexts which traditionally evoked its use. This preference results in a doctrinal advancement. It becomes more apparent that salvation is possible outside the Church of Christ and that the church as sacrament is the necessary sign of salvation wherever people are being saved through the grace of God in Christ. At times there are resonances of the former theology of ecclesial "influence," namely, that the grace of God flows through the church and so reaches men and women at a distance from the church. But there are only traces of this theology; the emphasis has shifted to the church as sign and finality.

The council furthermore advances an acknowledgement of the means of salvation outside the manifest boundaries of the Roman Catholic Church. It recognizes that the ecclesial realities of other Christian churches and communities serve as genuine sources of grace and salvation, though it claims that these realities belong by right to the Catholic Church.

While the council passes over entirely the question of the salvation of unbaptized infants who die before reaching the age of reason, it reiterates the traditional teaching that the possibility of salvation exists for all peoples even though they have not received the good news of Christ or have only received it inadequately. The grace of Christ is present to all, fostering a saving faith that ultimately is directed to full incorporation into the church. The grace of Christ, being social and communitarian, orients people toward the community of the church.

Chapter 3

Salvation Outside the Church
And Some Theologians

Having examined the documents of Vatican II as they relate to the axiom outside the church no salvation, we proceed to trace the thought of four twentieth-century Roman Catholic theologians on the same issue. All four theologians dealt with the axiom both before and after Vatican II; all four manifested a development of thought in regard to the axiom, less so in the case of Yves Congar and Karl Rahner whose theological careers began in the 1930's, and more so in the case of Gregory Baum and Hans Küng who appeared on the theological scene in the late 1950's and early 1960's.

1. Yves Congar

We turn now to Yves Congar, O.P., a pioneer in the fields of contemporary Roman Catholic ecclesiology and ecumenical theology. Since the early 1930's he has assiduously devoted his energies to the topics of church and ecumenism, topics to which he felt called as to a mission field. We select his writings for review because they span a period of four decades and have significantly influenced the church's view of itself.[1] His books and articles on the church contributed greatly to the advancement in self-understanding which the Roman Catholic Church attained in Vatican Council II. But the influence was also mutual, for we perceive that his writings during and after the council take up themes of the great conciliar decrees, especially the concept of the universal sac-

[1] Cf. his personal account of the attraction he felt for the work of ecumenical dialogue and an autobiographical sketch of his involvement in the movement from the 1930's through the 1950's: *Dialogue Between Christians* (London: Geoffrey Chapman, 1966), pp. 1–51.

ramentality of the church. Owing to various influences, including Vatican II, Congar broaches the subject of salvation outside the church more directly and clearly in his recent writings than in those of his early years.

In his influential study, *Divided Christendom. A Catholic Study of the Problem of Reunion*,[2] regarded by many as a classic of Catholic ecumenism, Congar devotes Chapter 7 to the ecclesial status of non-Roman Christians. In this context he occasionally enunciates principles which have a bearing on our subject.

He pursues the thesis that all the saved, even the unevangelized, belong in some fashion to the church. "Even among the 'unbelievers' there are people who are saved and who are consequently members of the mystical body."[3] If they enjoy the presence of grace, if they are justified and saved, they are joined to the body of Christ, the church. "The church is by definition the body of Christ. These souls belong to the church, and that which they have received of grace is not foreign to the church, which is the mystical body of the Lord."[4] Grace claims the unevangelized for the church. The same principle obtains with even greater reason for the separated brothers who believe in the Lord Jesus. Grace incorporates them into the mystical body of Christ:

Thus it is that the church has members who appear to be outside it. They belong to it invisibly and incompletely but they really belong. They belong to the church insofar as they belong to Christ, because what unites them to Christ is a fiber of his mystical body, a constitutive element of his church.[5]

It would seem to follow from this passage and others like it that the mystical body is not coterminous with the visible Roman Catholic Church — a teaching which Pius XII would reject six years later in his encyclical *Mystici Corporis*.

If it is possible for the unevangelized or the separated brothers to be joined to the mystical body in some fashion, it follows that the

---

[2] London: G. Bles, The Centenary Press, 1939. French edition: *Chrétiens désunis, principes d'un 'Oecuménisme' Catholique* (Paris: Les Éditions du Cerf, 1937). Translations are prepared here from the French since the published English version is quite free, and at times inaccurate.

[3] *Chrétiens désunis*, p. 278; *Divided Christendom*, p. 222. He realizes that the word "unbelievers" does not properly describe those incorporated into Christ by faith and love.

[4] *Chrétiens désunis*, p. 278: "Or, l'Église est par définition le Corps du Christ. Ces ânres, pour autant, appartiennent donc à l'Église, et ce qu'elles ont reçu de grâce n'est pas étranger à l'Eglise, qui est le Corps mystique du Seigneur." *Divided Christendom*, p. 222.

[5] *Chrétiens désunis*, p. 292; *Divided Christendom*, p. 234.

reality of salvation is not coterminous with the visible Catholic Church:

This is the reason, as it seems to us, why his real action as Savior reaches beyond the visible work of salvation, the unique ark upon mortal waters, which is his Catholic Church. It is the reason why the reality of his merciful action as Savior reaches beyond his visible kingdom and why the church too saves more [persons] than it rules and incorporates secretly more members than it can number as subjects.[6]

The Catholic Church remains the visible ark of salvation and the visible realm of Christ's kingship, but salvation does not necessarily demand a manifest enclosure in the ark or an evident subjection to the rule of Christ. Following the best of theological tradition, Congar refuses to interpret the image of the ark or of the kingdom in a rigid and exclusive fashion. Salvation is possible for those outside the visible ark. But those on the outside are still saved in an ecclesial fashion since they are incorporated secretly as members of the church. Thus the axiom holds: outside the church no salvation. Note however that Christ is operative salvifically beyond the visible confines of the church.

Later in the same chapter Congar refers once again to the efficacy of the church in the realm of salvation:

Precisely because one cannot be saved without an effective belonging to the church and because one cannot receive the Holy Spirit outside of the church, it must be said that anyone who is in error but actually in good faith really belongs to the church. . . . But this is clearly a secondary truth, true only when seen within the primary truth and presupposing the affirmation: *extra ecclesiam catholicam, nulla salus*.[7]

He presupposes that the Roman Catholic Church is the locus of salvation and of the action of the Holy Spirit. The person in good faith belongs to the church and can only find the Holy Spirit in relation to the church. "This incorporation in Christ and this salvation in him are not possible except through the ministry of a group [the hierarchy of the church] without which justifying faith would not be preached and the sacraments which incorporate would not be given."[8] He strongly stresses salvation in relation to the church.

---

[6] *Chrétiens désunis*, p. 280; *Divided Christendom*, p. 224.

[7] *Chrétiens désunis*, p. 294; *Divided Christendom*, p. 236.

[8] *Chrétiens désunis*, p. 88; *Divided Christendom*, p. 70. Cf. also: "Because God in his mercy extends the vivifying efficacy of the church's ministry beyond the visible bounds of the ecclesiastical body, we are not thereby dispensed from the primordial and serious duty of being rooted in the truth and entering the company of the

There is even an impression, common enough among Catholics of the time, that the Holy Spirit and all grace come to those outside by way of the church.

In an article published the following year Congar reiterates his thought that the life of the Holy Spirit is received only in the church:

On the one hand, indeed, the Holy Spirit, who is the Spirit of love, is the same in all the faithful; he dwells in them, animates them, and re-unites them all in one same body of Christ. On the other hand, since we do not lay hold of the life of the Holy Spirit except in the church, whose soul he is, since it is the church which explains the Christian life, and since it is the life of all which explains and establishes that of the member, a life of brotherly communion in love is for the faithful the condition, even more, the vital milieu of all that he can be and do as a Christian.[9]

Important for our purposes is the view that the life of the Spirit is possessed only in the church. In his later writings Congar will mitigate his language and allow for a looser relationship between the church and the Holy Spirit.

The mediatorship of the church is much in evidence in an article which he published some ten years later (1947). Given the fact that God deals with people in an incarnational, human, and social fashion, he insists that salvation comes to them in the same manner:

He [God] revealed himself to men and accorded them salvation by treating them humanly, socially, according to the mode which suited them — becoming incarnate, then associating with himself certain men for the salvation and illumination of the others. The church is the work of the Holy Spirit and of the apostles. After the ascension they and the Holy Spirit are charged with the realization of the work of Jesus Christ; and in his discourse after the supper (which may be called more exactly the discourse of his apostolic love), Jesus announced the sending of both the Holy Spirit (Jn 14; 16) and the apostles (Jn 17).[10]

The apostles and the whole church continue the work of Christ by mediating salvation and illumination. The Holy Spirit is part of the missionary team, but the extent of his influence is not stated here. It

---

redeemed whom he has willed to call and constitute visibly into a Church." *Chrétiens désunis*, p. 294; *Divided Christendom*, pp. 236f.

[9] "Je Crois en la Sainte Église. . . ," *Revue des Jeunes* (January 1938), pp. 85–92. Reprinted in *Sainte Église; etudes et approches ecclésiologiques* (Paris: Éditions du Cerf, 1963), pp. 9–17. The quotation is from the reprint, p. 13.

[10] "Apostolicité," *Catholicisme, hier, aujourd'hui, demain*. Ed. by G. Jacquemet. Vol. 1 (Paris: Letouzey et Ané, 1947), col. 728.

is not affirmed or denied that he is confined to the preaching of the apostles.

In 1951 Congar addressed himself to our subject directly in the popular magazine *Ecclesia. Lectures Chrétiennes.* A reader of the magazine requests enlightenment on the axiom and Congar responds with the suggestion that it would be better not to use the axiom since it is not self-explanatory, and a proper understanding of it requires much explanation. Congar explains that the adage is not designed to decide the subjective fate of individuals: "In its material or literal tenor it concerns the objective conditions of salvation, not the fact of salvation of this or that person."[11] Congar does not use the term instrument of salvation, but he approximates the concept by saying that God "has decided to save them [men] in and by his church."[12] The church is really involved in the salvation of individuals: "If Peter, Paul or John are saved, they are saved in and by the church, being dependent on it in a way that perhaps escapes us but which is nonetheless real."[13] The reason for this dependence is because "the church exercises through space and time the ministry of salvation which is in Jesus Christ alone."[14]

Individuals who recognize the church and Jesus have the obligation of entering the church. But good faith and invincible ignorance exist in the world. Still, for those being saved through good faith there is always some attachment to the church:

How does this salvation interiorly communicated by God lead to Jesus Christ and to his church? It is the task of theologians to find an explication. But none of them thus elaborated are imposed as Catholic dogma. It is enough for the faithful to know that all salvation of God passes through Jesus Christ and incorporates [a person] into the church.[15]

Four statements of position are of note in this short response. The first is the admonition to avoid the use of the axiom since it is generally misleading. Not only Congar but many other theologians will repeat this admonition. The second is that Congar requires some kind of real attachment to the church for salvation: those who are being saved outside the visible church are incorporated into the church in some real fashion. The third statement of position is that salvation really stems from Jesus and leads to the church. Apparently Jesus works outside the church to incorporate men and

[11] "Hors de l'Église pas de salut," no. 26, May 1951, p. 34.
[12] *Ibid.*
[13] *Ibid.*
[14] *Ibid.*
[15] *Ibid.*

women into the church. The fourth is that people are saved in and
by the church. Here Congar stresses more than he will later the
effective instrumentality of the church in the work of salvation. But
he refrains from providing details about the way in which the
church exercises the ministry through space and time.

In 1952 Congar outlined once again his view of the universal
efficacy of the church. It appears in the published notes of a course
he gave to the mother superiors of some religious congregations.
Speaking to the subject of the duality and unity of the church, he
finds occasion to interject an interpretation of the saving mission of
the church. "The church," he says, "has been instituted by God to
transmit to us the grace of Jesus. Thus we view the church as the
regulator of the means of grace."[16] Again: "The church has precisely this mission, to extend and to apply to all men the salvation
acquired in Jesus Christ as in its cause, to carry the seed of Easter
until it bears full fruit in the parousia."[17] The salvation of Jesus
reaches human beings through the missionary presence and activity of the church. The saving grace of the resurrection takes root in
the church, and through the Church of Christ individuals share in
its fruits. The mediation of the church simply conforms to the general manner of divine action in the world through tangible and
human instruments: God acts through intermediaries.

In another context he states: "There is no immediacy of God.
Sometimes the presence of God is made known to the soul in a
momentary touch, but it is momentary because we are actually in an
intermediate situation in which we do not have the immediate
presence or enjoyment of God."[18] It is significant that in spite of the
principle of mediation,[19] or perhaps because of it, Congar acknowledges a divine touch of the soul. It is significant because the divine
touch seems to be beyond the immediate effective instrumentality
of the church. It is another way of saying that God works outside the
immediate visible instrumentality of the church.

In the second edition of *Esquisses du Mystère de L'Église*,[20]
Congar again identifies the Holy Spirit and the apostolic
institutional church as the continuators of the work of Christ. While
he proclaims the freedom of the Holy Spirit in breathing where he

[16] "Position de l'Église. Dualité et Unité." The address was printed in *Forma Gregis* 4 (1952) and reprinted in *Sainte Église*, pp. 45–67, which we cite here: p. 46.
[17] *Ibid.*, p. 55.
[18] *Ibid.*, p. 62.
[19] Cf. *ibid.*, pp. 65f: "Thus it is, as long as we are earthly and sinners. Remote from God we cannot obtain the most intimate grace of union with him except by exterior means: liturgy, hierarchy."
[20] Paris: Les Éditions du Cerf, 1953.

will, that is, in not always working through the institution of the church,[21] Congar is not directly concerned about the work of the Spirit at a distance from the visible church. But at times he alludes to the traditional view of the instrumentality of the church. For instance, he cites the church as "the organism of the messianic work, the visible body of the means of grace."[22] Earlier he says that the Holy Spirit and the apostolic/institutional church have a common function: "to apply throughout space and time the universal cause of salvation, that is, the reconciled life realized in and by Jesus Christ."[23]

An alteration in position is perceptible in an article which Congar wrote in 1956. There he sketches the history and theology of the adage *extra ecclesiam nulla salus*. In his conclusion he notes Pius XII's teaching (*Mystici Corporis*) that those outside the visible structure of the Roman Catholic Church, even if they are endowed with divine grace, are not to be regarded as members of the body of Christ. Still, according to the encyclical, they are oriented (*ordinari*) toward the church:

That is to say that the realities of grace which are found in them are directed in themselves to be incorporated into the visible body of Jesus Christ, the whole of which is the *res* and *sacramentum* of salvation. Thus the salvation eventually assured these non-Catholics is not given *extra ecclesiam*. The Catholic Church remains the only divinely established and authorized institution (*sacramentum*) of salvation, and the grace that exists in the world is related to it by way of finality, if not by way of efficacy.[24]

As in his earliest works, Congar here holds that the grace of non-Catholics orients them to the Catholic Church, though this orientation cannot be called membership in the body of Christ, a terminology which Congar was willing to use before the appearance of *Mystici Corporis*. While grace is found outside the visible structure of the church, only the visible body of Christ is both the reality (*res*) and sacrament (*sacramentum*) of salvation. Since saving grace orients non-Catholics to the church, they are not saved outside the church (*extra ecclesiam*) but always with a reference to the church. This orientation is sufficient to ensure the ecclesial character of their salvation. Thus at this time Congar feels obliged to maintain

[21] E.g., p. 171; cf. the English translation: *The Mystery of the Church* (Baltimore: Helicon, 1960), p. 180.
[22] *Esquisses* . . . p. 157; *The Mystery of the Church*, pp. 168f.
[23] *Esquisses* . . . p. 155; *The Mystery of the Church*, p. 167.
[24] "Hors de l'Église, pas de salut." This passage occurs in an article written in 1956 and published in *Sainte Église*, pp. 431f.

and safeguard the axiom, while considerably reinterpreting its content.

He views the church as the divinely authorized and established *sacramentum* of salvation. Does this mean that all saving grace in the world must stem from the church as from its efficacious source? He does not seem to demand this. In scholastic fashion he draws a distinction between final and efficient causality. The church is not necessarily the efficient cause of all grace, but it is its final cause, its point of orientation, its term and model. Unfortunately Congar does not elaborate on this concept but merely tacks it to the concluding paragraph of the article. Nevertheless, the scanty evidence in this article seems to point Congar in the direction of not envisioning the church as the efficient cause of all grace in the world. This corresponds to his earlier recognition of the grace of the Holy Spirit outside the apostolic structure of the church.

The following year (1957), in a critical review of Riccardo Lombardi's book *The Salvation of the Unbeliever*,[25] Congar has occasion once more to appraise the content of the adage *extra ecclesiam nulla salus*. At the end of the review he specifies what he believes is the import of the maxim:

At the same time the meaning of the formula *Extra Ecclesiam nulla salus* (classical since the time of St. Cyprian) has been, if not exactly modified, at least made more precise. From the beginning it has indicated that grace cannot take its birth except through our Holy Mother the Church which is the second Eve and the Spouse of Jesus Christ; at the same time quite often we find the Fathers and medieval writers giving it a *personal* application and understanding it in such a sense as would exclude from salvation any individual not belonging to the body of the Catholic Church: Jews, pagans, heretics, schismatics, the excommunicated (exception being made, following St. Augustine, of those who had been injustly censured in this way). In the modern period, on the contrary, it is seen that its essence consists in the affirmation that God commissioned the Catholic Church, and it alone, as an institution for providing for the salvation for all men in Jesus Christ.[26]

In view of our historical sketch (Chapter 1) we would rather affirm that modern theologians have not just made the axiom more precise but have indeed modified it, for its classical formulation in Saint Cyprian is untenable. Judging from the last sentence of this passage, it would seem that Congar has stepped away from the more nuanced positions of his previous articles; for he seems to

[25] Westminster, Md.: The Newman Press, 1956.
[26] "Salvation and the Non-Catholic," *Blackfriars* 38 (1957), pp. 299f.

espouse what he calls the modern understanding of the axiom. Earlier in the article he speaks of an encounter with God outside the church:

Faith is presented in the Gospels as the outcome of a movement which has already begun, some time before the encounter with its object proper is made, in so far as there is present an inner disposition which can be summed up as humility of heart and a completely unegoistic openness to the promptings of the light whatever be the forms under which they are perceived. The soul, in fact, is faced with certain facts which in reality are so many messengers from God, even if they are not necessarily recognized as such, and invited to declare itself accordingly. But a man can miss encountering the positive fact of Christ without himself being at fault. Perhaps it is even possible never to encounter the fact of God as such, but rather give him other names and attain to him only under what amounts to a travesty of himself.[27]

Even before the encounter with the gospel of Christianity, a person can receive many facts which are "messengers from God." Apparently these facts — humility and openness of heart are given as the examples — do not derive even indirectly from the church. They are encountered in the many situations in which a person finds himself. A person may never encounter "the fact of God" (the true teaching about God in Jesus Christ?) but he can meet him in other names; he can even attain to him — and this is striking — in forms that are a travesty of God!

That Congar acknowledges as Catholic doctrine the gifts of light and grace existing outside the visible limits of the Catholic Church is enunciated clearly in his book *The Wide World My Parish. Salvation and its Problems*:[28]

Outside the Church, there is action of the Holy Spirit, but he is not given himself, in person; outside the Church, there are the gifts of righteousness and of life dedicated to salvation, but there is not the fullness of the good things of the Covenant — divine sonship, real incorporation in Christ, the Holy Spirit dwelling in us.[29]

In previous articles he acknowledged the presence and activity of the Spirit outside the structures of the church, but here in a manner reminiscent of Augustine he delineates more precisely the charac-

---

[27] *Ibid.*, pp. 296f.

[28] Baltimore: Helicon Press, 1961; French edition: *Vaste Monde ma Paroisse*; *vérité et dimensions du salut* (Paris: Temoignage Chrétien, 1959). A summary of the same material appears in "Hors de l'Église, point de salut?" in *Ecclesia. Lectures Chrétiennes*, no. 129 (December 1959), pp. 146–151, again as a response to a letter of inquiry.

[29] *The Wide World My Parish*, p. 111; cf. p. 120.

ter of this presence. It is an activity that falls short of real self-
donation and indwelling on the part of the Spirit. It is not clear
theologically how "the gifts of righteousness and of life dedicated
to salvation" can be present outside the church without the ensuing
gifts of "divine sonship, real incorporation in Christ" and "the Holy
Spirit dwelling in us." Perhaps Congar does not intend to deny
their presence altogether in those outside the church, but only their
fullness. Important for our purposes, however, is the recognition of
the action of the Holy Spirit and the gifts of righteousness outside
the church.

In another passage in the same book he again finds it necessary to
explain the axiom:

We have seen that that is the sense in which "Outside the Church,
no salvation" is now understood. A *wholly positive sense*, namely,
that there is in the world one and only one reality that shows forth
the gift given by God for the world's salvation, destining it to life in
fellowship with him: that gift is Jesus Christ, foretold by the prophets, suffering death and rising again for us, master of truth, who
entrusted to the Church, his Bride and Body, the treasure of the
saving word and the saving sacraments.[30]

Despite its negative formulation, the axiom bears a positive interpretation. Congar assumes that the positive sense of the formula
is the real meaning of the axiom. It symbolizes the church as the
clear manifestation of Christ, as the arrow pointing to the gift of
Jesus Christ, as the distinct light of Christ himself — themes that will
be taken up with great profit by Vatican Council II. Though Congar,
in this passage, states that Jesus "entrusted to the church, his bride
and his body, the treasure of the saving word and the saving sacraments," it does not follow that his word and saving grace reach
people only through the instrumentality of the church. The church is
"the institution to which universal salvation is committed."[31] The
church is the established institution of salvation for the whole
world but God works in salvific ways outside this church. A person
outside the church, he claims, can encounter God — even without
explicit reflection — in devotion to one's neighbor under these
causes: "Duty, Peace, Justice, Brotherhood, yes, and Human
Progress, Welfare," or even "Humanity, Freedom, Science."[32]
Idolatrous self-delusion and self-seeking can always creep in, but
these eventualities do not invalidate the possibility of encountering

[30] *Ibid.*, p. 112.
[31] *Ibid.*, p. 139.
[32] *Ibid.*, pp. 124, 127. Cf. "Au sujet du salut des non-Catholiques," *Sainte Église*,
p. 436; cf. original article in *Revue des Sciences Religieuses* 32 (1958), pp. 53–65.

God in such "tangible" realities outside the church. He does not claim that these fraternal causes must stem from the church.[33]

Congar again touched the subject of outside the church no salvation in a rather lengthy encyclopedia article.[34] He recounts the history of the axiom, providing an overview which is both well documented and clearly perceptive of the historical development of the issues. By and large, however, his summary rarely surpasses the positions of *Mystici Corporis* and the Holy Office letter of 1949. It gives only slight evidence of the ecclesial stirrings of Vatican II already in session. Still he reviews the important teaching that implicit and salvific faith may be inherent in the pursuit of such causes as justice, truth, fraternity, peace.[35] At the end of the article, pointing up especially the uses of the word *ordinari* in *Mystici Corporis*, he speaks of an attachment to the church at least by way of final cause:

Realities of grace which are found in them [non-Catholics of good faith] tend of themselves to incorporate them into the visible body of Jesus Christ, altogether the *res* and *sacramentum* of salvation. Thus the salvation eventually assured these non-Catholics is not given *extra ecclesiam*. The Catholic Church remains the only divinely instituted and commanded institution (*sacramentum*) of salvation, and the grace which exists in the world is attributed to it by finality if not by efficacy.[36]

This statement, which closes the article, is memorable for at least three reasons: it stresses the sacramentality of the church, a concept which achieves great prominence in Vatican II; it teaches that all the saved are related to the church at least in some fashion, by way of final if not always by way of efficient causality; and the church always remains the direction toward which the saved are turned as to their goal, model, and fulness. The church is a "cause" of salvation at least in the sense of finality. Congar returns to this notion in later articles.

[33] The salvific task of the church is also clear in this passage: "The Church is something more than a mode of sanctity; she has a mission for the world. She was set up first of all by an act of God, or a series of acts of God, as a divine institution, at one and the same time a complex of the means of salvation — Revelation, sacraments, powers of the apostolic ministry — and as Life in the supernatural communion with God, through His grace, built on faith." "The Council, the Church, and the 'others'," *Cross Currents* 11 (1961), p. 245. Original article: "Le Concile, l'Église et 'les Autres'," *Lumière et Vie* 45 (1960), pp. 69–92; reprinted in *Sainte Église*, pp. 327–349.

[34] *Catholicisme, hier, aujourd'hui, demain.* Ed. by G. Jacquemet. Vol. 5 (Paris: Letouzey et Ané, 1963), cols. 948–956.

[35] *Ibid.*, col. 954.

[36] *Ibid.*, col. 955.

In recent articles Congar turns more and more to the concepts of the people of God and the sacrament of salvation as descriptions of the church. Admittedly, he depicted the church in these terms even before the 1960's; in fact, his writings had no small influence on the fathers of Vatican II. Or perhaps it might be more correct to say that the inspiration was mutual: Congar influenced the conciliar decrees but they in turn instigated his deeper investigation of the reality of the church as the people of God and the sacrament of salvation. Both of these themes appear in an article which Congar wrote shortly after the promulgation of Vatican II's *Dogmatic Constitution on the Church*:

It is the People of God structured in this way, which continues the mission and represents in the world *the sign of salvation* that God established definitively, totally, adequately *in Christo et in Ecclesia*.

The People of God is, in the world, the sacrament of salvation offered to the world. By this we mean to say that God who has willed (according to an antecedent will) the salvation of all men, has placed in the world a cause, of itself sufficient to achieve this purpose effectively.[37]

Here as in articles of the 1950's he uses the term "cause" to describe the power of the church. The church is a sufficient and effective cause of the salvation of men and women. But apparently it is not the only cause of salvation.

He becomes more precise in another article of the same year (1965).[38] In this article, "The Church, the Universal Sacrament of Salvation," his most significant and informative article for our purposes, Congar proposes to elucidate the concept of church as sacrament, a concept accorded a place of privilege in the decrees of Vatican II. It is from the perspective of the church as the universal sacrament of salvation that he undertakes to identify the locus and extent of God's grace in the world and to reject the use of the axiom *extra ecclesiam nulla salus*.

As the universal sacrament of salvation, including within itself the individual sacraments and the apostolate, the church communicates to people the salvific benefits of the incarnation. The church functions as a mediator of grace to the people of the world, but only

[37] "The Church: The People of God," in *The Church and Mankind*. Ed. by E. Schillebeeckx, O.P. *Concilium*, Vol. 1 (New York: Paulist Press, 1965), pp. 25 and 20–21.

[38] "L'Église, sacrement universel du salut," *Église Vivante* 17 (1965), pp. 339–355. The same article appears as Chapter 2 in *Cette Église que j'aime* (Paris: Éditions du Cerf, 1968). English translation: *This Church that I Love* (Denville, N.J.: Dimension Books, 1969).

as a minister of Christ, the sole mediator between God and mankind, and of his Spirit.

Does the universality of redemption in Christ mark all men and women as the people of God? Congar sketches three possible definitions of the people of God: 1) they are exclusively those who belong to the authentically revealed and instituted religion, the people of Israel and the Christians of the new covenant; 2) besides the community of Israel and Christians the people of God include those who are actually saved but remain outside the limits of the instituted and revealed religion; 3) the people of God embrace the whole of mankind that is objectively saved in Jesus Christ.[39] Unlike Rahner, who at one point can understand the people of God in sense 3), Congar prefers not to make the people of God coextensive with mankind. The church, the messianic people of God, "though it does not actually include all men and may at times look like a small flock, is nonetheless a most certain seed of unity, hope and salvation for the whole human race."[40] Both Rahner and Congar can find support in the scriptures for their respective positions. Rahner stresses God's universal regard for all peoples and the universal significance of the incarnation, while Congar (without denying these concerns) underscores the significance and mission of a special people. We need not pursue further their preferences; important is the fact that both endeavor to explain the universality and effectiveness of God's favor.

Another thought which Congar pursues is the sacramental value of each person. In a sense each person is or can be a sacrament of Christ and of salvation for his neighbor. "The sacrament of the neighbor" can be an authentic encounter with Christ, an occasion of meeting God's presence and love. Congar finds a scriptural illustration of the sacramentality of the neighbor in the famous judgment scene of Matthew 25. He concludes that even without consciously adverting to the fact, a person can encounter and serve Jesus in the hungry, the thirsty, etc. Besides this gospel proof (which some scholars would find unacceptable since the scene may refer to Christians only) Congar sets down two other reasons for the sacramentality of the neighbor. The first is the incarnation itself: "In becoming man, God has taken every man for a brother, and the mystery of the Son of Man is reflected in the whole of humanity."[41] The second is the very structure of the human person. By creation

[39] Cf. "L'Église, sacrement universel du salut," pp. 348f.

[40] "The Church. Seed of Unity and Hope for the Human Race," *Chicago Studies* 5 (1966), p. 39; cf. pp. 27f. Cf. Vatican II's *Dogmatic Constitution on the Church*, Art. 9.

[41] "L'Église, sacrement universel du salut," p. 350.

we are such that only love can be the adequate determination of our relationship to the other, a relationship which is at the same time an indication of our attitude toward God.[42]

Though Congar propounds the potential sacramentality of every person, his chief interest is the universal sacramentality of the church. The visible church remains the great sacrament of salvation, "the bearer of the positive revelation of his truth and of the means of grace instituted by him. Thus, she is the public and universal sacrament of salvation, while the encounter of the other is only a private, particular and occasional sacrament."[43] The church alone is the visible assembly of the people of God, the body of Christ and the temple of the Holy Spirit. It alone is necessary for the God-willed unity of mankind.[44] At this point Congar does not indicate which sacramentality is the normal and more universal way for people to encounter the saving God: the private sacramentality of persons or the sacramentality of the church.

Must the church be the mediator for every occasion of grace, for every encounter with God in the world? Congar in this article addresses this question more clearly than previously and his answer is more decidedly in the negative:

Every Catholic admits and must admit that there have existed and exist gifts of light and grace working for salvation outside the visible boundaries of the church. We do not even deem it necessary to hold (as is nonetheless commonly done) that these graces are received *through* the church; it is that they are received in view of the church and that they orient people toward the church or that they incorporate them invisibly into it.[45]

The saving grace accorded persons outside the visible limits of the church, and not necessarily accorded *from* the church, is ecclesial in character because it directs them toward the church as to the fulfilment of their relationship with God in Jesus Christ and the Spirit. This is a clearer formulation of Congar's thought than that which appeared in the previously examined article of 1956. There he used the terminology of final and efficient causality; here he expresses the same concept in less technical and more lucid terms.

---

[42] *Ibid.* Cf. *The Wide World My Parish*, pp. 124–126.

[43] *Ibid.*, p. 350.

[44] Cf. *ibid.*, p. 353.

[45] *Ibid.*, p. 351: "Tout catholique doit admettre et admet qu'il a existé et qu'il existe des dons de lumière et de grâce travaillant pour le salut, en dehors des limites visibles de l'Église. Il ne nous paraît même pas necessaire de tenir, comme on le fait cependant communément, que ces graces soient recues *par* l'Église: il suffit qu'elles le soient en vue de l'Église et qu'elles orientent vers l'Église ou qu'elles y incorporent invisiblement."

Congar concludes his article with the suggestion that we abandon the formula *extra ecclesiam nulla salus* because it cannot be taken literally, and because a proper understanding of it requires a long explanation. He does not reject the axiom as meaningless, for he can find the following biblical truths contained in it: "The church is the only institution created and commanded by God to obtain for people the salvation which is in Jesus Christ; the church has received from her founder and Lord all that is necessary to obtain the salvation of the whole of mankind." [46] Congar discovers the same content in the formula "the church, the universal sacrament of salvation"; thus he recommends this latter formula as a replacement for the traditional and easily misunderstood *extra ecclesiam nulla salus.*

After Vatican II Congar continually returns to the concept of sacramentality to explain the axiom, for indeed his recommendation to discard the axiom does not eliminate his need to speak of it. The axiom means:

The Catholic Church is the only one legitimately commanded to be the sign and instrument, that is, the sacrament of salvation for the whole world until the end of history. Beginning with and according to revelation and Jesus Christ it is the historical shape of the plan by which "God wishes all men to be saved and to come to a knowledge of the truth" (1 Tm 2, 4). This means also that the Catholic Church holds within itself by the grace of its Savior the means to procure the salvation of each and every man, no matter what his time, country, or milieu. In short, the true meaning of "Outside the Church . . ." is the idea — enunciated many times by Vatican II — that the church is the universal sacrament of salvation.[47]

The church is directed to all peoples, is their sign of salvation, and possesses the means of salvation for all. Congar states that the Catholic Church is the only legitimate or God-appointed sign of

[46] *Ibid.*, p. 354. Cf. this passage in *The Wide World My Parish*, p. 98, where there is a similar explanation but no rejection of the formula: "Briefly, it is no longer a question of applying the formula to any concrete person whatever, but of stating objectively that the Church of Christ is commissioned and qualified to carry salvation, brought by Jesus Christ, to all men; and that she alone, as Christ's Church, is so commissioned and qualified. So the formula is no longer to be regarded as answering the question 'Who will be saved?' but as answering the question 'What is it that is commissioned to discharge the ministry of salvation'?" Cf. also, p. 112. Similar ideas are found in *Le Concile au jour le jour. Session 3* (Paris: Les Éditions du Cerf, 1965), especially pp. 143–176.

[47] "La signification du salut et l'activité missionnaire," *Parole et Mission*, no. 36 (1967), pp. 72–73.

salvation. But he would not deny, especially after the decrees of Vatican II, that other Christian churches and communities share in the one sign of the Church of Christ.

Another passage from the same article clarifies to some extent Congar's understanding of the relationship between the visible church and the people of faith outside the church. The church as means of salvation and germ of unity is related to the people of faith "outside" as the *res* is related to the *sacramentum*: "Faith and charity on the one hand, and knowledge of Jesus Christ and entrance into the church on the other, are related somewhat like the reality (*res*) and sign (*sacramentum*) of classical theology."[48] The realities of faith and salvation can be present before actual reception into the church, but at the same time the church exists as the sign and goal of the realities wherever they exist.

But he immediately points to the reality of salvation that is dynamically directed toward the church. Salvation effected by Christ and the Holy Spirit has as its concrete and complete terminus the church, which is at once the people of God and an institution. He can even suggest the presence of a church before and outside of the church:

There exists already from the church and before the church a church in inchoative act or rather in tendency, as Cardinal Journet says. This church is precisely the sum total of saved individuals and of the elements which prepare them for the church; it is a church that exists outside of explicit and total attachment to the positive institution of salvation: Jesus Christ and his church.[49]

Congar still refers to the church in terms of "institution" and "means of salvation," but he allows for an operation of salvation outside the church which is oriented dynamically to the one institution of the church. He plays with the idea of a church outside the church; but such a reality is church only insofar as it is the sum total of individuals who are being saved and directed toward the church as to their completion and goal. The church as means of salvation is understood as the goal of salvation for those outside or before the church. In the same year, elucidating Vatican II's uses of the phrase "universal sacrament of salvation," Congar calls the church "the historical and positive form of the covenant of grace, a hope and a germ of unity for the whole of mankind."[50] The word "germ"

[48] *Ibid.*, p. 70.

[49] *Ibid.*, p. 74.

[50] "Église et Monde dans la perspective de Vatican II," in *L'Église dans le monde de ce Temps, Constitution Pastorale Gaudium et Spes.* Ed. by Y. Congar, O.P., and M. Peuchmaurd, O.P. (Paris: Les Éditions du Cerf, 1967), Vol. 3, p. 27. Cf. Vol. 2, p. 316.

would seem to indicate that the church is the locus out of which the hope grows for the whole of mankind. The direction is from church to world.

To sum up, in his early writings Congar taught that people being saved outside the Roman Catholic Church are nevertheless incorporated into the one church. Later he abandoned this terminology. He acknowledged explicitly the presence of many graces outside the visible boundaries of the church: the sacrament of the neighbor, the grace dimension of human strivings for peace, justice, brotherhood, etc. At first it was still unclear whether he ascribed all these grace movements among peoples to the instrumentality of the church. His recent writings indicate, however, that while all grace need not derive from the church it nonetheless directs a person toward the church. Thus all grace in the world has an ecclesial dimension, at least in the sense that it is oriented toward the one, visible Church of Christ. For a time he strove to reinterpret the traditional axiom, but in the end he advocated its abandonment and replacement by the concept of the church as the universal sacrament of salvation.

2. *Karl Rahner*

The many-sided dimensions of the church in the modern world — its self-understanding, spirituality, extent, and future — all receive elucidation from the tireless pen of Karl Rahner.

In his strikingly personal solutions to a wide variety of theological issues Rahner has repeated recourse to his underlying theological anthropology. His view of a person's basic, ontological relationship to God determines the way in which he approaches most theological problems. It will not be possible here to attempt any more than an outline of his anthropology, but we need to remind ourselves of its fundamental importance in his ecclesiology, especially in his view of a person's relationship to the church.

A person's spiritual and bodily being in the world, his or her knowing and loving, is not limited to the strictly material. By God's positive design, the human make-up includes a transcendental orientation to the divine and the supernatural. This orientation, this limitless openness to the transcendent, is called a "supernatural existential" for it describes the actual, concrete situation in which a person finds himself or herself. The individual stands open to divine grace, to revelation, and to God's self-communication in the Logos. A person's ontological orientation is not in itself sufficient to ensure his or her ultimate perfection in the beatifying presence of God, for the grace of God in Christ Jesus is always necessary in the actual history of salvation. But the orientation is present whether or not an individual consciously reflects upon it, whether or not it is ultimately perfected and actualized in justification and beatitude. It is this supernatural existential which constitutes a basic unity of all people.

The Son of God became enfleshed in the man Jesus Christ and thus entered into the real, ontological unity of mankind. He thereby effected the radical and ontological salvation of everybody — not that everyone is automatically saved by being born but that the radical source of salvation is already present in the world. It is present before any conscious effort and reflection on the part of the individual. Men and women are thus constituted and situated by the person of Jesus whether they know it or not, whether they desire it or not. People have the real and ever-present possibility of turning to the personal center of mankind and of finding forgiveness of sins, atonement, and union with God. We need not detail here the reflexive and unreflexive ways in which this possibility is actualized.

A revelation has taken place in and around the person of Jesus Christ. A human being who is by nature a listener for a possible revelation can turn to the unique history of Christ and of Christianity and there find the historical revelation of God. In a discussion of the uniqueness of the Christian revelation Rahner cites — for the first time, to my knowledge — the axiom *extra ecclesiam nulla salus*:

We can speak of an historical revelation of God only if this historical manifestation is the cause of a claim to *"extra ecclesiam nulla salus."* This is a claim that is the sole historical, visible entity which to the exclusion of all others is the place where a free God can adequately be found.[51]

His use of the axiom here is oblique since he does not address himself to the question of salvation within or without the church. He cites the axiom merely to express the conviction that God has uniquely revealed himself in Christ and Christianity. The oblique reference does indicate, however, how seriously he understands the axiom (and the church), for he can use it to describe a unique revelation of God.

It is important for our purposes to note that Rahner, especially in his earlier writings, preferred to call mankind (so constituted, situated and unified in the person of Christ) the people of God:

God sees all human beings as brothers and sisters of his incarnate Son "in the midst of the Church" (Heb 2, 10-11), as the people of

[51] *Hearers of the Word* (New York: Herder and Herder, 1969), p. 179.

God with whom he has concluded that new and eternal covenant by that union between God and creature which we call the hypostatic union. By the gracious comings of the Logos in the flesh, in the unity of the race, in the one history of humanity, mankind as a whole has become a consecrated humanity, in fact the people of God.[52]

This usage, which is broader than that found in the scriptures and in the documents of Vatican II,[53] underscores the filial relationship that exists between God and the whole of mankind, a relationship that derives from the incarnation. This understanding of the people of God is akin to the notion that through the incarnation all the descendants of Adam become brothers and sisters of the God-made-man, a concept which is espoused by Pius XII in his encyclical *Mystici Corporis*.[54] Rahner does not consistently promote this concept of the people of God. He can also call the church more strictly "the people of God to which belong all those who are baptized and who have the true faith." [55] But the broader usage appears again in a recent writing (1966), though here the words are placed in quotes, an indication, it would seem, that he consciously employs the phrase in an extended sense.[56]

A further question concerns his specific definition of the church. If the people of God are co-extensive with mankind, is the church equally as far-reaching? In an early writing (1942) Rahner approximates this idea:

The order of human history to which Christ belongs is already "Church;" not yet indeed in the sense of a visible society which continues the making-visible in Christ of the salvific will of God and which was authoritatively organized as visible by Christ himself, the society of those who have existentially ("believing") submitted to the demands made by this reality; but certainly in the sense that the *historical* order of man's existential decision has become, before any visible organization of the Church, through the Incarnation and the Cross, already quite different from one in which Christ did not exist; we must say, therefore, that the visible

[52] *The Church and the Sacraments* (New York: Herder and Herder, 1963), p. 13. Cf. "Membership of the Church according to the Teaching of Pius XII's Encyclical *Mystici corporis Christi*," in *Theological Investigations*, Vol. 2 (Baltimore: Helicon, 1963), pp. 82–84.

[53] Cf. *Dogmatic Constitution on the Church*, Art. 2.

[54] Cf. *Acta Apostolicae Sedis* 35 (1943), p. 198.

[55] "The Church of the Saints," in *Theological Investigations*, Vol. 3 (Baltimore: Helicon, 1967), p. 97.

[56] K. Rahner, N. Greinacher, H. Schuster, and B. Dreher, *La Salvezza nella Chiesa. Strutture fondamentali della mediazione salvifica* (Rome: Herder, 1968), p. 12.

organization of the Church does not first create this order but is
called into being by it and is no more than its necessary expression.[57]

The quotation marks around the word "church" indicate an extended use of the term. Mankind redeemed in Christ is already
"church," but not in the full sense of the word, since the church is
properly speaking the visible manifestation of the Christian word,
sacrament, and life.

Generally his description of church is more traditional, one
confined to the visible, institutional community established by
Christ:

If we speak in modern terminology of the Church, we mean the
community of the faithful organized socially and juridically by
Christ, under the hierarchical direction of the Pope, and the
bishops in union with him, in a common outward profession of
faith, in a common cult, and in the life of the faithful as hierarchi-
cally directed in other respects.[58]

This definition is reminiscent of the one elaborated by Robert Bellarmine and assumed by Pius XII in *Mystici Corporis*. It stresses the
unmistakable and unique character of the church. In his recent
writings Rahner shifts from the broader to the narrower notion of
church. He places the emphasis on the sacramentality and visibility
of the church. "The church is nothing else than the historical presence of the gift which God makes of himself to the creature in
Christ and the historical verifiability of the effects of this gift of God
in Christ to humanity."[59] Humble in extent and appearance, the
church is nevertheless based in history and is discernible as a sign
of God's eschatological and saving gift to men and women.

To be sure, Rahner acknowledges the ecclesial values of the
other Christian churches and communities which do not meet the
strictest stipulations of the above definitions, but he claims with
some persistence that only the Roman Catholic Church meets the
most genuine qualifications of the church.[60] Only the Catholic
Church has the authentic tradition of the Church of Christ, even
though features of the church may be cultivated better in non-
Roman Christian communities. Thus Rahner does not advocate the

[57] "Priestly Existence," in *Theological Investigations*, Vol. 3 (Baltimore: Helicon,
1967), pp. 247f.
[58] *The Christian Commitment. Essays in Pastoral Theology* (New York: Sheed
and Ward, 1963), p. 41.
[59] *La Salvezza nella Chiesa*, p. 11. Cf. *Do You Believe in God?* (New York: Paulist
Press, 1969), p. 58: "Nor does the Church exactly coincide with sanctified mankind."
[60] Cf., e.g., "On Conversions to the Church," in *Theological Investigations*, Vol. 3
(Baltimore: Helicon, 1967), pp. 373–384.

kind of pan-Christianity which indiscriminately claims the equality of its broken parts. The oneness of the church, the perfection of which is an object of hope, is already a present reality and a manifest sign to the world. But Rahner's view of the way in which non-Catholic Christian communities and churches are related to the Roman Catholic Church is not our concern here. He experiences no difficulty in recognizing Christian graces and values in these communities. More directly related to our subject is the source and medium of these graces, not only in all Christian communities but also in the life of every person.

That grace exists outside the church is unquestionable. Theologians and the ecclesiastical magisterium have long interpreted the axiom outside the church no salvation in such a way as to respect the extra-ecclesial graces accorded to all peoples. It is heresy to believe otherwise:

Why should we not today alter to our use, quite humbly and dispassionately, a saying of St. Augustine's: Many whom God has, the Church does not have; and many whom the Church has, God does not have? Why, in our defeatism, which springs from a muddled feeling of pity for mankind, do we forget that it is not the truth but a heresy that there is no grace outside the Church?[61]

God's grace is not confined to the sacraments of the church nor to the whole church viewed as a sacrament.[62] Even where the word of the church has reached the free decision of an individual, there is still a free self-communication of God, a grace which insofar as it is efficacious, cannot be given or administered by the church but simply stems from the free giving of God.[63]

The offer of God's grace is not a rare happening. The generosity of God continually and abundantly confronts a person in his or her whole spiritual life; it provides an individual with the opportunity of deciding for or against his or her openness to the divine, for or

[61] *The Christian Commitment*, p. 35.

[62] Cf. *The Christian of the Future* (New York: Herder and Herder, 1967), pp. 96f.

[63] "Secular Life and the Sacraments," *The Tablet* 225 (March 6, 1971), p. 237: "But is another approach to the sacraments possible? There is such an approach and it is based on the simple truth of faith that what we call sanctifying grace and divine life is present *everywhere* — wherever, in fact, man does not close himself to the God of salvation by culpably rejecting His grace. For we know that this grace is being communicated, even though in ways which are partially anonymous and hidden, within the concrete reality of history and human life: and we know that grace is present wherever the struggle of human life and dying takes its course, provided the end of this struggle is not mortal guilt. . . . Grace is simply the last depth and the radical meaning of all that the created person experiences, enacts, and suffers in the process of developing and realizing himself as a person." Cf. *La Salvezza nella Chiesa*, p. 13.

against the horizon of transcendence. God's presence to a person who decides in favor of his or her whole human existence and orientation makes it possible for him or her to act in a salutary manner. The morally good act takes place in the *de facto* history of salvation, in the presence of the gracious God and thus is a supernatural act that is fruitful for salvation. The individual need not be reflexively conscious of all the implications of an action; he or she need not have specific knowledge of the orientation of the gift of grace. The grace-filled condition of the person can remain in the more general realm of inarticulate consciousness without being expressed or interpreted in a distinct fashion.[64] It is this situation which Rahner calls "anonymous Christianity":

The grace of God has always been there ahead of our preaching; a man is always in a true sense a Christian already when we begin to commend Christianity to him. For he is a man, already included in God's general will for salvation, redeemed by Christ, with grace already living and working in his innermost heart at least as the proffered possibility of supernatural action.[65]

More recently, in response to opponents of the phrase "anonymous Christianity" as a depiction of people who are implicitly justified in Christ, Rahner proclaims his allegiance to the *reality* of attachment to Christ rather than to the descriptive phrase "anonymous Christianity." He shifts his terminology from "anonymous Christianity" to "anonymous faith," which is dynamically oriented toward explicit faith and which under the usual conditions is sufficient for salvation.[66]

Grace, faith, and salvation are thus not confined to the external structures of the church. It follows that Christians generally cannot be accused of narrowness and sectarian haughtiness. They acknowledge their explicit profession of faith but claim no monopoly on God's extensive goodness. Today, more than in centuries past, Roman Catholics and Christians generally realize that their numbers in the world are small, that the vast majority of men and women live and find justification (insofar as they do achieve it) outside the boundaries of the church. The majority's means of attaining to justification, therefore, can hardly be called exceptional,

---

[64] Cf. "Nature and Grace," in *Theological Investigations*, Vol. 4 (Baltimore: Helicon, 1966), pp. 179–181.

[65] *The Christian Commitment*, p. 103. Cf. "Anonymous Christians," in *Theological Investigations*, Vol. 6 (Baltimore: Helicon, 1969), pp. 390–398.

[66] Cf. "Anonymous Christianity and the Missionary Task of the Church," IDOC-North America, New York, 1970, pp. 70–96; "Anonymer und expliziter Glaube," *Stimmen der Zeit* 99 (1974), pp. 147–152.

for more people are presumably (that is, presuming the abundance of God's mercy and human co-operation) saved in this extra-ecclesial manner than within the confines of the institutional church. This being the case, Rahner joins an increasing number of contemporary theologians who regard the achievement of salvation outside the church as normal and ordinary and that within the church as extraordinary.[67]

If theology insists on the presence of grace outside the visible structure of the church, one might be left with the impression that the extra-ecclesial grace is structureless and invisible. Rahner counters this impression with a reference to the incarnational principle: God has chosen to deal with people in a concrete, historical, human fashion. This principle is verified primarily in the Word-made-flesh but by extension in every offer of grace. Speaking of the diaspora situation of the Christian of the future Rahner says:

The Church for him is something like the uniformed units in God's array, the point at which the inner character of man's divinized life is manifested in tangible historical and sociological form or, rather, in which it is most clearly manifested because, to the enlightened gaze of faith, grace does not entirely lack visible embodiment even outside the Church.[68]

God's saving grace is embodied primarily and authentically in the church but every grace "has, in a certain sense, an incarnational, sacramental and ecclesiological structure."[69] Every grace is either publicly and officially embodied in the church or privately and unofficially incorporated in the private life of the individual. In the church it takes on concrete, social, and historical form; in the individual outside the church it is still visible in some external mode of existence, but only in a non-official manner.[70]

The sacramental quality of all grace, even that outside the boundaries of the church, implies another truth which touches our sub-

---

[67] Cf. *The Church After the Council* (New York: Herder and Herder, 1966), p. 53; H. Schlette, *Towards a Theology of Religions* (New York: Herder and Herder, 1966).

[68] *The Christian of the Future*, p. 84. Cf. *On the Theology of Death* (New York: Herder and Herder, 1965), p. 73. Cf. also "The Sacramental Basis for the Role of the Layman in the Church," in *Theological Investigations*, Vol. 8 (New York; Herder and Herder, 1971), pp. 57f: "The function of the Church is rather to provide an outlet by which grace breaks out into the world, into history, into the social and communal life of man."

[69] "Membership of the Church according to the Teaching of Pius XII's Encyclical *Mystici corporis Christi*," p. 68. Rahner is paraphrasing here the teaching of the encyclical.

[70] Cf. *The Church and the Sacraments*, p. 17.

ject: the salvation of one person through another. Rahner proclaims
the solidarity of mankind: the close union of all peoples in the
concrete history of the world and of salvation.[71] In fact, his thesis is
that the concrete, existential intercommunion of all persons forms
the basis of the mediatorship of Christ. It is because individuals are
dependent upon each other, responsible to each other in all matters, including those of salvation, that Jesus the man can be a personal means of salvation for the others.[72]

Important for our subject is the understanding that one person is
responsible to another in matters of salvation, that one's concrete
acknowledgement of the offer of grace has repercussions on the
way in which others respond. One person's life of grace is not
lacking in meaning for his or her neighbor, for no one is so isolated
from the other that his or her concrete decisions have no influence
on another human being. One's justification has real meaning for
the salvation of others; one's actions and words, one's manner of
life, have salvational value for other people in the world. All grace,
in other words, has an efficacious and sacramental value, even
when it is found outside the church. Can we call this grace ecclesial?

Rahner can state on occasion that all grace is ecclesial: "Every
grace has analogously the same structure as its source, viz., the
structure of the Word become *man,* and all grace is grace of the
Church, i.e., all grace has an ecclesiological structure."[73]

In another place Rahner says: "To deny the ecclesiastical character of all grace and redemption would either imply that grace is not
always related to the incarnation, to history, and so to the Church, or
else it would imply that one can attain salvation without the grace
of Christ."[74] Here Rahner clarifies the sense in which he views the
ecclesial dimension of all grace. His argument stems from the close
association of Christ and the church. Since all grace is Christic,
incarnational, and historical, it is consequently ecclesial. It cannot
be Christic without being ecclesial. Christ and the church are so
interwoven in life and purpose that one cannot receive the grace of
salvation without being related to both, though of necessity the

[71] It was one of his major arguments in the defense of monogenism, a teaching he
no longer regards as necessary. Even without a basis in monogenism he insists on
the basic unity of mankind.

[72] Cf. the elaboration of this theme in *Der eine Mittler und die Vielfalt der Vermittlungen* (Wiesbaden: Steiner, 1967).

[73] "Personal and Sacramental Piety," in *Theological Investigations,* Vol. 2 (Baltimore: Helicon, 1963), p. 113.

[74] *The Church and the Sacraments,* p. 22.

relationship to the church admits of degrees. Rahner sums up his position in these words:

> If it is true to say that the Church as the continuance of Christ's presence in the world, is the fundamental sacrament of the eschatologically triumphant mercy of God, then salvation is offered and promised to the individual by his entering into positive relation to the Church. This positive relationship may possibly have very different degrees and grades of intensity, but if the individual is to attain salvation, can never entirely be lacking. God's life is offered to men plainly and once and for all in Christ, through whose incarnation the people of God exists. This has socially organized form in the Church, which is consequently the abiding and historically manifest presence of this saving grace in Christ, the fundamental sacred sign or sacrament of this grace. From this the necessity of the Church for salvation — at root it is the necessity of Christ himself — directly follows. Its necessity as a means is also clear, the kind of necessity which is presupposed by the question of a moral claim to men's obedience.[75]

Moreover all grace has an ecclesial structure because, as the church itself is structured with concrete, visible, and historical lineaments, so grace, wherever it is found in the world, bodies forth in some visible, tangible form. All grace is of the church because it is patterned on the human/divine model of the church.

Another sense in which all grace is ecclesial is developed in terms of orientation. All grace is directed to the church as to its model and goal. This view of grace appears in one of Rahner's earliest writings (1934): "Grace has also an inner orientation to the visible Church."[76] A similar passage appears in a later discussion of penance:

> In so far as this very grace [divine grace in the Christian sinner] is grace of the Church, since all grace is grace of the Body of Christ (i.e. from this Body and directed towards it), and in so far as it is given as a gift to this baptized sinner *qua* member of the Church (as her vital force), the personal penance of the baptized person is a manifestation of grace both as divine and as of the Church.[77]

This passage again indicates the church orientation of all grace, though it remains to be determined what Rahner understands by the affirmation that all grace is from the body of Christ, the church.

[75] *Ibid.*, p. 21.

[76] "The Meaning of Frequent Confession of Devotion," in *Theological Investigations*, Vol. 3 (Baltimore: Helicon, 1967), p. 186, note 14.

[77] "Forgotten Truths Concerning the Sacrament of Penance," in *Theological Investigations*, Vol. 2, p. 162.

Is it sufficient to say that all grace is ecclesial because it is oriented to the church or is structured on the visible/invisible character of the church? Does the quotation intimate that the church is a channel of all grace? Is all grace mediated by the church? Here we strike the core of the problem.

Our understanding of the problem may begin with a discussion of the Holy Spirit, who is personal grace *par excellence*. Is the grace of the Holy Spirit always bound up with the church? Rahner's answer is affirmative. In a 1956 article, whose revealing title is "The Church as the Locus of the Sending of the Spirit," Rahner holds that the church is not only the extension of the historicity and visibility of Jesus but also the point of reference for the Spirit in the world: "In ecclesia posuit deus . . . universam operationem spiritus. 'God ordained that the entire work of the Spirit should take place in the Church.' And where the Spirit is active, there, at any rate remotely, a state is achieved in the construction of the visible Body of the Church."[78] Again he says, "There is no Holy Spirit apart from the holy Body which is the Church."[79] The church and the Holy Spirit are so closely associated that one is always tied to the other. The church is the visible manifestation of the Spirit so that where the church is there is the Spirit and where the Spirit is working there also is the formation of the church. "The Holy Spirit and the Body of Christ belong together in the one Church. Anyone who belongs to her, has her Spirit and is sanctified by belonging to her and by having her Spirit through her mediation."[80] A similar thought is expressed in *Encounters With Silence*:

Your Holy Spirit blows where He will — where *He* will, not where I will. He is not simply always there, whenever and wherever a man wants Him to be. We must go to Him, there where He chooses to give His grace. And that's why your salvation is bound up with Your visible Church. That's why Your grace comes to us in visible signs.[81]

For our purposes it is important to note that God chooses to make his Spirit dwell in the church and that the church is the locus of the Holy Spirit, the place from which he is effective in the world.

---

[78] "The Church as the Subject of the Sending of the Spirit," in *Theological Investigations*, Vol. 7 (New York: Herder and Herder, 1971), p. 189. The article first appeared in 1956: "Die Kirche als Ort der Geistsendung," *Geist und Leben* 29 (1956), pp. 94–98. Irenaeus is the inspiration of this passage.

[79] *Ibid.*, p. 190.

[80] "Forgotten Truths Concerning the Sacrament of Penance," in *Theological Investigations*, Vol. 2, p. 138.

[81] Westminster, Md.: The Newman Press, 1965, pp. 69f.

These passages are likely to give the impression that the church functions as some giant vessel from which the Spirit of God is let loose upon the world. The impression only partially corresponds to the activity and place of the Holy Spirit as envisioned by Rahner. It is true that the Spirit is associated intimately with the visible church, with its sacraments and offices. He can say this about the Christian order of grace:

[It is] the order of the Word of God *become man*, the order of the Church, and of the eschatologically indissoluble union of the pneuma and the ecclesiological corporeality of the Spirit. The office and the grace of office belong together in the eschatological situation of the Church, in which the tangibility of the Church and of her possession of the Spirit in its totality can never be again torn apart; the grace of office, since it is the grace of God become man and the grace of the visible Church, always presses of its very nature towards some concrete tangible form and sign.[82]

The Spirit is not so chained to the offices and institutions of the church that it cannot be found elsewhere or that it cannot be influential apart from them. There are non-institutional charisms and visitations.[83] But these are not unrelated to the church. Wherever the Spirit is active in the world — and who can confine his presence and influence — there is the drive toward corporeality and thus a positive, embodied orientation toward the visible church:

For if it is ecclesiastical Nestorianism to enumerate only those marks within the total concept of the "Church" which belong to the social and external structure of the Church and to leave the inner "animation" of the Church by the Holy Spirit out of this concept, then it cannot be said that those are absolutely outside the Church who possess this Spirit and hence are governed by that supernatural "formative principle" which — if it attains its full effect — forms members of the visible Church.[84]

Thus the church as the place of the Spirit may be understood also (akin to the extra-ecclesial graces mentioned above) as the point of orientation of the presence, activity, and embodiment of his grace throughout the world.

To answer the question concerning the universal mediatorship of

[82] "The Theology of the Restoration of the Diaconate," in *Theological Investigations*, Vol. 5, (Baltimore: Helicon, 1966), pp. 287f.

[83] Cf. *La Salvezza nella Chiesa*, p. 38.

[84] "Some Theses on Prayer 'In the Name of the Church'," in *Theological Investigations*, Vol. 5, p. 425. Cf. "The Spirit that is over All Life," in *Theological Investigations*, Vol. 7, p. 195.

the church we need also to examine Rahner's understanding of the church as the *sacrament* of salvation and his view of the church as the *means* of salvation.

We may consider the church as a sacrament first, acknowledging that its sacramental character is closely associated with its role as a means of grace. "The Church," he says, "is in a certain sense the Proto-Sacrament; this means, however, that she is in her whole concrete, visible and juridically verifiable appearance, a real sign and embodiment of the salvific will of God and of the grace of Christom."[85] The church is patterned on the nature of Christ himself. Just as he combines the human and the divine in unmixed unity, so the church unites within itself a visible and divine reality. Rahner thus views the church as the "continuation, the perpetual presence of the task and function of Christ in the economy of redemption, his contemporaneous presence in history, his life, the Church in the full and proper sense."[86] An affirmation of union between the church and Christ is even more pronounced in this passage: "If Christianity, then, *is* Christ, the absolute action of God for man, in which God gives his very self, then Christianity — the Church — cannot renounce its claim to absolute character and universal mission."[87] This union, not to say quasi-identity, is important for understanding Rahner's view of the sacramentality of the church, for its efficaciousness derives precisely from its union with Christ. The church, then, can be called a sacrament since its external, human form is an efficacious sign of its internal, divine reality. All the sacraments of the church are really individual manifestations of the one, primal, sacramental life of the church itself. The church is logically and effectively first in any consideration of the sacramental presence of the divine reality in the world.

As the primordial sacrament the church is the historical, concrete, societal, and communitarian embodiment of the saving grace of God. It is the eschatological and visible sign of the forgiveness of sins in the person of Jesus Christ. It is the evident manifestation of the saving love of God. As sacrament the church signifies the grace of redemption, not only the grace that finds its necessary and culminating representation in the community of the church, but also the extra-ecclesial grace that comes to expression in the limitless variety of modes in the peoples and religions of the world. For all the expressions of grace in the world the church as sign and sacra-

[85] "Membership of the Church," p. 73.

[86] *The Church and the Sacraments*, p. 13. Cf. pp. 18, 21.

[87] *The Church after the Council*, p. 53. Cf. p. 55 where the church is termed the historical permanence of Christ.

ment is the summational representation. The church exists as the
light of the world, as a sign among the nations pointing out the
genuine direction of the manifold gifts of God.

The concept of the church as sacrament undergoes historical development in Rahner's writings, but the basic position is already
found in his earliest articles.[88] More recently (1965) he expressed
the concept in these succinct terms: "Whatever the change [in the
church], however, one thing endures: the nature of the Church as
the presence in social form of God's grace *in Christo*, in doctrine,
worship and life."[89] The church is the enduring sacrament and sign
of the gift of redemption in Christ. It is the form of redemption but
it must not be identified with the very reality of redemption. In his
later writings Rahner carefully distinguished between the sign of
saving grace and that which is signified by the sign:

The Church is only a sign of God. It can never affirm that what is
signified (God's grace), is present only where the sign is, i.e. in the
Church's historical reality as doctrine, sacrament and society.
There is a grace of justification for the "non-Christian." And yet the
Church is *the* sign (the primal sacrament) of this grace for the whole
world, the sign in which God gives himself not simply to the
Church and to those in the Church, but to the world and to all men.
Also, all salvation seeks its concrete manifestation in the Church. In
this double sense there is no salvation outside the Church. . . . In
everything it is and does the Church is a sign which functions by
pointing away from itself to God, to God alone, to God as mystery.[90]

Rahner strikes a de-triumphalizing note in this passage. However
exalted and glorious it is, the church is nevertheless only a sign of
the grace of Christ. It cannot be erected as an idol to which the
people of the world bend the knee of worship. There is extra-
ecclesial grace; there are embodiments of this grace outside the
visible structure of the church: the church is dependent upon the
grace and Spirit of Christ, the source of redemption and forgiveness.
Thus the church is only a sign and sacrament, but one that is filled
with the effectiveness of the Spirit.

If the church is the proto-sacrament and the sign of divine grace,
must its sacramentality enter into salvational activity wherever
people are actually being saved? Rahner would respond in the
affirmative:

[88] Cf. "Priestly Existence," in *Theological Investigations*, Vol. 3, p. 255. *The Church and the Sacraments*, p. 21.

[89] *The Christian of the Future*, p. 35. Cf. pp. 81–85.

[90] *Theology of Pastoral Action* (New York: Herder and Herder, 1968), p. 46. Cf. *La Salvezza nella Chiesa*, p. 25.

The question of whether there is an empirical, "sacramental" embodiment of God's self-communication and of human movement toward God, an embodiment which is non-ecclesiastical and yet necessary for salvation — this problem essentially depends on a solution (ultimately a merely terminological one) of the question of the factors which constitute the Church. If only those elements are taken into consideration which in the actual circumstances of history distinguish the Roman Catholic Church from others, it would have to be said that there is of course no human being whose transcendental relation to God is not mediated historically, and that this mediation (as freely accepted) is necessary for salvation. We would have to add, however, that such mediation (as really operative and not merely *in voto*) is not necessarily ecclesiastical. If, however (and this is objectively and terminologically more correct), the bond of mankind and other factors of human reality are counted among those which go to make up the Church, then it can also be said that the Church fundamentally exercises a sacramental function absolutely necessary for salvation even when a man does not belong to it in a sociologically perceptible way.[91]

This passage is of utmost importance, for it indicates how Rahner can uphold and explain the traditional teaching of the church for salvation. Extra-ecclesial graces and extra-ecclesial manifestations of graces (e.g., concern for human unity and justice) are sacramentally patterned on and in a real initial sense constitute the church, though not the full, perceptible church evident in the sociologically discernible Church of Christ. If it is necessary for such grace to manifest itself sacramentally and thus become modeled on the sociologically perceptible church, then the necessity of the church can be vindicated for any salvation in the world.

If Christ is the source of all grace, and if the church as the sacrament of salvation is patterned on the model of Christ, is it then necessary to conclude that the church is the source of all justifying grace and salvation? If sacramental actions are sources of grace, is the church as sacrament the source of grace for all of mankind?

There is no doubt, first of all, that the church is often a medium or means of grace in a very perceptible fashion. It communicates the word and celebrates the sacraments, actions that expressly transmit the grace and favor of God (though, of course, their ultimate effectiveness depends upon the immediate presence of God and a person's free decision):

For there can be no doubt about the fact that the visible and hierarchical Church as such contributes in many ways to the transmission

[91] *Theology of Pastoral Action*, pp. 47f.

and increase of the divinizing grace of man: by guidance, admonition, prescriptions, communal prayer, the sacraments, good example, the visible and hierarchical Church influences the granting and increase of grace (both as part of and outside of prayer itself) and in this way influences also the value prayer has before God.[92]

That the church is the only source of salvation is stated rather baldly and sharply in one of Rahner's earlier (1947) works:

Once more, this Church as she is in the concrete is *the* Church, the only Church, the Church of God and of his Christ, the home of our souls, the place where alone we find the living God of grace and of eternal salvation. For this Church is one with Christ and the Spirit of God — not confused with them but inseparable from them. From this Church there is no escape which could lead to salvation.[93]

There is no doubt about his intention to uphold the traditional teaching concerning the unicity of the church and its necessity for salvation. There is only one church of Jesus Christ which alone leads people to salvation. In spite of the fact that the church includes sinners in its midst, that it fails in its ideal of holiness, it remains "the bride of Christ and the vessel of the Holy Spirit, the only means of grace."[94] It remains to be determined how Rahner understands the church as a means of salvation. Does he understand means in a rather physical and concrete sense?

In an article of 1952 Rahner clearly disavows a materialistic understanding of the efficacious function of the church:

By positing the material, outward sign and expression of grace in space and time through her ritual action, which is the action of Christ, she [the church] obtains a really efficacious mode of presence for the grace thus signified in this historical moment of time. By the fact that Christ acts on man through the Church by giving his grace the form of a constitutive sign, it is *he* who renders his grace inwardly efficacious in man, and not his servant nor the recipient of the sacrament. This is the meaning of the term *opus operatum*,

---

[92] "Some Theses on Prayer 'In the Name of the Church'," in *Theological Investigations*, Vol. 5, p. 426. Cf. "The Church and the Parousia of Christ," in *Theological Investigations*, Vol. 6, p. 305. Also "Forgotten Truths Concerning the Sacrament of Penance," in *Theological Investigations*, Vol. 2, p. 150, where he can speak of life and divine love issuing from the vital principle of the church. In "Remarks on the Theology of Indulgences," in *Theological Investigations*, Vol. 2, p. 194, he can speak of grace and forgiveness granted to men in view of the moral works of Christ and of others in his grace. Again, *Theology of Pastoral Action*, pp. 66f, where he teaches that the *whole* church has the task of being "a channel of salvation for all others."

[93] "The Church of Sinners," in *Theological Investigations*, Vol. 6, p. 265.

[94] *Ibid.*, p. 261.

which has therefore nothing to do with the imagination of any kind of physical effectiveness of a material occurrence which would appertain to this occurrence independently from its nature as a sign, so that this occurrence would only be "incidentally" "also" a sign of grace.[95]

Grace is rendered efficacious insofar as it is signified by the church and insofar as the church itself is a sign. Grace is efficacious insofar as it is a sign of Christ's action, for he alone can make grace inwardly efficacious. The action of the church is a physical and tangible action, but it is efficacious because of the conjoined activity of Christ. The action of the church is a sign of Christ's activity, and only as a sign is it efficacious. Thus while Rahner avoids the impression of a mechanical transmission of grace, he propounds the visible dimension of grace which itself is a sign of Christ's activity. It is clearer in other writings that all grace is tangible in some sense or other and that this embodied grace becomes a sign of Christ's activity and is equally related to his visible church.

A discussion of the individual in the church and his prayer is another context in which Rahner speaks of the mediatorship of the church:

Each man is to go into his room and shut the door and pray to him in secret as his God; he gives himself by grace to each directly, without anything whatever coming between, and this in spite of, or rather *because of*, the mediation of all grace through Christ the mediator and his church, whose purpose is not to come between God and man in the manner of the neo-Platonic or Areopagitical cosmic hierarchy of mediators, but to give each man immediate access to God.[96]

There are traces of tension in this passage. On the one hand Rahner insists on a person's direct access to God in prayer, on the other hand, on the necessity of Christ and the church as mediators. Apparently, though the paragraph lacks clarity in this matter, the mediators do not block access to God but form a link to him. In any event he proclaims the mediatorship of the church even for an action so personal and private as prayer in secret.

At the beginning of the 1960's Rahner continued to use terminology that carried with it physical or power-mediating implications. In a discussion of Latin as a church language, for example, he re-

---

[95] "Personal and Sacramental Piety," in *Theological Investigations*, Vol. 2, p. 124.
[96] *Nature and Grace. Dilemmas in the Modern Church* (New York: Sheed and Ward, 1964), p. 18. Cf. "The Apostolate of Prayer," in *Theological Investigations*, Vol. 3, p. 218, where he mentions the "vocation of prayer for the salvation of the whole world."

ferred to the church's "capacity as the one channel for the salvation of all, without being ultimately dependent on a single human or sacred language."[97] In a 1961 article Rahner assumed traditional terminology and concepts: the church as the ark of salvation; the dogma of the necessity of the church for salvation (*necessitas medii*); the universal salvific will of God. But while the terminology is traditional, the solution of the tension is sought in terms of the church as sacramental sign of salvation:

The Catholic must experience and see the Church as the "vanguard," as the sacramental sign, the historical tangibility of a saving grace which goes beyond the sociologically tangible and the "visible" Church, i.e. the grace of an anonymous Christianity which "outside" the Church has not yet come to itself but which "within" the Church is "present to itself," not because it is simply not present outside but because, objectively speaking, it has not yet reached full maturity there and hence does not as yet understand itself in that explicit way and reflex objectivity of the formulated profession of faith, of the sacramental objectification and of the sociological organization which are found within the Church herself.[98]

The mechanical notions of mediatorship are absent here, and the necessity of the church is seen according to its function of signifying all grace of Christ. The church as the sacramental sign of grace is designed to signify the grace of God anywhere in the world, even where the organized church is not yet present. The grace of God is powerfully at work where the church is not yet present, but it is precisely for this grace that the church is a sacramental sign.

In another essay Rahner maintains that the hierarchy of the church does not and cannot direct all the salvific and grace-inspired activity of the laity; here he explicitly cites the universal effectiveness of the church:

Without prejudice to the basic necessity of the Church for salvation, the Church as actually existing, understood in this full sense [the socially and juridically organized church under the hierarchical direction of the pope and bishops and with an outward creed and cult], is identical neither with the influence and effect of God's grace nor with the total life of the Christians who are her members. For according to Catholic teaching there is grace, and justifying grace, outside the Church too, true though it is that this grace does, in an effective sense, originate within the Church and "orders" a man to the true Church whether he realizes it or not.[99]

[97] "Latin as a Church Language," in *Theological Investigations*, Vol. 5, p. 369.

[98] "Dogmatic Notes on 'Ecclesiological Piety'," in *Theological Investigations*, Vol. 5, pp. 356f.

[99] *The Christian Commitment*, p. 41.

God's salvific work is more widespread than the activity of the church. Yet the church is necessary for salvation, so necessary in fact that all justifying grace effectively originates with the church and directs a person to it. There is a tension here between the universal effectiveness of the church and the universal activity of God's grace. How does all grace originate effectively with the church? Surely not in the sense that the church intervenes in every divine act of justifying grace. Rahner explicitly rejects this notion of effectiveness:

The significance and purpose of the Church is not merely or exclusively to make possible or to facilitate the attainment of salvation in the sum total of many individual cases. For while the Church could be regarded as making a useful and significant contribution to this end, her existence is not absolutely necessary for it in view of the fact that this purpose is in fact often achieved even without any evident intervention on the Church's part.[100]

A person's salvation can be achieved without an evident intervention on the part of the church. The church facilitates the attainment of salvation but it is not absolutely necessary for it. Why then is the church necessary and in what sense does all grace originate with the church?

In union with Christ the church is the primary and first grace of God. It is the manifest beginning of God's salvific activity in Christ. As such it always exists to exhibit the saving activity of God in Christ. It sacramentally portrays the grace of God that is present throughout the world. The effectiveness of God's grace takes its beginning in Christ's body, the church, and it is manifested outwardly through the church. Perhaps Rahner's choice of words is not felicitous, for the terms "effective" and "originate" can lead to the misconceptions of direct intervention and mechanical contact. But they are traditional words in sacramental and ecclesial theology; he develops their use and deepens their content.

Rahner continues this thought in an encyclopedia article on church membership:

Where somebody is justified without baptism, in faith/love and through the *votum implicitum* of the church, there is not (yet) given a real church membership but indeed a condition which seeks with objective and existential tendency its historical, communitarian embodiment in church membership and which thus already orients

---

[100] "The Sacramental Basis for the Role of the Layman in the Church," in *Theological Investigations*, Vol. 8 (New York: Herder and Herder, 1971), p. 56.

the man to the church; as a consequence the salvational significance of the church is maintained for him.[101]

The pre-Vatican II terminology of *votum implicitum* is used to express the thesis that anyone justified at a distance from the church and without an explicit desire to enter the church is nevertheless in a state of positive orientation toward the church. Such a person's situation of justification abides in tension, for it is dynamically turned toward its fulfillment in real and communitarian attachment to the church. This, Rahner holds, is sufficient to safeguard the salvational importance of the church (*die Heilsbedeutung der Kirche*). Here again the extra-ecclesial grace orients the person toward the church, but there is no indication that the church mechanically channels the grace to the person.

A clearer answer to this question emerged after Vatican II. In a section of his book *The Church After the Council* he deals with the subject of the church as the sacrament of the world's salvation and points up an antithesis in the documents of Vatican II: the possibility of salvation outside the church, and the necessity of the church for salvation.[102] Since the council employed sacramental terminology in referring to the place of the church in the world, Rahner assumes the same manner of speaking to resolve, as far as possible, the antithesis:

Taken earnestly, the word describing the Church as the sacrament of the world's salvation means this: that the Church is the concrete historical *appearance* in the dimension of history become eschatological, in the dimension of society, for the unique salvation which occurs, through God's grace, across the length and breadth of mankind.[103]

A sacrament of word and action is visible and concrete. So too the church as sacrament is present in history as the concrete "appearance" and sign of God's salvational grace. In itself this statement does not transcend the explanations embodied in his earlier writings. But he continues his explanation of the power of the sacraments. It is traditional teaching that one may receive the grace of a sacrament even before its actual reception, and conversely one may receive the sacrament without receiving its grace. Now if the church is viewed as a sacrament of salvation, this must mean that a person may receive the grace of the sacrament (the church) before

---

[101] "Kirchengliedschaft II," in *Lexikon für Theologie und Kirche*, 2d ed. Vol. 6 (Freiburg: Herder, 1961), cols. 224–225.

[102] Pp. 51–53.

[103] Pp. 53f.

he actually receives the sacrament, that is, before he becomes the church in an explicit fashion:

We may safely say, therefore, that the grace of God gives assurance through the individual sacramental sign; that it is everywhere powerful, even where this individual sacramental sign as such does not yet reach those very men in whom we may hope that the grace of God is very powerfully at work.[104]

In another article of post-Vatican II vintage Rahner continued to depict the church in terms of mediatorship: "It is the Church which is to bear credible testimony, before that world, to God's truth, mediate the grace of God to that world, be the sacrament of salvation for that world."[105] Using language of traditional sacramental theology, Rahner characterized the church as "the sign of grace which brings what it expresses," a necessary and visible efficacious sign of salvation for all peoples of the world, whether they are visibly joined to the church or not, whether they lived before or after the incarnation.[106] It would seem, judging from his general pre-Vatican II terminology, that Rahner does not advance his thought appreciably after the council. He repeats the concept of the sacramentality of the church with greater frequency because the council itself assumed this theme, for which he was not a little responsible.

That the church is in the world as an efficacious sacrament is acknowledged in an article published in *Sacramentum Mundi*. "Above all, however, the Church is precisely its [the world's] special fundamental sacrament, i.e., the eschatological and efficacious manifestation (sign) in redemptive history that in the unity, activity, fraternity, etc. of the *world*, the kingdom of God is at hand."[107] The church functions as an efficacious sign of the kingdom of God; it manifests and points to the kingdom of God present in the unity, activity, and fraternity of the world. "Efficacious" may be understood in terms of sacramental sign and symbol.

Addressing himself to the universality of the church in the same *Sacramentum Mundi*, Rahner limits himself to the word "manifestation" to designate the church's mission:

---

[104] P. 65. Cf. p. 54. Also Rahner's commentary on the *Dogmatic Constitution on the Church* where he says that the church is "the means of salvation and the primordial sacrament for the world"; "Dogmatic Constitution on the Church. Chapter III, Articles 18–27," in *Commentary on the Documents of Vatican II*. Ed. by H. Vorgrimler Vol. I (New York: Herder and Herder, 1967), p. 186.

[105] *The Christian of the Future*, p. 36.

[106] *Ibid.*, p. 83. Cf. pp. 8, 76, 89, 90, 95.

[107] "Church and World," in *Sacramentum Mundi*, Vol. 1 (New York: Herder and Herder, 1968), p. 348.

This sense of universality (Church as universal *potentia et des-tinatione*) implies two facts. In the first place the Church is for *all* men the *sacramentum salutis*, whether they belong actually and fully to the visible unity of the Church or not. In other words, the grace of God in Christ, without which absolutely no one finds supernatural salvation in God's triune life, has its historical and eschatological manifestation (even for the unbaptized) in the Church. Secondly, no human being can in principle be exempted from the obligation of belonging to the visible unity of the Church. This second point follows immediately from the necessity of the Church and of baptism for salvation.[108]

Here Rahner again recalls the teaching that the church is the sacrament of salvation for all people, and he interprets it in the sense of manifestation — the church is the historical and eschatological manifestation of God's saving grace in Christ. Rahner thus stresses the *sign* value of the church, its presence as an indicator of God's work of salvation in Christ. Thus even in this relatively recent writing he still insists on the traditional terminology of the necessity of the church and of baptism for salvation; he both repeats and surpasses the traditional doctrine. The repetition stems from a continued respect for the traditional teaching on the place of the church in the world.

A third article in the same *Sacramentum Mundi* is extremely explicit on the need for belonging to the church and for sharing its grace:

We must therefore take both truths together: the necessity of Christian faith and the salvific will of God's omnipotent love. This we can only do by affirming that somehow or other all must be able to be members of the Church, not just in the sense of an abstract possibility, but historically and in the concrete. But this means that there must be degrees of membership . . . going from the explicitness of baptism down to a non-official and implicit Christianity, which nonetheless can and should be called Christianity in a valid sense, even though it cannot call itself such or refuses to do so.[109]

Salvation requires membership in the church, even a minimum degree of attachment to the church. Such an attachment arises from faith, explicit as well as implicit faith in Christianity. Implicit faith results from a person's acceptance of himself or herself in grace, an acceptance of God in a historical and existential situation (cf.

[108] "Church. IV. Universality of the Church," in *Sacramentum Mundi*, Vol. 1, p. 330.
[109] "Missions. II. Salvation of the Non-Evangelized," in *Sacramentum Mundi*, Vol 4 (New York: Herder and Herder, 1969), p. 80.

Rahner's concept of supernatural existential). Grace is always necessary and it is the grace of Jesus Christ. "This in turn is the grace of his [Christ's] Church, which is none other than the prolongation of the mystery of Christ, his permanent visible presence in our history."[110] The grace that saves a person is ultimately ecclesial because of the close relationship between Christ and the church. It follows that grace is always through the church, and thus the doctrine of the necessity of the church is safeguarded.

In summary, Rahner's theology of church and salvation is both traditional and forward looking. He abides by the traditional teaching that the church is necessary for the salvation of people. The church is the locus of the Holy Spirit and of all saving grace. All grace is ultimately ecclesial, because it is operative through the church, because it is always expressed according to the divine/human pattern of the church, and because it orients toward the church. It does not follow that everyone belongs to the church in the fullest sense of the term, that is, in the sense of adhering to the creed, cult, hierarchy and discipline of the church. There are degrees of attachment to the church, but nevertheless some form of attachment is required for salvation. The incorporation may be implicit in other acts of faith and commitment, but it needs to be inspired by grace. Moreover, such grace is operative only through the Church of Jesus Christ. In the final analysis the intimate association between Christ and the church demands the teaching of the necessity of the church for salvation.

Rahner makes little mention of the axiom *extra ecclesiam nulla salus* in his more recent writings. In regard to salvation outside the church, his theology develops very little over the years. In the earlier writings, it is true, the language is more peremptory and decisive, e.g., he speaks of the church as the means of salvation or as the place of the Holy Spirit. Subdued strains of this language reverberate in his later writings, and the emphasis shifts to the sign and manifestation value of the church. Drawing upon the sacramental themes of Vatican II, Rahner characterizes the church as the sacrament of salvation. The church is the clear proclamation of universal divine grace, the more definite and sure heralding of God's saving will that finds only halting and uninterpreted expression outside the church. The expression of grace in the church acts as a pointer to the generosity of God whose gracious presence is the source and end of the whole history of salvation.

On the one hand his explanation of the axiom is traditional, in the sense that he requires an ecclesial dimension of all grace and salva-

110 *Ibid.*

tion. On the other hand it is a developed explanation, in the sense that the church is regarded as an effective symbol of all grace and salvation, not necessarily intervening in every case of God's activity.

3. *Gregory Baum*

The third theologian whose thought we wish to explore on the subject of church and salvation is Father Gregory Baum, O.S.A., a professor of theology at Saint Michael's College, Toronto. He is one of the noted ecumenists and ecclesiologists of North America, a theologian whose thought is particularly significant because it bears evidence of profound change in the decade of the 1960's. In his earliest theological writings (pre-1960) he remained close to the traditional teaching on the place of the church in the work of salvation. But in later writings, those appearing approximately at the time of Vatican II, he pursued new modes of thought. And in his more recent works he manifested an almost complete reversal of position. Three aspects of his thought are of specific concern for our theme: his concept of the church; his view of the instrumentality of the church in the work of salvation; and his approach to grace outside the Church of Christ.

In his doctoral dissertation, a study of ecumenism and unity in recent papal documents, Baum assumed a relatively restricted (though broad enough for the times) definition of the Christian:

By a Christian we mean a man who acknowledges Jesus Christ as God and Saviour. This definition excludes many who like to think of themselves as Christians, but in denying that the eternal Word has become flesh in Jesus Christ they do not step out of the circle of what may at best be called a human wisdom.[111]

An ecumenical study of a few years later continues the relatively traditional understanding of the Church of Christ and its salvational task in the world. A representative passage appears early in the work:

This work of his divine redemption is perpetuated by the Church which he founded. In her, Jesus continues to act on men as the Savior of the world. Through her voice, he makes himself known; through her sacramental gestures, he transforms our sinful hearts; through her rule, he leads us on the steep road to holiness.

But in reconciling the world with his eternal Father, Jesus, the crucified and risen Lord, has chosen men to be his helpers. These

---

[111] *That They May Be One. A Study of Papal Doctrine (Leo XIII-Pius XII)* (Westminster, Md.: The Newman Press, 1958), p. viii.

men, called and redeemed by him, become organs of the very redemption which has given them life. The brothers he elects to have
a share in his divine vitality become his instruments in choosing
others. Redeemed and united to himself, the followers of Christ
make up a holy community in which the saving acts of the
Redeemer are rendered present to mankind. In his Church, Christ
remains in history. To him who believes, the Church is the community of God's choice in which the redemptive acts of Christ are
present to all men.[112]

With the death and glorification of Christ the church becomes the
voice and form of Jesus. As the living instrument of the Lord the
church extends in time and space the redemptive works of Jesus.
This task of the church is universal in scope and presumably,
though here Baum is not explicit, the church is the only community
so empowered to act in the world, in fact, the only means of salvation for mankind. A later passage from the same work partially
confirms this judgment. Commenting on 2 Cor 5, 18-19, Baum observes: "In connection with his doctrine of universal reconciliation,
the Apostle Paul clearly states that the Church's ministry is to extend this reconciliation to the world."[113] Later he describes the
church as the unique community of salvation embracing all of humanity:

By the catholicity of the Church theological writers usually understand the universality of the Church in regard to place and people.
The Church is sent and established as the unique community of
salvation embracing all of humanity, and hence she is not bound to
any particular people, to any race or country, to any cultural or
social class.[114]

From other passages in the book it is clear that the phrase "embracing all of humanity" does not mean that the church is actually the
whole of humanity but rather that it is directed to the whole of
humanity. Already here there could be the beginning of the inver-
sion which his thought undergoes at the end of the decade: the
view that at least in one sense the church truly embraces the whole
of mankind inasmuch as it is graced by the word of God. At this
time, however, Baum still views the church as the elect of the
Father burdened with the task of continuing the reconciling work
of the Son, and it stands over against the rest of mankind. The
church is the holy and saving community which perpetuates the

---

[112] *Progress and Perspectives. The Catholic Quest for Christian Unity* (New York:
Sheed and Ward, 1962), pp. 3f.

[113] *Ibid.*, p. 20.

[114] *Ibid.*, p. 199.

redeeming acts of Christ, who, of course, is the sole source of forgiveness wherever it occurs.[115]

In a 1963 article Baum reiterates the traditional teaching but with
a nuance of expression that points in the direction of identifying the
church and the world of men touched by grace. He begins the
article with this summary of faith: "The question of Church membership is difficult because, according to Catholic belief, the
Church is at one and the same time an institution containing the
means of grace (Gospel and sacraments) and a fellowship of men in
union with Christ."[116] Here the church is pictured both as an institutional means of grace and as a fellowship of people who are
united to Christ. Is the church the unique and universal means of
grace in the world? Apparently such is his position. A subsequent
passage is more explicit in this regard:

The more profound our theological approach to the Church and the
more ready we are to regard her as the universal means of redemption in the world, the more necessary it becomes to acknowledge
several ways of belonging to her, i.e. to consider membership as an
analogous concept. To assert the universal mediation of the
Catholic Church and to regard membership as a univocal notion,
i.e. to reject membership in various degrees, would ultimately lead
to a sectarian position.[117]

In this article Baum still speaks in terms of membership and he
argues his case for an analogous concept of membership. To his way
of thinking, the analogous concept of membership is the only view
that can be reconciled with another truth: "the universal mediation
of the Catholic Church." The Catholic Church is the one means of
salvation in such a manner that anyone who is saved must be joined
in some fashion to this church. Salvation is possible for those outside
the explicit Catholic and Christian faith, but it is possible only because of some bond of union with the church:

The particular theological advantage of this position over the first
[that is, the analogical concept of membership as opposed to the
univocal] is that it clearly distinguishes the salvational situation of
Orthodox and Protestant Christians from the situation of men who
do not have the Christian faith though, being touched by God's
grace and having submitted to the divine will in their hearts, they
are also attached to the body of salvation in the world.[118]

The person who is saved without an explicit profession of the

115 Cf. *ibid.*, p. 19.
116 "Who Belongs to the Church?" *The Ecumenist* 1 (1963), p. 49.
117 *Ibid.*, p. 50; cf. p. 51.
118 *Ibid.*, p. 50.

Christian faith is nevertheless attached to the church, the only means of salvation in the world. But we note the way in which he describes the conversion of this person's heart: being touched by divine grace he submits his or her will to God. He does not say specifically that the touch of grace comes through the church as through a mediating community. A problem regarding the church as the unique means of salvation is present here, but Baum does not face it directly; rather he still repeats the traditional teaching that some bond of union with the church is necessary for salvation.

Toward the end of the article Baum poses the question of whether Vatican II should define the boundaries of the church. He favors a negative answer and adds: "One might even go further and say: The Church that claims to be universal should refuse to define its own boundaries in the world."[119] This suggestion is not clear. Does he mean that since the church is universal it has no boundaries except those of mankind itself? Or does he only intend to say that since the church is directed to the whole of mankind it ought not to define its limits? That he is tending toward an identification of the church and the world of men touched by grace is apparent from the subsequent paragraph:

The Church was created by what Christ did for us on the cross, and since the people purchased by Christ on the cross was the whole human family, there exists a basic identification between the Church and the humanity into which she is sent. This identification is acknowledged constantly by the Church in her faith and her prayer. Because of the intentional unity between the Church and humanity, the grace of Christ is active everywhere in the world. Even though the means of grace are concentrated in a singular and complete fashion in the visible Church, all of humanity has been touched by the redemptive work of the Lord and his saving grace appeals to the hearts of men everywhere, preparing and initiating the kingdom.[120]

On the one hand he speaks of the basic identity of the church and mankind arising from the universal efficacy and presence of Christ's redemptive grace — an identification confessed in the faith and prayer of the church. On the other hand he acknowledges a distinctive and visible community called the church where "the means of grace are concentrated in a singular and complete fashion." Grace is present outside the visible church, yet the church is the singular means of grace. Presumably "singular" means "unique" since he held earlier that the mediation of the church is

119 *Ibid.*
120 *Ibid.*

universal. Baum does not reconcile these two strains of thought. But at this time he is drawn more to the phenomenon of the visible church which is distinguishable from the church of the whole of mankind.[121]

In 1965 Baum published a brief commentary on Vatican II's *Dogmatic Constitution on the Church*.[122] Elucidating the text of the constitution Baum manifests his own perspective on the subject of church and salvation. The fathers of Vatican II describe the church as "the sacrament or sign and instrument, both of a very closely knit union with God and of the unity of the whole human race" (Art. 1). Baum comments:

In the Church we discover what is the destiny of mankind: to be one and to be reconciled with God. And as God never limits his grace to the visible sacraments but offers mercy to those whose heart he touches, we may firmly hold that the grace of reconciliation which is manifest in the Church is also active among men who have not heard of Christ or have misunderstood and therefore rejected the message we have preached.[123]

Where the *Dogmatic Constitution on the Church* speaks of the church as sacrament, Baum more specifically refers to the individual sacraments of the church. His main points are, however, that grace is not confined to the church and that the church manifests intelligibly mankind's goal of unity and reconciliation with God. He does not comment on the passage in terms of universal efficacy and mediatorship.

His commentary on Chapter 2 of the *Constitution* is even more indicative of the grace of God outside the church:

Conscious that the Holy Spirit sent to men by the risen Christ, is also at work in the world, the Church presents the urgency of her missionary action not as if, without her preaching, men would go to eternal perdition; rather, basing herself on the explicit command of

---

[121] Cf. this statement from an address of the same year: "This movement [the missionary movement] was responsible for much theological insight into the universality of the Church and the realization that divine grace is present in the whole of humanity preparing the ground for the establishment of God's kingdom;" "Theological Reflections on the Council," in *Ecumenical Dialogue at Harvard. The Roman Catholic-Protestant Colloquium*. Ed. by Samuel H. Miller and G. Ernest Wright (Cambridge, Mass.: The Belknap Press of Harvard University Press, 1964), p. 76.

[122] "Constitution on the Church," *Journal of Ecumenical Studies* 2 (1965), pp. 1–30; we will quote from the reprint in *De Ecclesia. The Constitution on the Church of Vatican Council II*. Ed. by H. Peters, C.S.P. Foreword by B. C. Butler, O.S.B. Commentary by G. Baum, O.S.A. (Glen Rock, N.J.: Paulist Press, 1965).

[123] *Ibid.*, p. 20.

Jesus to go and to preach to all nations, the Church sees in her missionary endeavor an appointed ministry to lead other men to explicit and declared faith in divine mercy, to join them to the family of the faithful, to protect them from the threats to grace they experience, and to heal and consolidate the good which God has already produced in them. The presence of divine grace outside of the Church is no reason to abandon the missionary activity; on the contrary, the action of God outside the Church is a preparation for the full presence of the Gospel and hence invites the action of the Church to supply the cooperation necessary that the divine initiative come to its full fruition.[124]

Baum acknowledges that the church has a missionary task even though God works outside its boundaries. Sensitive to the missionary preoccupations of the council fathers themselves, a concern only hinted at in the text of the *Constitution*, he supplies here a number of reasons for the missionary activity of the church.

Baum's thought develops further in his book *The Credibility of the Church Today. A Reply to Charles Davis.*[125] Davis's departure from strict adherence to any particular Christian church, while remaining broadly within the Christian tradition, draws a response from Baum, a response which forces him to think through more carefully his understanding of the reality of the church and its assigned function in the world.

Baum elaborates a view of the church in the direction of its identification with the whole of mankind. He calls the church "the community of men who believe that there is hope."[126] Or again, "In a strictly doctrinal sense, therefore, we may call Church the community of men, extending as far as the human race, who are open to the Spirit and in whose hearts God creates good will."[127] There is not a strict identification of church with every person in the world, because not every one has hope and not everybody is open to the Spirit and has a God-created good will. Thus while the church does not coincide with the whole of mankind, it does include everyone who is responsive to the grace of God and properly related to him. This is certainly a broader notion of church than that (or those) developed in the documents of Vatican II, but it compares with the suggestions of other contemporary theologians, e.g., the anonymous Christianity or faith celebrated by Karl Rahner. It is significant, however, that Baum does not simply identify the church and the peoples of the world.

[124] *Ibid.*, p. 30.
[125] New York: Herder and Herder, 1968.
[126] *Ibid.*, p. 17.
[127] *Ibid.*, p. 25.

Apparently what prevented a simple identification was his assumption and elaboration of a new model to describe the reality of the church. He turns to a movement-within-society model, one borrowed from the field of sociology. In this perspective the church becomes an outer-oriented movement in the midst of society.[128] For our purpose here we need only note that the church is a movement within society and that not everyone belongs in fact or by commitment to the movement.

As a movement the church has a mission and a plan of action:

Since the Gospel reveals the sickness of society and makes available the sources of well-being, the Church's mission is a movement of humanization. The Gospel is a critique of human life. The mission of the Church, therefore, is to serve mankind with this Gospel and to help the redemptive presence of God among people to triumph in terms of unity, reconciliation, social justice and peace.[129]

Understandably, not all people benefit from the judgment and corrective nature of the church since it is not a movement that is present throughout the world. But this fact does not annul their chances for redemption. Grace is certainly present outside of this movement. "Good News," Baum affirms, "is that God is redemptively present wherever people are."[130] Again, "In the power of the Spirit God is at work in human life: he summons and graces men to become more conformed to the perfect manhood that is in Jesus Christ."[131] Or even clearer is this passage: "A mystery is at work wherever people come together. As they engage in conversation and seek to solve the problems of life together something happens which we acknowledge as divine grace or a mystery of reconciliation."[132]

There is no question here about the existence of grace outside the limits of explicit Christianity, and it can even be called ecclesial grace. "Divine grace creates fellowship. For this reason theologians have said that wherever grace is given to men, from the very beginning of history, it has an ecclesial character."[133] He does not say that the grace must come through the Christian movement or the visible Church of Christ, but it does form fellowship and orients a person to the community of the church. Thus the church is as exten-

---

[128] Cf. *ibid.*, pp. 196f.

[129] *Ibid.*, p. 198; cf. p. 158.

[130] *Ibid.*, p. 14.

[131] *Ibid.*, p. 17; cf. pp. 24 and 37.

[132] *Ibid.*, p. 46.

[133] *Ibid.*, p. 47.

sive as those who have responded favorably to the saving word of God which enters into the life of every single person.[134]

The revealing word of God confronts every person in the world. Baum insists on the universality of the word in his book *Faith and Doctrine. A Contemporary View*,[135] which for the most part recapitulates the positions espoused in his book *The Credibility of the Church Today*:

What God has said in Christ, he continues to say to the Church. This Word of God, addressing Christians today, creates divine faith in them and in this way constitutes the Church as the community of believers. More than that, this on-going divine self-communication is not confined to the Church in which it is proclaimed, acknowledged and celebrated; it is offered to men, wherever they are, and orientates them away from their sin toward human growth and reconciliation.[136]

It is evident from this passage that for Baum the church is not identified with the totality of mankind, for he affirms that on-going revelation is not confined to the church but is directed to everybody. The church is the community of believers, the gathering in which the word of God is expressly acknowledged, celebrated, and proclaimed. It is the place where divine revelation is interpreted, translated, and explained for the world. "In short, the Church is a necessary hermeneutical principle for understanding divine revelation."[137] The church is necessary as the community of believers which penetrates the meaning and direction of the saving word of God and proclaims this openly for the benefit of the world.

We turn now to a brief article which discloses a radical rethinking of the reality and mission of the church.[138] The reality of the church is expanded beyond the recognizable limits of the professedly Christian community to include anyone touched by divine grace:

When we say church, we do not even think exclusively of the Christian community. Ecclesiology, in the new perspective, does not deal first and principally with the ecclesiastical community of believers and then only, as an afterthought, with the rest of humanity. Ecclesiology brings out the manner in which salvation comes to men everywhere and hence has to do with human life in community. Church, then, in this new perspective, is the whole of mankind inasmuch as it is touched by divine grace.[139]

[134] Cf. *ibid.*, p. 183.

[135] Paramus, N.J.: The Newman Press, 1969.

[136] *Ibid.*, pp. 106f.

[137] *Ibid.*, p. 119.

[138] "The New Ecclesiology," *Commonweal* 91 (October 31, 1969), pp. 123–128. The issue is entitled *Commonweal Papers: 4. The Church in the Year 2000*.

[139] *Ibid.*, p. 123.

The church is as wide as mankind because the whole of mankind is touched by grace, by a grace that comes to people in and through the community:

Divine grace is offered in community. . . . Thanks to God's presence to human life the community becomes the matrix out of which we come to be redeemed people. This is the ecclesial mystery. . . . The ecclesial mystery, proclaimed in Jesus Christ, makes the human community the mother of salvation. Outside the church there is no salvation.[140]

Baum safeguards the axiom *extra ecclesiam nulla salus* by extending the notion of church to the human community throughout the world. No one can come to be or grow outside the community, and this is particularly true of a person's approach to the redeeming grace of God. It is offered to everyone in community and it enables him or her to be saved in the church. Since there is no salvation outside the church, that is, if the maxim is to be retained, the church must extend to the human community everywhere.

In this new perspective the mission of the Church of Christ is not defined in terms of an indispensable means of salvation or a unique instrument of redemption. The church functions as the visible manifestation of the redemption that is present to the whole community of mankind. This is a thought which Baum expressed in previous writings. The church explicitly professes belief in the saving designs of God in Jesus Christ; it celebrates these designs and proclaims them to the world. Moreover, it exercises a ministry of healing and reconciliation:

The church's mission, we are now able to say, is to promote communication among people born into estrangement. The church tries to detect the demonic in the present age; and then seeks to discern the structures of healing present in the wider community and to serve these structures so that the obstacles to fellowship and growth will be overcome. . . . This mission is a ministry of the Word: for it is God's Word that enables the church to detect the demonic in society, to recognize the patterns of renewal already at work among people, and to engage in a dialogue with others that fosters reconciliation.[141]

In the rest of the article Baum explains his view of the church as an outer-oriented movement rather than as a society set over against other societies, a subject which he pursued at great length in *The Credibility of the Church Today*.

Another statement appears in a dialogue between Baum and Dr.

[140] *Ibid.*
[141] *Ibid.*, p. 124.

Rosemary Ruether held under the auspices of the *National Catholic Reporter*. His position here is not so much changed as nuanced, for he acknowledges diverse definitions of the church:

Well, for me the church is a multi-valued reality; that is, I think there's a way in which the church could mean the whole of mankind inasmuch as it is touched by divine grace; this is traditional, too. It's possible to think of all men as God's people and that wherever people are touched by divine grace, love, friendship and truth, this is the church emerging. That's one meaning of church.

And there's another meaning of church and that would be the community of Jesus, the people who celebrate, who believe in him, live with him in liturgy and worship, people who acknowledge a kind of mission in regard to other people. . . . And then I would say another meaning of church for me is the Roman Catholic community, the church which has attempted to be a local and universal church and has enriched the kind of tension between the local and the universal — never abandoning the ideal. . . . I feel that the other churches — while I regard them as sisters — nonetheless have at some particular point in history abandoned this dream of being the universal church.[142]

It seems that Baum's *Commonweal* article (1969) reveals better his true preferences. In this dialogue he is more careful to present the wider spectrum of definitions of the church. The church emerges wherever people respond to grace. Baum calls this view traditional. This is true of recent tradition, especially if he means that all grace is ecclesial and that it procures some form of attachment to the church.

God's grace in Christ touches people the world over, promoting liberation and forgiveness. The mission of the church is to proclaim this liberation and forgiveness:

I regard the church, the Christian church, as a community where this mystery of which I've spoken is proclaimed in Jesus, and is celebrated when the people gather around the eucharistic table and celebrate this mystery which is present everywhere.

But while I say this, I would want to add immediately what I call the irony of the gospel, that is, it's always possible that the gifts which Jesus gives in the church exist with greater intensity outside of it.[143]

There is no indication here that the Christian church is the unique source of the grace which exists in abundance outside its limits.

---

[142] Vol. 6, no. 20, March 18, 1970, p. 6.
[143] *Ibid.*, p. 6.

The church points up and celebrates Christ's work of redemption in the world. Moreover, according to Baum, the limits of the Christian church need not be as sharply defined as in the past:

I have a different sociological model for church; I think what has taken place is that the church has gone from being a society with definitive boundary lines, with a government and jurisdiction of the people, and is coming to be a movement. A movement is another sociological reality which is institutional because a movement has organization. But in a movement you don't have clearly defined boundary lines and people associate themselves with a movement according to their own responsible choice. I think this is what's taking place.[144]

In his recent book, *Man Becoming. God in Secular Experience*,[145] Baum acknowledges an explicit Christian church whose boundaries are more or less clearly marked out by an outward profession of redemptive faith in the Lord Jesus Christ. The whole of mankind is not church in this express and articulate manner, though it is not easy to determine boundaries between church and world. The redemptive grace of Christ and the Spirit of God are operative throughout the world bringing people to faith and reconciliation, but the church's task centers around the conscious proclamation and celebration of the mystery that is present to humans everywhere. Moreover, the church serves to create community in the world, to unify and socialize the human race. The church acts as a dialogue partner with the world, witnessing to the gospel of Christ, identifying the religious values in the world at large, criticizing the harmful movements, but also learning from the world:

[In sum, the church is] a movement in human society with open boundaries not always clearly visible, appointed as divine catalyst of a spiritual and social transformation, a movement drawing men into dialogue and even conflict so that the whole human family may become more open to God's self-communication and proceed on the way to growth and reconciliation. The acknowledgment of a graced humanity, therefore, does not invalidate the Church's mission. The mission of the Church sets up an inexhaustible dialectic in humanity by which all men are summoned to greater consciousness of the divine mystery operative in their lives. The Church is the visible instrument, the extension of Christ, by which the divine Word elevates humanity to the ever-to-be-renewed awareness of God's presence in its own self-creation.[146]

[144] *Ibid.*, p. 7.

[145] New York: Herder and Herder, 1970. Cf. especially Chapter III, "The Church in the New Perspective."

[146] *Ibid.*, p. 88.

According to Baum, therefore, the church is not the only medium of grace to the world at large, for the redemptive grace of Christ and his Spirit are effective outside the limits of the church. Baum states: "The New Testament gives witness to the Church as the unique instrument of salvation and at the same time acknowledges the universality of God's salvific care for his people." [147]

Baum moves away from the identification of the church and mankind. He propounds an explicit and visible church whose limits are not always clearly defined, and he ascribes some instrumental function to the church. He abandons the conceptual framework of viewing the church as uniquely necessary for salvation, but still he allows the church a task in the world and he accepts the doctrine that people are redeemed outside its boundaries.

This direction of Baum's thought is articulated more clearly in "Toward a New Catholic Theism." [148] Baum notes certain ecclesiological shifts since Vatican II, especially those regarding the place and role of the church in the world:

There is no way of denying that this is a radical shift in the Church's self-understanding. The Church is constituted by the explicit awareness of the mystery present in all men in a hidden way. This awareness is produced by the Christian message. The Church is, therefore, not needed for individual salvation; what counts for salvation is man's response in faith to the divine voice present to him in his life. But the Church's awareness, created by Christ, appoints her to enter into dialogue and cooperation with other people, to serve the mystery of redemption present among them, to effect the formation of a new consciousness in humanity and thus to create a more truly human future for mankind. [149]

While Baum is here summarizing the views of other ecclesiologists, he seems to agree with the broad features of these views. What was implicit in his book *Man Becoming* becomes explicit in this article, namely, that the church is not necessary for the salvation of an individual. The church's task is to bring to consciousness the salvific mystery present in man's life (a theme he developed at greater length in *Man Becoming*).

In the same article, criticizing Richard McBrien's use of the words church and kingdom, Baum cites the opinions of other theologians:

They prefer to use the word Church in an analogous sense: Church refers to the Christian community, but in an analogous sense it may

---

[147] *Ibid.*, p. 79.
[148] *The Ecumenist* 8 (1970), pp. 53–61.
[149] *Ibid.*, p. 54.

also refer to the fellowship created by God's redemptive presence to men. In this terminology it is possible to say that there is Church beyond the Church. In this perspective the Church's mission is to serve the redemptive mystery present in the human community. The differing terminologies do not express an actual theological difference.[150]

It would seem that Baum numbers himself among the theologians who use the word church in an analogous sense, though in his *Man Becoming* he favored a narrower use of the term and applied it to explicit Christians.

In a matter of a few years, therefore, Baum's view of the church and its mission has undergone considerable evolution, from the traditional picture of the Christian community functioning as the unique means of salvation to the progressive concept of the Christian church as the express movement of reconciliation and of interpretation of the divine mystery in the world. At times he expands the notion of church to include the whole of mankind inasmuch as it is touched and moved by the redeeming grace of God. In the latter view it is not difficult to accept the axiom *extra ecclesiam nulla salus*, for salvation would always be within the church. But more recently Baum prefers the explicitness of the church as constituted by Christian belief and he holds that this church is not necessary for the salvation of the individual, even though it has a task of reconciliation and community building in the world.

4. Hans Küng

The renowned Tübingen theologian, Hans Küng, directs his attention to the axiom with more force and incisiveness than does any other Catholic theologian since World War II. This is understandable, given his predilection for ecclesiological topics and his talent for asking vital questions of the church. His references to the axiom are few but they indicate a substantial evolution of thought.

The first reference appears in *That the World May Believe*, a book that is set in the literary form of letters to a seminarian.[151] In "Outside the Church No Salvation?" (Letter 7) Küng broaches our subject directly:

What it [the axiom] asserts is that there are not two or several true

---

[150] *Ibid.*

[151] New York: Sheed and Ward, 1963. An earlier allusion may be found in a brief reference to the traditional teaching of salvation through the church: "God chooses Himself in His Son to achieve the salvation of all men through the Church." *Justification. The Doctrine of Karl Barth and a Catholic Reflection* (New York: Nelson and Sons, 1964), p. 134.

Churches in which Christ is given to us, but only one: one great all-embracing one. Only those are excluded from her who do not believe because they are against Christ, not by ignorance but by malice; for these unbelievers there is no salvation. All men of good will believe in her, who truly believe in Christ and work for him in love. True, there are different ways of believing, different ways of belonging to the Church. It's true that a Protestant Christian, who rejects the Petrine office which was willed by Christ, does not belong to the Church in the same way as a Catholic does. But the Protestant Christian does belong, if he is in good faith, to the same one Church, the one ark of salvation for all. God does not let anyone be lost except through their own fault; he let his Son die for *all* men, and wills that *all* men should be saved. But whoever is saved is saved through Christ in the Church, and thus belongs in some way (often a very hidden way) to the one Church. Thus the Church is here for all men who are in good faith and of good will. Thus she is the one Church for the salvation of all true believers, outside which there is no salvation but only damnation and unbelief.[152]

In this early writing Küng utters not a word against the traditional axiom nor dissuades the seminarian from citing it. Adhering to the customary theological approach, he merely offers a clarification of the maxim, noting especially the qualifications that must be invoked in order to understand it properly. The axiom means that there is only one church of salvation. This church is the unique locus of salvation, so much so that anyone who is saved must belong to it in some way. Attachment to the church varies according to the individual's type and extent of faith. But the ultimate thrust of his statement is that all people of good will belong to the church and consequently are saved *in* the church (through Christ, of course). Thus Küng safeguards the axiom, though in a qualified sense, and he extends the church to those of good will who are attached to it in some hidden fashion.

Letter 7 is silent about the manner in which the church graces persons of good will. Apparently a mediational function of the church is not necessary, for in Letter 8, titled "What Happens to Pagans," where he describes the salvation of "unbelievers" in the customary fashion, we find this statement: "But what if we suppose, seeing that it is God's merciful will that *all* men shall be saved, that Christ's grace reaches right out beyond the visible Church to embrace the whole of mankind?"[153]

In 1964 Küng delivered a paper at a conference on "Christian Revelation and non-Christian Religions," held under the auspices

---

[152] *That the World May Believe*, pp. 100f.
[153] *Ibid.*, p. 114.

of the International Eucharistic Congress (Bombay).[154] It exhibits a remarkable reversal of position. Küng no longer attempts to preserve and explain the axiom as he did in his letters to the seminarian. He traces the origin of the axiom to the image of the ark of Noah which is cited in 1 Peter 3, 20 to portray salvation through baptism. Here he finds a positive indication of salvation *in* the church, not a negative indication of no salvation *outside* the ark. Thereupon he outlines a history of the axiom from Ignatius of Antioch to Pius XII and he discovers that "whenever this axiom in its *negative* formulation has been taken in the absolutely literal sense of the words, it has led to heresy."[155] While he realizes that dogmatic theology must continue to study the axiom, he recommends its abandonment in preaching and practical instruction. For it invariably leads to an impression of duplicity or intolerance: duplicity, because its literal implication is that no one is saved outside the church while in fact the church teaches that people can be saved outside the church; intolerance, because it is often understood in the literal and rigid sense that no one is saved outside the church.[156] At the same time he expresses a dislike for the extension of the concept of church to a vague community of people of good will; the reasons are essentially those repeated later in his book *The Church*.

Salvation is ensured for those outside the church. In fact the way of salvation for the peoples of the world religions can be called ordinary: "As against the 'extraordinary' way of salvation which is the Church, the world religions can be called — if this is rightly understood — the 'ordinary' way of salvation for non-Christian humanity."[157] Implied in this statement is a positive evaluation of non-Christian religions; they cannot be regarded, as they were at some times and in some circles, as products of the spirit of evil but as manifestations of the Spirit of God working with people all over the world. Of course this judgment does not exclude the possibility and reality of deviations in these religions:

Despite their errors, the religions teach the truth of Christ when they recognize man's need of salvation: when they discern the loneliness, the helpless and forlorn state of man in this world, his abysmal fear and distress, his evil behaviour and false pride; when they see the cruelty, perdition and nothingness of this world, and

---

[154] The paper, "The World Religions in God's Plan of Salvation," is published in *Christian Revelation and World Religions*. Ed. by J. Neuner, S.J. (London: Burns and Oates, 1967), pp. 25–66. It was first published in a special number of *Indian Ecclesiastical Studies*, IV: 3–4 (July-October, 1965).

[155] *Ibid.*, p. 31.

[156] *Ibid.*, pp. 34f.

[157] *Ibid.*, pp. 51f.

the meaning and meaninglessness of man's death; when, because of this, they look for something new and long for transformation, rebirth and redemption for man and his world.[158]

Themes from this paper are taken up repeatedly in subsequent writings whenever, in fact, Küng broaches the subject of church and salvation.

That Christ's grace reaches right out beyond the visible church is in particular true of the Spirit of Christ. In a different context, though not unrelated to the subject of the mediational role of the church, Küng extols the freedom of the Spirit:

This Spirit emerges neither from the Church nor from the Christian, but only from God himself. He is not the bestowal and gift, the power and strength of the Church, but of God. He acts *on* the Church, manifests himself *to* the Church, comes *to* the Church, establishes and maintains the Church. But he does not become the Church's own spirit. He remains God's own Spirit. Therefore he is and remains the *free* Spirit.[159]

The Spirit of Christ is free, neither arising from the church nor depending on the church for its existence and operation. Thus it is clear — and this is the only reason for citing the passage here — that the church is not the mediational source of all grace, specifically the grace of the Holy Spirit.

Küng returns to a study of the axiom in a brief article prepared for a *Festschrift* in honor of G. C. Berkouwer.[160] Since it adds little to the paper of 1964, a passing notice of it will suffice. Included in his historical sketch of the use of the axiom is an interpretation of 1 Peter 3, 20, one of the significant scripture texts that stand behind the adage. He understands the passage to mean that there is salvation in the ark, not that there is no salvation outside the ark.[161] Included also is a criticism of Cyprian's negative formulation of the axiom: "Here we already experience that which later too would always prove to be true, namely, that when the *negatively* formulated axiom is taken exactly according to its literal meaning, it always leads to heresy."[162] Our historical sketch (Chapter 1) bears out the validity of this observation.

[158] *Ibid.*, p. 53.
[159] "God's Free Spirit in the Church," *Freedom and Man*. Ed. by John Courtney Murray, S.J. (New York: P.J. Kenedy & Sons, 1965), p. 18.
[160] "Anmerkungen zum axiom 'Extra Ecclesiam nulla Salus'," in *Ex auditu verbi*. Ed. by R. Schippers, G. E. Mueleman, J. T. Bakker, and H. M. Kuitert (Kampen: Uitgeversmaatschappij J. H. Kok N. V., 1965), pp. 80–88.
[161] *Ibid.*, p. 80.
[162] *Ibid.*, p. 81.

One way to safeguard the axiom is to extend the notion of church to include anyone being justified and saved and thus to provide for his salvation within the limits of the church. Küng now disagrees with this argument. He does not align himself with those theologians who wish to stretch the notion of church to non-Christians for this or any other reason. He prefers to restrict the concept of church to the lineaments provided in general by the New Testament; the church there is composed of well-defined believers, those who profess the Lord Jesus Christ and celebrate his name in word and sacrament.[163] This does not imply, of course, that there is no salvation outside the church; there is salvation outside the church, but it does not follow that those saved outside the church are in fact church.

Should the axiom be committed to oblivion or declared heretical? Küng simply recommends that dogmatic theology continue to study the axiom but that Christian preaching abandon it entirely.[164]

Küng's most complete and carefully reasoned statement on the axiom is found in his award-winning book *The Church*.[165] But the space allotted to it is relatively small, and much of it is a recapitulation of his previous articles. Nevertheless it is an incisive and bold statement of position. He depends upon other studies, to be sure, but he cuts through much historical and dogmatic red tape to expose the center of the problem.

Noteworthy is his reference to the demographical dimension of the origin of the axiom — the presumption that the Christian message had gone out to most of the inhabited world and that people had an opportunity to accept or reject faith and baptism (cf. Mk 16, 16). Also, he underscores the multiple misunderstandings and ill-feelings engendered by the axiom, especially because of its negative formulation:

The words are interpreted more often as either intolerance or duplicity: as intolerance when they are understood literally and exclusively in accordance with the old tradition; as duplicity when it means on the one hand that no one will be saved outside the Catholic Church and on the other hand does not exclude the fact that people outside the Catholic Church are saved, in fact millions and billions of them, the greater part of mankind.[166]

Küng rejects the attempt to "save the axiom" by stretching the notion of church to a vast number of invisible members, to

---

[163] Cf. *ibid.*, pp. 84–87.
[164] *Ibid.*, p. 88.
[165] New York: Sheed and Ward, 1967, pp. 313–319.
[166] *Ibid.*, p. 316.

everyone of good faith. He prefers to define the church more narrowly, as he does in this section:

The concept of the Church can rightly be applied to the Christian
Churches which compose a community of baptized Christians
united by the message of the New Testament, believing in Christ
the Lord, celebrating the Lord's Supper, trying to live according to
the gospels and wishing to be regarded by the world as Church.[167]

Thereupon he submits four reasons why he elects not to extend the
notion of church to those outside the believing and confessing
community: 1) it is contrary to the evidence of the New Testament
and the tradition based on it; 2) an extension of the notion of church
is not necessary to account for the salvation of non-Christians; 3) the
broad notion of the church renders missionary work unnecessarily
difficult, for it presumes that people of good will already belong to
the church; 4) it offends non-believers to be told that they are Christians, at least in implicit desire, and they reject such theological
speculation.[168]

Küng concludes, as in a previous article, with some advice about
the use and non-use of the axiom. Those who insist on the negative
formulation should not use it to condemn people outside the church
but rather they should apply it to themselves: there is no salvation
for *them* except in the church. The positive formulation — salvation
in the church — can be applied to others. Dogmatic theology must
examine weaknesses and limitations of the axiom, stressing especially the fact that there is salvation in Christ. Küng gives con-
tradictory advice to the preacher:

In preaching the phrase should be passed over and used as little as
possible, since today it is either not understood or misunderstood.
. . . For the sake of this very faith the formula "no salvation
outside the church," which is so open to misunderstanding and so
damaging to the Church's mission in the world, should no longer
be used in the preaching of the word of faith.[169]

The second sentence seems to express better the whole tenor of the
passage, namely, that Küng advocates the elimination of the axiom
in the preaching of the church.

This judgment is borne out by a statement in a later book, *Truthfulness: The Future of the Church:*[170]

She [the church] is the believing, confessing, inviting vanguard of

---

[167] *Ibid.*, p. 317.
[168] *Ibid.*
[169] *Ibid.*, p. 318.
[170] New York: Sheed and Ward, 1968.

mankind, knowing by faith what is involved for all. But, precisely for the sake of this faith, she ought no longer to use in her proclamation the axiom which today has become deceptive and misleading.[171]

His other statements here on the understanding of the axiom take up themes contained in *The Church* and in previous articles, but manifest more sharply the impropriety of repeating the formula literally when its theological content today implies just the opposite.[172]

Küng's position requires no summary, for it is brief and clear. But an evaluation is in place. His decisive opposition to the axiom is based on a grasp of the New Testament church and of the history of the axiom. He places the adage in its proper historical perspective and perceives the religious malaise which it engendered over the centuries. He proceeds with confidence against the continued use of the saying, and at the same time he establishes a theology of salvation outside the church which no longer requires the support of the adage. Thus he opens up fresh areas of theological investigation: the salvation of those who are truly outside the church, and the mission of the Christian church in the vast non-Christian world.

---

[171] *Ibid.*, p. 149; cf. pp. 143–154.

[172] There is only a brief reference to the subject in his *Infallibility? An Inquiry* (Garden City, New York: Doubleday, 1971), p. 65, note 1.

Chapter 4

Church Models and Salvation Outside the Church

Scientific disciplines commonly use models to organize, analyze, explain, and explore a vast amount of empirical data. As conceptual tools drawn from everyday experience either directly or through a process of elaboration, models assist the investigating mind to grasp the whole of a specified subject and/or the interrelation of the subject's many particulars. Models are only more or less successful in bringing to light aspects of the reality under investigation. One model makes manifest certain features of the subject, another model, other features. Usually a variety of models must be used to uncover the richness of a reality.[1]

Christian writers, ancient and modern, have used many images, metaphors, and models to elucidate the reality of the church.[2] Obviously these are never exhaustive since the reality of the church is complex, combining the perceptible and the mysterious. But they are helpful instruments of exposition and discovery.

This chapter is designed as a systematic presentation of some of the ecclesial models which have been or are assumed in the resolution of the question of the Church of Christ and the salvation of non-Christians. The ecclesial models range from the scriptural model of the body of Christ to the sociological model of a movement within society (these are not necessarily the extremes). The various descriptions of the church, drawn as they are from diverse and independent realms of human thought, determine to a great extent the type of answer that is given to the question of the relationship

[1] Cf. Max Black, *Models and Metaphors. Studies in Language and Philosophy* (Ithaca, New York: Cornell University Press, 1962).

[2] Cf. Avery Dulles, S.J., *Models of the Church* (Garden City, New York: Doubleday and Co., 1974).

122

between the church and salvation. Since we cannot examine here all models of the church that appear in the scriptures and in theological writings, we will select a few dominant models from recent theology. We propose to sketch out a description of the model, then to place the axiom within the model. Our purpose is to determine what happens to the axiom when it is seen against the backdrop of various models.

It is acknowledged that no theologian uses any one model of thought to the exclusion of the rest and that the use of a variety of models augments the conceptual grasp of the reality of the church. But it is also recognized that generally one particular model or image prevails in the mind of a theologian or in the ecclesiology of a certain period. It is a matter of history, for instance, that the body of Christ model dominated the ecclesiological scene of the 1940's and 1950's.

For the sake of clarity we reiterate the thrust of our investigation and the focus of our question: we wish to determine whether the Church of Christ is a medium of salvation for everyone actually being justified and saved. It is assumed that the church can be and is an effective locus of salvation for those who profess belief in Jesus Christ and pursue a life of love. Specifically then, what is the relationship between the church and the salvation of those "outside" its explicit boundaries? If the church is not a *universal* reality, what is the relationship between the church and the saved "outside" its visible limits? How does the axiom *extra ecclesiam nulla salus* fare when placed in the framework of ecclesial models? Finally, what models of the church best account for the relationship between the church and those saved "outside," if indeed they are saved "outside" the church?

Before turning to the individual models, we need to clarify briefly an issue that pervades all of them: the question of the boundaries of the church. The ecclesial models presuppose or explicitly embrace various solutions to the question of the extent of the church; in fact, some of them are chosen by theologians precisely because of their possibilities in this regard. Some of the ecclesial models assume or specifically demand a widening of the boundaries of the church; others, a narrowing of its limits. Some models expand the notion of church so that it includes countless numbers of people outside an explicit profession of faith in Christ; others contract the notion to include only professed Christians, or even professed Roman Catholic Christians.

The manner in which ecclesiologists use ecclesial models and thus expand or contract the notion of the church is crucial for our question of the relationship between the church and the salvation of those "outside." Who are those saved "outside" the church? Is anyone saved "outside" the church? If one is saved, is he or she saved by being *in* the church? Or if one is saved, is he or she saved *through* the church? Or if one is saved, is it with a minimum of orientation to the church? Or finally, is one saved without any relationship to the church? There are basically three approaches to the solution of this set of questions.

1) One approach is to widen the notion of the church to the extent that it embraces all who are *de facto* being saved by the grace of God in Christ Jesus. It is assumed that not all those being saved exhibit a profession of faith in Christ; but it is stressed that non-Christians who are being saved belong to the church in some implicit and hidden manner. They are church; they are saved in the church, not outside of it. This approach may include the idea that the grace of salvation comes to non-Christians through the church in an anonymous fashion. It may also include the idea that people are joined to the church in a variety of ways: from full participation in church life to a tenuous, unknowing but real attachment to the church. (In the past some spoke in terms of belonging to the soul of the church and not to its body, or in terms of belonging invisibly to a visible church.)

2) A second approach is to confine the notion and extent of the church to professed Christian believers, those who receive the word of the gospel, are baptized, and lead a Christian life of worship and service. Salvation for these is effected precisely in and through the church. The boundaries of the church are well-defined so that it is relatively easy to trace the extent of the church. With this definition of church the theologian can then frankly admit that grace and salvation are present outside the boundaries of the church, not of course outside the redemptive life of Christ. Those saved outside the boundaries of the church are simply saved through the grace and merits of Jesus Christ, not through or in the Church of Christ. The church is not regarded as a medium of grace and salvation for those totally outside its boundaries. It may be conceded that those saved outside the limits of the church assume some orientation toward the church, in the sense that the visibility of their grace-filled lives (morally upright conduct, professed belief in God, etc.) is comparable in varying degrees to that of professed Christian believers.

3) A third approach is to define the church in terms of explicit Christian believers and to acknowledge that the church is involved in the salvation of those outside its visible boundaries. The

church's involvement can range from a near mechanical mediator-ship of grace to the less obvious spiritual assistance of prayer and worship.

Ours is a version of this third approach. We confine the church more narrowly to explicit believers in Jesus Christ, and we assume that the fullest and most authentic tradition of Christianity is found in the Roman Catholic Church. We also assume that the ecclesial realities of other Christian traditions manifest the Church of Christ. Thus in this chapter we wish to relate the Christian churches in this broadest sense to the salvation of those outside of explicit Christian belief.

The point at issue in this chapter is the manner in which the thrust of a particular model throws light on the relationship be-tween the church and the salvation of those outside the church. The question is this: what kind of relationship between the church and those outside does a particular model indicate? What kind of a relationship does it demand?

1. *The Church and Christ*

Undoubtedly Catholic ecclesiology of the recent past has favored the christological model. We witness the popularity of the image of the body of Christ, the chief example of this model. This image of the church, prominent in the Pauline epistles, was extolled by au-thors of the past century, beginning with Johann Adam Moehler (d. 1838) and culminating with Pius XII (cf. his *Mystici Corporis* of 1943). It ceded its position of privilege to no other image during the 1940's and 1950's; even Vatican II accorded it a respected place in its *Dogmatic Constitution on the Church* (1964), though now it had to share the honors with other images, notably that of the people of God.

According to the christological model the church is viewed in its intimate relationship to Christ. Christ and the church, while retain-ing their separate identities, are closely joined and mutually in-volved. Biblical images such as the body of Christ, the bride of Christ, the vine and the branches, bespeak a union that is at once an intimate mutual sharing and a respectful duality. Evidently the im-ages convey various degrees of intensity of union and separateness. For instance, the bride of Christ image highlights better than most images the separateness of Christ and the church together with their loving union. The vine and branches image extols the com-mon life that Christ shares with his church.

The christological model incorporates these and similar images in order to proclaim the union between Christ and the church. The church is seen primarily against the personal outline of Christ; the features of the church are viewed in Christ, and vice versa. Some theologians, especially those with a homiletic bent, press the description of the union, if not to the point of identity, at least to that of quasi-identity. This is not to say that their descriptions are entirely devoid of scriptural precedent (e.g., "Saul, Saul, why do you persecute me?" Acts 9, 4); but it is to affirm that their preoccupation involves the bonds and forces that manifest the unity of Christ and his church.

The union is drawn out in terms of similar features and characteristics. Just as Christ joined within himself the divine and the human, so also the church is structured along the lines of the divine and the human. The human appears in both Christ and the church, but it is the human that leads symbolically and effectively beyond the visible to the invisible realities within. Thus with the death and glorification of Jesus the church extends in time and space the visible manifestation of the activity of Jesus. To a certain extent the church already participates in the glory of its Lord, already shares his triumphs. As a continuation of his life and activity on earth it assumes his regal, priestly, and prophetic functions. It is the teacher of truth, proclaiming the word and preserving it from corrosion and oblivion. It is the overseer, setting up with firmness and care a pattern of Christian living. It is the priestly community, offering up sacrifices of praise and thanksgiving for itself and mankind. It is the church without spot and wrinkle, advancing from victory to victory over the forces of sin and evil in the world.

It cannot be denied that the church does in fact show forth the features of Christ and does in a wonderful manner carry out the functions and activities of Christ. But it is also true that generally the glorious and triumphal aspects of this privilege receive the bulk of attention from Catholic ecclesiologists (at least those of the recent past) who operate mainly within the christological model of the church. They cannot deny the sinful character of the church, but this aspect is customarily set in terms of sinful *members* in the church, thus portraying the church itself as some kind of glorious reality above human sinfulness and corruption. Again, we cannot deny that holiness is a mark of the church, especially in virtue of its union with the sinless Christ and his Spirit, but this fact does not allow the one church to be divided into two realities, one covered with sin and the other bedecked with holiness. The one Church of Christ is both washed in the saving waters of baptism and standing in need of continual purification from its sins.

To approach our question more specifically, the christological model underscores the close union of Christ and the church. Consequently this model is prone to view the activity of the church as the continuation of the saving and redemptive functions of Christ.[3] According to this model the church is the extension of the incarnation precisely so that it may effectively bring salvation to the men of all times and places. It would be easy to multiply quotations from theological writers who advocate this salvific function of the church. Let two witnesses stand for all: Pope Paul VI, while still the archbishop of Milan, wrote these words about the church:

The mission of the Church is the continuation of Christ. . . . We must therefore understand very well how Christ's mission becomes transformed into the Church's mission, for exactly in this lies the act whereby the Church comes into being, and in this lies its efficient cause.[4]

And Peter De Rosa:

Whoever is saved by Christ has felt and benefited from the power of the Church's influence. The Church's influence is as far-reaching and as incalculable as Christ's own. . . . It is only in the Church that the grace which abounds in Christ is communicated to this world for she is "the sacrament of salvation" (*Decree on the Missionary Activity of the Church*, paragraph 5). It is for the Church to give men a share in the plenitude of Christ and to ensure that everything that has happened in her head may be reproduced in his members.[5]

The more the church is viewed as bound up with the person and activity of Christ, the more it is regarded as the effective means of salvation. This christological view of the church carries with it both

[3] Cf. F. Holböck, "Das Mysterium der Kirche in Dogmatischer Sicht," in *Mysterium Kirche in der Sicht der theologischen Disziplinen*. Ed. by F. Holböck and T. Sartory, O.S.B. Vol. 1 (Salzburg: Otto Müller Verlag, 1962), pp. 327f. Also C. Journet, *The Church of the Word Incarnate*, Vol. I (London: Sheed and Ward, 1955), p. 513.

[4] G. Montini, *The Church* (Baltimore: Helicon, 1964), pp. 23, 25.

[5] *God Our Savior. A Study of the Atonement* (Milwaukee: Bruce, 1967), pp. 136, 142. The chapter in which these passages appear is significantly entitled "The God who saves us in the church." Cf. also Y. de Montcheuil, *Aspects of the Church* (Chicago: Fides, 1955), p. 144. E. Schillebeecks, O.P., "The Church and Mankind," in *The Church and Mankind, Concilium*, Vol. 1 (New York: Paulist Press, 1965). F. X. Lawlor, S.J., "The Mediation of the Church in Some Pontifical Documents," *Theological Studies* 12 (1951), pp. 481–504. The whole article is important, but note especially this statement on pages 484f: "We may say then that there is a solidarity in the salvific order between Christ and His Church, between Head and Body. One cannot, so to speak, 'unchurch' Christ the Savior, and adhere to Him apart from that visible and social communion so consciously precious to the early centuries of Christianity." Cf. too O. Semmelroth, S.J., *Church and Sacrament* (Notre Dame, Ind.: Fides, 1965), p. 32.

advantages and disadvantages. Some advantages: it points up the redemptive life of Jesus; it speaks loudly for the utter dependence of sinful mankind on the person of Christ; the presence of the church is a continual incentive for us to fix our eyes on Christ's redeeming life and activity. The salvific relationship to Christ is necessary; and the church is the abiding sign of this relationship.

The model also has its disadvantages. It carries with it the tendency to minimize the differences that exist between Christ and the church. It passes over too easily the imperfect nature of the church, its struggles with error and sin within its midst, its continual need for purification, its proneness to domination over the lives of people, its self-exaltation in triumph and splendor. This model of the church, precisely in the question of salvation, does not explain sufficiently the communication of saving grace by a sinful and imperfect church — sufficiently, we say, because while it acknowledges the valid and fruitful ministrations of a sinful minister, it does not extend this explanation adequately to the church as a whole and especially to the church in its quasi-identity with Christ.

There is another aspect of the christological model which should be broached here, though it ties in with the anthropological model which we will take up later. The aspect in question is anthropological, deriving both from the "man" perspective of Jesus Christ and from his influence on the whole human community. Since the Word became flesh, took on a human form, and thereby entered the human community, his influence permeates the whole of mankind. In their relationship to God men and women bear the impress of the God-made-man; it is a salvational impress in the sense that it opens up the possibility of grace and holiness, of reconciliation and proper orientation toward God.

To the point at issue: what does this view of Christ and his salvational influence on human beings mean for the question of church and salvation? Does it imply that if people realize the possibility of grace and holiness in their personal and moral lives (a possibility which most theologians acknowledge) they are consequently within the realm of the church, at least in a latent or hidden sense? Does the possibility of grace and salvation which accrues to them as a result of Christ's presence within the human community mean that they have become anonymous Christians or anonymous believers (cf. the position of Karl Rahner)? Does the actualization of grace at a distance from the visible church mean that the actualization is also effected through the power of the church and not just through the power of Christ? Is the church's influence on people to be compared with Christ's influence, so that the church's influence extends instrumentally as far as and in the same measure as Christ's?

Some suggest that the church shares or enters into the work of redemption in the sense that it participates in the priesthood of Christ; it unites itself with the sacrificial action of Christ and so profits all mankind.[6] Traditional theology could not deny that the life, death, and resurrection of Christ is all-sufficient for the redemption of the world, but it puzzled over the place of the church in the work of salvation. A passage in Colossians was a conundrum: "Now I rejoice in my sufferings for your sake, and in my flesh I complete what is lacking in Christ's afflictions for the sake of his body, that is, the church" (1, 24). Some were wont to stress the meritorious and complementary character of the sufferings of Paul and the church. But more likely (though the passage is not altogether clear) Paul refers to the sufferings of the apostolic ministry, the sufferings endured in the task of preaching where Christ did not preach and also the sufferings caused by the persecutions and divisions resulting from a people's acceptance or non-acceptance of the gospel.[7]

It is apparent that the church's activity cannot derogate from the universal effectiveness of the Christ event. If the church participates in the redemptive sufferings of Christ, this can only mean that the worth of its sufferings is relative to and dependent upon the work of Christ. Ultimately then the event of Christ remains the all-important and all-embracing factor in the work of redemption. And the church, confined as it is to a restricted area of the world, shares his sufferings through the office of evangelization. Thus one cannot speak of participation in Christ's redemptive sacrifice without the introduction of urgent qualifications which safeguard the unique and universal effectiveness of Christ. The church profits the whole of mankind, therefore, only in and through Christ, not directly through any preached word, celebrated sacrament, or Christian style of life. The question is this: what effect does the church have on those who are profiting from the work of Christ as a distance from the church? Or again, how in fact does the church profit these people? God looks with favor, to be sure, upon the sacrifices of the Christian community, especially upon its celebration of the word and the sacraments.

[6] Cf. A. Bea, *The Church and Mankind* (Chicago: Franciscan Herald Press, 1967), pp. 71f; p. 134.

[7] Cf. J. Grassi, M.M., "The Letter to the Colossians," in *The Jerome Biblical Commentary*. Ed. by R. E. Brown, S.S., J. A. Fitzmyer, S.J., and R. E. Murphy, O. Carm. (Englewood Cliffs, N.J.: Prentice-Hall, 1968), p. 338.

Thus perhaps the weightiest argument in support of the universal effectiveness of the church in the salvation of those outside its boundaries is the matter of prayer to the Father in Christ Jesus. The prayer of the faithful, whether in solemn liturgies or in private aspiration, is addressed to the Lord God on behalf of all men. It is prayer to the Father *through* Christ. According to traditional Christian teaching the Father urges us to pray and is affected by prayer. It can be argued persuasively, therefore, that the church exercises through its mission of prayer some effectiveness in the process of salvation.

The effectiveness of the christological model to explain the role of the church as a means of saving grace for those "outside" increases as the union between Christ and the church is intensified to the point of quasi-identity. Conversely, the effectiveness of the model diminishes the more the differences between Christ and the church are pointed out. We maintain that the church cannot have the same effectiveness as Christ precisely because the church is not Christ, is not the Savior but the saved, is not the Lord but the sinful servant. It cannot share the same universality as the saving effect of Christ. Here we only wish to deny traditional theology's excessive identification of Christ and the church, and the exaggerated consequences of this identification: a rigid and wide-ranging instrumentality of the church in the work of salvation for those in fact being saved. If we accept a narrower view of the church, we must acknowledge that it is not universal, even while admitting the principle that it is directed toward every person. If it is not universal in fact and in many other ways deviates from the universality and effectiveness of Christ, it is more logical to hold that the church is not a universal locus of salvation, that Christ's effectiveness extends beyond the boundaries of the church to bring people into a saving relationship to God and to orient them in a graceful sense toward the church. Thus we are constrained to say that many people are brought to the church by Christ rather than that the church brings Christ to all peoples:

It is undoubtedly the will of Christ that his fullness should be present in the Church as an institution. But today men seem to come to the Church through Christ rather than to Christ through the Church. A man who is attracted by the grace and person of Christ may finally realize that his fullness on earth is to be found in the Church, whereas it seems much rarer that men, fascinated by the Church, finally find Christ in it. This is generally true of all separated Christians.[8]

---

[8] A. Mueller, *Obedience in the Church* (Westminster, Md.: The Newman Press, 1966), p. 140.

Thus the thrust of the christological model is the union between Christ and the church as well as their difference. The salvific effectiveness of Christ is universal, but insofar as the church is not coextensive with the human community nor identical with the person of Christ, its salvific power is not as extensive as that of Christ.

2. *The Church as Sacrament*

Sacrament is another conceptual model of the church. This traditional view of the church, based as it is on the scriptures and rendered explicit by the fathers of the church, depicts the church as the fundamental and primordial sacrament, as the great mystery of divine redemption. We omit here a sketch of the historical development of this model, since it will be sufficient to note its popularity in the late 1950's, a popularity which resulted in its use by the fathers of Vatican II.[9]

It is not difficult to ascertain how this model could be used to establish or undergird the teaching that the church is the universal medium of salvation. As a sacrament conjoined to the person of Jesus, the church is viewed as an instrument of grace, conveying the message and life of Christ to mankind. It is the living sacrament joined organically to the living Christ. Generally the use of the sacramental model of the church contains resonances of the theological explanations of the effectiveness of the seven sacraments. The types and forms of sacramental causality, if not explicitly cited, are at least presumed and form a backdrop for the whole discussion.

Undoubtedly there are many advantages in the use of this theological model. As in the christological model, the intimate, even organic, union between Christ and the church is underscored; clearly, the church is not an absolute entity but depends totally upon the life and power of Christ. The model utilizes another principle that pervades the whole economy of salvation, namely, that God touches men and women through other human beings and through the tangible events of this world. It is easy to argue, therefore, as many have traditionally argued, that God effects the salvation of all persons through the Church of Christ; that the church is the appointed instrument and sacrament of salvation for the whole of mankind; that it thus becomes the hands and mouth of Jesus, communicates his word, perpetuates his consoling ministrations, forgives sins in his name, prepares the eucharistic banquet, and channels his Holy Spirit to people.

---

[9] Cf. S. Jáki, O.S.B., *Les tendences nouvelles de l'ecclésiologie* (Rome: Herder, 1957), p. 246, who notes that many theologians assumed the *de fide* character of the efficacious sacramentality of the church.

But there are also disadvantages in the use of this model. The "instrument" mentality that invariably insinuates itself into this understanding of the reality and function of the church is often freighted with mechanical implications. The functional relationship between Christ and the church is likely to appear too mechanistic, and to the extent that it does it becomes less personal. Certainly theologians are solicitous about stressing the *living* character of the union of Christ and the church, the *living* character of the instrumental effectiveness of the church; but the very terminology often fails to avoid the pitfalls of mechanism.

Moreover, an unfortunate concept of grace is frequently bound up with the notion of the church as a sacrament. The instrumental effectiveness of the church often engenders a quantified concept of grace; the grace of the sacraments of the church takes on a physical aspect, especially when the seven sacraments are regarded as sources of grace with varying marks and qualifications. Each sacrament imparts its own peculiar type of grace. We do not wish to dispute here the fact that the dimensions of Christian grace are multiple and rich; we only wish to point up the dangers of mechanism that often accompany its description. Admittedly recent theology has revised its notions of Christian grace; it has moved from the fluid and impersonal to the relational and personal. But a continued use of instrument or organ terminology in ecclesiology runs the hazard of misconceiving both the reality of grace and the relationship between Christ and his church.

How does the sacramental model fare more specifically in our question of church and salvation? As the model is generally used, even by the fathers of Vatican II, the church assumes the role of the universal instrument of salvation. Christ establishes his church as the primary sacrament which effects saving grace in the form of word and sacrament. Every grace that comes to humans bears the impress of the church just as the coins of a realm bear the stamp of its government. It is admitted, of course, that grace extends beyond the visible boundaries of the church, but it is assumed that grace remains ecclesial. This general economy of grace is common in ecclesiologies that exalt the notion of the church as the universal sacrament and instrument of salvation. Sometimes the sacramental role of the church is put even more baldly in terms of a channel of grace.

Particularly problematic is the way in which the church as sacrament is *universally* effective of salvation. How does the church reach into all times and places and effectively contact those who are actually being saved by the grace of Christ? This is not an insoluble problem for those who extend the notion of church to the anonymous or latent believers, though in their explanations, too, theological maneuvering is necessary to account for the instrumental character of the church in the actual communication of grace. The question of distance looms large, however, for those who assume a narrower definition of the church. If the Church of Christ is marked by a conscious profession of faith, a celebration of the sacraments, and a life according to the gospel, how is it instrumental in effecting the salvation of people living perhaps at a great physical or psychological distance from the church? The professing church cannot claim more than a small fraction of the world's population, and though a larger fraction has come into some contact with the church, it is often insufficient for adequate knowledge of the church or for conversion to her profession. It must be recognized that literally millions of people have not heard of Christ or the church. If the church is the universal means of salvation, as the proponents of the sacramental model often presume, how does it function as mediator for those being saved beyond its limits?

One explanation takes its point of departure from the theology that has been elaborated around the sacrament of baptism. Traditional teaching maintains that the grace of baptism may be acquired through the actual reception of the sacrament or through a desire to receive it: baptism *in re* or *in voto*. However traditional theology further defines the notion of desire. It may be an explicit desire for baptism and entrance into the church or it may be only an implicit desire, bound up with other moral and religious acts that when analyzed in detail are logically directed to baptism and entry into the church.[10]

This elaboration of the manner in which people may be saved by implicit desire (and any elaboration of how grace may be received before the sacrament) is used by some theologians to explain the manner in which the church as a sacrament is effective at a distance.

According to theological tradition the effective celebration of the seven sacraments required specific dispositions on the part of the recipient and designated activities on the part of the ministers of the church. The celebration of the sacraments is an ecclesial event in which the church realizes itself. Even when the church is not actualizing itself solemnly in the celebration of the seven sacraments, it remains an event with discernible activities (e.g., the communication of the word or the exercise of charity).

[10] Cf. the 1949 letter of the Holy Office to Archbishop Cushing (DS 3870).

Now if the church is the universal and instrumental means of salvation, we might ask how in fact the church actualizes and realizes itself (and thus communicates the grace of Christ) in the case of those who are not conscious of its ministrations and whom the church is not addressing in any "eventful" manner. It does not seem that the church is consciously plying its ministry in their regard since it is not present to celebrate the sacraments, to proclaim the word, or even to manifest a life of charity. It is true that people at a distance who receive forgiveness and holiness in Christ manifest this grace in some external fashion; grace has its visible aspects for them, and it orients them toward the Church of Christ. It is not clear how these people come to grace through the sacramental ministrations of the church.

The sacramental model, however, might be understood in a more modest and less mechanical sense than was customary in traditional theology. The church as sacrament may mean only that the church exists in the world as the visible sign of the saving grace that God is effecting through Christ at a distance from the visible church. The church mirrors, articulates, and makes intelligible the process of salvation that is being accomplished anywhere in the world. Thus the church is not necessarily effective in the sense that through its ministrations words of forgiveness, the message of peace, the sacred actions of grace, etc., are communicated to people. In this sense the church as sacrament exists to show forth the riches of God's mercy in Christ. It is a universal sacrament of salvation in that it becomes a sign of God's salvific activity in Christ wherever this occurs in the world. The thrust of the sacrament model of the church leads to an understanding of the church as visible event and concrete manifestation of God's grace effecting salvation of people anywhere in the world.

The church as sacrament is a church of worship and prayer. It lauds the Father for the work of salvation in the person of Jesus Christ. It also prays to the Father for the salvific well-being of all mankind. Prayer for the whole of mankind is both commanded by scripture (cf. 1 Tm 2, 1–4) and urged by the disposition of Christian charity. Here is an instance in which the church is involved in the salvation of all people. It is true that the prayer is directed to the Father in the name of Jesus and his Spirit, but it is an evident concern and activity on the part of the church for the salvation of all persons. People are saved outside the limits of the church but not without the prayer dimension of the church, a dimension which pertains to the essence of the church and which becomes absorbed into the deep mystery of a person's prayerful relationship to God.

3. *The Church as the People of God*

The eminently scriptural and patristic description of the church as the people of God received merited attention from the fathers of Vatican II. In fact it emerged from the council as the choice designation of the church, overshadowing the body of Christ image.

We cannot outline here the historical development of the privileged status of the people of God model. It will be sufficient for our purposes to note the many advantages of this image. The people of God model is closely allied to the ecclesial themes of the assembly or gathering of God, the election and covenant, and the kingdom of God. It points up the continuity between historic Israel and the Christian church. It indicates, furthermore, that the church is first of all a community of persons, not an impersonal institution. It describes the condition of the whole assembly of believers, not just the hierarchy.

The people of God model underscores the fact that the church is planted solidly in history and in the nations of the world. It is not simply a spiritual reality, remote from the lives of men and women. As a historical phenomenon the people of God are subject to change and renewal, are subject to imperfection and sin. They cannot pride themselves on being a perfect society (*societas perfecta*). As a historical phenomenon the people of God are a pilgrim community, dynamically oriented to a goal that lies in the future; they are not perfect or complete but yearn for the perfection and completion that comes with the eschatological times and the fulness of the kingdom. The people of God are present to serve mankind; they manifest the destiny of human beings and promote peace and reconciliation among all nations.[11]

The notion of the people of God is bound up with the representative character of the church. The people of Israel as well as the people of the church are chosen not for isolated glory and esteem but for service and mission. The people of God are not precisely identified with the whole of mankind but are a representative sign of God's loving concern for all men and women. God's special and covenanted involvement in the history of Israel and the church is indicative of his designs for the whole of mankind. All nations enter into the salvific plan of God but the people of God interpret this plan and communicate the revealed word that is received in community. Without doubt God manifests and reveals himself in many ways to the people of the world, but the people of God are chosen

---

[11] Cf. Y. Congar, O.P., "The Church: the People of God," *The Church and Mankind, Concilium*, Vol. 1 (New York: Paulist Press, 1965), pp. 11–37.

for the task of authenticating the divine word. The people of God are gathered together as the perpetual representative of the whole world community, showing forth and lauding the purposes of God.

The advantages of the people of God model far outnumber the disadvantages, but disadvantages and limitations there are, just as with any other conceptual model of the church. To speak of the people of Israel or of the church as the people of God can, though need not, result in divisive implications for the rest of mankind. This designation of the church would seem to imply that other people outside the church are not beloved of God, are not his people. In point of fact, however, there is a real sense in which everyone is the object of God's love and election, for he wills the salvation of every person. This objection to the use of the people of God model is not intended to deny the special place and representative function of Israel and the church in the mystery of salvation; its aim is to point up a deficiency in the model, a deficiency that can result in real misunderstandings when the exclusiveness and particularity of Israel and the church are overstressed.

Our problem, more specifically, is to determine how this model fares in the question of church and salvation. Are the people of God charged with the task of bearing the gifts of salvation to all men and women? Does their representative character imply that the saving word comes to them first, and only through them to the rest of mankind? If so, in what manner? Commentators on the history of Israel and the Church of Christ have recourse to the scriptural examples in which God dealt representatively with people through a king, a family, or a nation. The destiny of some persons was determined by the lot of a nation, a king, or the father of a family. Could not this "divine economy" be applied to the relationship between the church and the rest of mankind?

An argument against the rigid application of this economy is found within scripture itself. The principle that the sins of a king or of a father can be visited upon the nation or the family must be counterbalanced by the equally scriptural principle that each person is responsible for his or her own sins (cf. Ez 18). Thus the moral character of the people of God or the majority decision among them does not spell automatic salvation or damnation for everyone "outside."

To speak of the church as the people of God, therefore, does not necessarily imply that the church is the universal locus of salvation. Its representative and interpretative function in the world does not mean that in every single instance, not even in the majority of instances, the church is the communicator of God's grace leading individuals to salvation. It can be assumed that the saving word of God in Christ reaches people in many ways outside the interpretative and revelatory function of the church. The reason for this assumption is that in fact countless numbers of people have not so benefited from the mission of the church, have not had their own revelations and moral insights purified by the word of God spoken to the people of God, have not associated with the elect people of God, have not been numbered among the privileged people of God, neither in actuality nor in desire.

As the people of God, however, the church acts as the representative of all persons who are achieving salvation anywhere in the world. The church not only interprets the meaning and direction of the process of salvation throughout the world; it also exists as the pattern of salvation for anyone in the world. The people of God, understood in this way, certainly are not the exclusive realm of salvation espoused by traditional theology, but our conclusion indicates that the church has at least a "minimum" representative function in regard to those saved outside its visible boundaries.

4. The Human Church

According to an anthropological model the church is viewed as a community of persons, either gathered together in local assembly or dispersed in society at large. It is a community of men and women professing a well-defined doctrine, proclaiming a manifest gospel, celebrating a patterned liturgy, and pursuing a specific way of life. The perspective of the model is the human person; it underscores the church's relationships to other men and women in the world.

Anthropology is a dimension that pervades the whole of theology. It is well-known that recent theologians, notably Karl Rahner, have taken pains to lay bare the anthropological character of all theology and to employ (theological) anthropology to serve as the point of departure for the systematic development of all theological subjects.

The human dimension of the church forms a bridge of contact between the church and the rest of humanity. The men and women of the church, planted in the concrete vicissitudes of history, assume a complex of human relationships in all areas of interchange, economic, political, sociological, and religious.

Obviously the anthropological perspective is present in other models of the church. The people of God model characteristically involves an assembly of men and women charged with a special mission to mankind. The anthropological dimension is less apparent in the sacramental model of the church, though here too the sacramentality of men and women is of major importance. The perspective of anthropology is most evident in the christological model.

To come to the point of our investigation: what is the relationship between the community of Christian believers, viewed from the standpoint of their humanness, and the people saved at a distance from the church? Does the human church add a salvific dimension to the human community by the mere fact that it exists in the world community and sets up many points of contact with men and women? Is the human church on a par with the humanity of Christ whose salvific influence permeates the whole world? We have argued that the church cannot be portrayed with privileges equal to those of Jesus. The church as a human community has limited contact with the whole of mankind. Thus there does not seem to be sufficient evidence that the human dimension of the community of believers is so universal that it can form the point of salvific contact with all people who are in fact being saved. It is not enough to say that since the church is rooted in the human community and since those being saved pertain to the human community, the church must therefore be the instrument or source of their grace and salvation. For it is not clear that the influence of the church as a human community is universal, whereas it is a doctrine that the salvific power of the risen and eschatological Christ is all-pervading.

5. *The Church as Community*

The human person is communitarian by nature and cannot avoid societal ties in some form or other.[12] He or she is born into a human community, grows in community, discovers language and meaning in community. The human person is destined to live his or her whole life in society with its organizational procedures and forms of political action. In varying degrees of intensity and involvement a person participates in the art, mechanics, and viewpoints of society. Without community the individual enjoys neither life nor meaning.

Human community or society may function as a model of the church. For the church is a community where persons become involved in a set of human relationships. People are born into the community of the church, grow in the community, participate in the rituals and viewpoints of the community, find meaning in the community.

The church as *societas perfecta* is one form of the communitarian

[12] The sociologist distinguishes between the more intimate and traditional *Gemeinschaft* (community) and the more rationally self-interested *Gesellschaft* (society).

model. According to this traditional and juridical model the church would be the perfect society equipped with its own laws and its own resources to achieve its goal; it would be an ecclesial society set over against the general society of men and women. We do not accept this form of the model because the church is an imperfect and evolving community, immersed in and yet distinguishable from the human community at large.

Another variation of the community model is the simple identification of the church and the whole of society or all societies of the world. The church would be co-extensive with the world community. There would be no essential difference between the church and human societies, except that the church could be realized in various degrees of explicitness. Some men and women would manifestly profess a belief in Christ and his church; others would not, though they might profess a belief in God and express this belief in other ways and pursue a moral life comparable to the explicitly Christian mode of life. The church, however, would be as broad as human society, and human beings would belong to it whether or not they would actualize the grace that is theirs in community. We also must reject this form of the community model.

A third variation of the communitarian model would indeed extend the notion of church to all societies of the world but only to those men and women who are actually and properly oriented to God, that is, only to those who are responding to the grace present to them, who have a belief (however implicit) in God, and who are leading a life in accord with this belief. We are not in agreement, finally, with this third variation of the model.

According to our last two variations of the community model, the salvation of the individual would be effected in and through the community or society of the church. The revelation of God's word and other forms of grace would proceed from and through the human community. The forgiving presence of God in Christ, the power of reconciliation and new life would reside in society; and individuals could not avoid them. In other words, the offer of grace and salvation would proceed from God through the human community, and the human community itself would be the medium of this grace. The divine grace would be discerned in the human community's concern for the welfare of the person, its dedication to justice and peace, its communication of moral values, its provisions for the worship of God, etc. The saving and loving grace of God would come to an individual in the innumerable ways in which people dialogue with each other, are concerned about each other, and seek the human good for each other in society. Our task here is not to draw up a detailed list of ways in which the community is a locus of grace but only to acknowledge the existence of these ways.

With these broad notions of the church it would be relatively easy to account for the axiom *extra ecclesiam nulla salus*. The church would be as wide as the human society and the grace of salvation would come through the society. Salvation would always be in and through the community of the church. In this way the axiom would be safeguarded and the possibility of salvation would be accorded every person, since everyone must live and grow in society.

How should we evaluate the communitarian model of the church? It must be granted, first of all, that the model accents a prominent and important feature of divine grace, namely, that grace is present in the whole human community in a rich variety of forms. The question is precisely whether as a consequence of this fact the human community itself should be termed church.

We hold that one need not "save" the axiom in this fashion, that the axiom itself can be altered or discarded. The concepts of the church in the New Testament do not extend the reality of the church to the whole of human society. It would seem more biblical, historical, and reasonable to allow for salvation outside the church rather than to widen unduly the notion of the Church of Christ.

We grant, however, that salvation is communitarian in structure, wherever it is realized. Salvation in the church itself is communitarian. And since all grace and reconciliation take shape in the human community, form community, and are related to the community of the church, it may be maintained that all salvation has a communitarian base. It does not follow, however, that all communitarian salvation is the express community of the church or stems from the church as community.

6. *The Church and the Spirit*

The primary perspective of the charismatic model is the Spirit dimension of the church. Since the glorified Lord sends his Spirit upon the church to animate it, to confirm it in truth, to provide it with multiple charisms of service, and to ensure its growth and unity, the Church of Christ is viewed in the first instance as the locus of the operation of the Spirit in the world.

Irenaeus provides the classical text of this view of the church:

Where the Church is, there is the Spirit of God; and where the Spirit of God is, there is the Church and all grace. Now the Spirit is truth. Wherefore they who have no share in that Spirit are neither nourished from the breasts of their Mother unto life, nor do they receive of that clear stream that flows from the body of Christ.[13]

Just as the christological model tends to identify the church and Christ so the charismatic model is inclined to identify the church and the Spirit. In fact, the latter identification is dependent upon the former. The more one stresses the unity of Christ and the church, the more one must emphasize the unity of the Spirit and the church, for the Holy Spirit is the Spirit of Christ. The Holy Spirit is the other advocate who stands with the church as its guide and strength. He receives from what is Christ's and communicates it to the church.

The charismatic model highlights an aspect of the church that often received short shrift from theological writers in the last four hundred years. Their preoccupation with the visible features of the church detracted from its Spirit dimension. Often they stood in fear and hesitation in the face of Spirit manifestations. They thought that too many enthusiastic deviations have emerged with the alleged support and inspiration of the Holy Spirit (e.g., the Montanists, Joachim of Flora).

The early drafts of Vatican II's *Dogmatic Constitution on the Church* were, for all practical purposes, devoid of the Spirit. Though it was improved through the suggestions of some observers and council fathers, the final text still lacks a coherent and systematic pneumatology. Fortunately, however, contemporary ecclesiologists generally take the Spirit dimension of the church seriously and no longer shun the manifestations of the Spirit in the life of the church.

The Spirit dimension of the church is not opposed to good order and sobriety. The Spirit of Christ is not a Spirit of chaos and wild enthusiasm; it is a Spirit of service, directed to the building up of the whole community in love. There is the danger, of course, of promoting the role of the Spirit to the point of diminishing other important features of the church: its articulate word and message, its visible structures of administration and of worship, its human features, especially failure and error.

Turning to the specific question at hand, we may ask whether the charismatic model supports the contention that the church is the medium of all grace. Is the church the only locus of the Spirit's activity in the world? Is the Spirit tied to the structures of the church in such a way that it is given only where the church itself is present?

[13] *Against Heresies*, Bk. 3, Chap. 24, 1 (PG 7, 966).

Here again we must respond in the negative. Understandably our answer hinges on our view of the church, on whether it extends to the world-wide community or not. We opt for the narrower view of the church and thus must conclude that the church is not the only locus of the operation of the Spirit. The Spirit breathes where he wills, and he is present to people of all times and of all places. His inspiration provides them with the opportunity to turn to God in belief and moral rectitude. This is not to deny that the church is indeed driven by the Spirit, that it is the home *par excellence* of the Spirit, but it would be a trace of triumphalism to hold that the Spirit operates only within the confines of the church.

7. The Existential Church

What happens to the axiom when placed in an existentialist model of the church? Does this model demand the mediation of the church in the case of everyone who is saved?

Briefly, an existentialist model of the church draws upon the thought categories of existentialist philosophies. In point of fact the contemporary existentialist philosophies of Jean-Paul Sartre, Albert Camus, Martin Heidegger, and Gabriel Marcel are not without ties with the Christian past (e.g., the bible, Augustine) and especially with the writings and personality of Søren Kierkegaard. It will not be possible here to sketch the distinctive position of each of these men, though it must be realized that existentialism is not of a piece. Each author develops his own brand of existentialism, his own view of human existence. Still, it is possible to detect certain trends which may be called existential. We wish to cite these trends, determine how they can influence one's view of the church, and apply our findings to the matter of church and salvation.

The existentialists set themselves against any encroachment of human freedom and self-determination. They oppose both the completely rational and ordered world of a Hegel and the entirely determined world of certain positivists and empiricists. Men and women are free. According to Sartre, they are condemned to freedom. They are set within the forces of the world as free agents, determining their position in regard to objects and other persons through a process which can be termed creation and self-transcendence. Rather than finding themselves fixed in a pre-arranged pattern of action determined by God or other humans, they are set the task of carving out an existence for themselves, of determining their relationships to others and of transcending themselves through decision. Humans find themselves in a world in which they must choose. Heidegger calls this condition the "thrownness" of man. Men and women are thrown into the world where they freely create themselves, strive for the understanding of Being, but are all the while existing as beings unto death. Through decision they choose death (according to Heidegger); or they choose the reconciliation of the objective and subjective sides of themselves (according to Sartre). The mystery of life appears to humans in a poignant fashion; they suffer the freedom of existing in the midst of an absurd life, alienated from the cosmos and from the world of their fellows. Human life is not cut off from the future; to a certain extent it is oriented to the future, for the future is open to the possibility of decision. But in fact the drive is less for future possibilities than for freedom now: in a certain sense the view of the future, the eschatological moment, is thrown back to the present moment, the moment of terrible freedom.

It cannot be denied that many existentialist trends have had their impact on the current views of the church. This is not to say that the contemporary church understands itself only in existentialist terms, nor that the complete transfer of any particular existentialist system (if such it may be called) is compatible with the biblical and traditional concepts of the church. It is apparent that atheistic forms of existentialism are not compatible with Christian theologies of the church.

What results, however, if some existentialist features are drawn into service to describe the church? In many ways, it would seem, some features provide a rich concept of the church, a deepened sense of self-understanding. For instance, the church cannot be regarded as an indiscriminate crowd of people, an unthinking body of disjunct members, a society determined by internal and external forces. However much men and women are determined by factors which are beyond their control — birth at a particular time, of specific parents, with poor or excellent opportunities for development — they remain free to decide for or against the person of Christ. Their decision now, in the present moment, renders them a confessing Christian or not. In a very real sense (allowing for the priority of God, grace, and word) they determine themselves, create their relationship with Christ, transcend themselves by becoming personally related to Christ. Existing in a state of alienation they discover the power to create a Christian life by positive attachment to the person of Jesus and his church. It is true that they continue to exist in a state of mystery and of faith; they are still oriented to physical death, the mystery and dread of which are not removed because of their decision. But most important is the continual decision to belong to Christ and his church, to create themselves anew day by day, and to maximize their awesome freedom.

The point of departure in the existentialist view of the church is not the huge reality of a universal church, not even the unwieldly community of the local church. It is rather the person in his or her subjective, unique circumstances. The church is viewed in the first instant from the standpoint of the individual, and only in the second instant from the perspective of the persons who are like-minded in decision and commitment. In this view the person is considered first, the larger reality of the union of persons, only secondarily.

Morever, the existentialist view of the church is actor oriented, not spectator oriented. It is the view from within the person freely transcending himself or herself through personal decision. Thus this model of the church bears the mark of personal pathos and anxiety.

Existentialist themes, then, can profitably enter the self-conception of the church, can underscore and strengthen authentic dimensions of ecclesial living. This is not to claim, of course, that the themes are without the burden of serious deficiencies: e.g., the atheistic presuppositions or consequences of certain existentialist systems; the devaluation of the historical church in favor of the church that is created now through personal decision; the stress on the individual and his or her freedom rather than on the community as a whole; the problem of an eschatology that is essentially thrown back into the present moment and personal decision; an atomistic view of the church which exists from moment to moment through personal decision; a self-transcendence that derives more from self than from outside forces (specifically, the grace of Jesus Christ). Obviously any use of existentialist themes cannot be exclusive. They must be refined with the sharp critical tools of other models and concepts of the church.

What happens, now, when a predominantly existentialist view of the church is espoused and one uses it to elucidate the problem of the church and salvation? Does the church need to mediate salvation to the individual who is being saved? It seems apparent that in the existentialist conception of the church the individual makes a personal decision for or against Christ, for or against the church. The thrust of the movement is from personal decision to attachment to the community. This thrust does not of course rule out a proclamation on the part of the church. But it is the person who creates his or her union with the body of believers through a decision. In the case of one who has not heard the proclamation but who nevertheless makes a decision for God (in the many ways in which this can be accomplished), it is even more apparent that the church is not the medium of salvation and that the salvational relationship to God is created through the self-determination of the person and not through the church.

The dimension of personal decision is crucial for the person who is being saved at a distance from the church, and for this situation the existentialist themes of personal resolve and self-determination are valuable and necessary. The existentialist view of men and women makes it more apparent how someone could decide for God (and salvation) at a distance from the church and still not receive the invitational service of the church. That person's decision counts. It orients him or her toward God and the community of Christian believers.

8. *The Church as Prophet*

The designation of the church as prophet captures the imagination of many Christians today. They compare the church to the prophets of the Old Covenant who as God's spokesmen lashed out against the unfaithfulness and injustice of the people. The prophets called the people back to the initial agreements and covenantal stipulations, to the promises of loyalty to Yahweh. The prophets' way of life was often perilous; many had to bear the persecutions and misunderstandings of their own people. But in spite of opposition the prophets gathered up the religious experience of Israel and expressed it in word and action. Their message was frequently unpleasant but it served as a reminder of past commitments and as a source of enlightenment. It was designed to make the whole of Israel prophetic, manifesting a God-centered way of life to the surrounding nations.

Christ too was a prophet, the prophet *par excellence* who proclaimed the word of the Father in truth and fidelity. The church as prophet cannot do better than pattern its prophetic work on that of Christ.

The church (the whole church but especially its teachers) exercises a prophetic role, pondering and proclaiming the word of Jesus. Its word is often consoling, drawing attention to the work of salvation and forgiveness in Jesus Christ. It proclaims the unprecedented good news of God's favor and kindness. But its word is also critical, condemning the demonic and idolatrous in the world. It condemns, for instance (often all too hesitatingly); injustices in society, failures of governments or institutions to take up the cause of the oppressed and dispossessed. Its prophetic role results in both admiration and opposition. It is extolled for its courage and maligned for its incursion into mundane affairs. It is a sign of contradiction in society, an accusing presence that is felt but little understood.

To turn to our specific question: how does the notion of the church as the medium of all salvation fare in the prophet model of the church? Has this model been used to promote the notion of the church as mediator and is it an apt model to express such a function? The historical evidence of Chapter 1 leads us to conclude that the prophetic role of the church was acknowledged from the beginning but that it was not frequently selected as the crucial model to explain the salvational status of the people of the world. It is true that the proclamation role of the church was always considered necessary, even under the assumption that the divine word was somehow present in all the world (cf. the theology of Justin Martyr). It was thought that by and large the word of the gospel had gone forth to the ends of the earth and that most people had come into contact with it.

With Europe's discovery of new peoples, it became apparent that the word of the gospel had not gone out to all nations on earth. Thereupon theologies were elaborated to account for the ways in which people could achieve salvation without explicitly hearing the proclamation of the gospel. For over a century now the papal magisterium itself has proclaimed the possibility of salvation outside the express announcement of the Christian message.

Our position is that the prophet model of the church does not support the traditional interpretation of the axiom outside the church no salvation. When we use the prophet model to describe the church, we do not automatically imply the axiom; nor do we imply that all salvation stems from the prophetic function of the church. It is common teaching of the Roman Catholic Church that people can achieve salvation without encountering the prophetic dimension of the church. They can be saved without hearing the express proclamation of the good news in Jesus Christ. The church does not touch them in its proclamation of the word of Christ. It does not follow, however, that no word reaches the people who are being saved. The word of God can reach people in ways other than through the community of Israel, the historical Jesus, and the church. It can come through contact with other people in society, through personal reflection on human society and natural wonders. Our point is that in fact people can be saved without an explicit hearing of the word of Christ and of the church, and that in spite of this situation the church as prophet has an authentic role to play in the world.

9. *The Church and Eschatology*

The eschatological model has the best chance of accounting for the pilgrim character of the church and for the salvation of those outside the church. It is a model that corresponds appropriately to a prevailing dimension of theology today, namely, its direction toward the future in hope and expectation.[14] Contemporary theologians such as Jürgen Moltmann and Johannes B. Metz isolate the "promise" and "not yet" character of revelation, both that which developed in the history of Israel and that which surrounded the person of Jesus and the early church. The eschatological aspect is not a side issue of theology, not an appendix to systematic theology, but a vital strain that pervades the whole. No part of theology is complete without a serious confrontation with the eschatological phenomenon.

When the church is viewed in an eschatological framework, some of its most authentic features come to light. It is seen not as a perfect society graced with glory and splendor but as a journeying people of God. The church is temporal, subject to the grime and sweat of history, and at the same time moving on toward the fulfillment of a promise. It is not a static institution but a dynamic, living assembly waiting eagerly for the fulfillment of its expectation. The church is a people that lives in lively hope and expectation of a promise that indeed is theirs, accorded them in the person of Jesus and his Spirit, but one that remains substantially in the realm of the "not yet."

The eschatologically oriented church is steeped in confidence, but it is a trust that is acquainted with the sufferings, failures, and sins of the present. Its solid basis in the present prevents it from diminishing into a utopian church, ever looking to the future and deceiving itself about present conditions and opportunities. The church's locus of optimism is ultimately God himself and his promise in Jesus Christ. It is equally the Lord who is both the present reality of salvation and the point of personal return.

The eschatological character of the church does not imply that salvation is totally absent from the present time. The forgiveness of sins and the impartation of the Spirit (and everything else that is denoted by the concept of grace in the New Testament) form an essential part of the present reality of the church. But this is not a fixed, perfect, unchanging, and absolute salvation. It too shares in

[14] Cf. G. A. Lindbeck, *The Future of Roman Catholic Theology* (Philadelphia: Fortress Press, 1970), Chapter 1. Also "A Protestant Point of View," in *Vatican II: An Interfaith Appraisal*. Ed. by J. H. Miller (Notre Dame: University of Notre Dame Press, 1966), pp. 228f.

the ongoing and dynamic character of the whole people of God, since it is not complete in its present form. Salvation shares the dynamic tension of the church since it is enjoyed now only in part, but a part that cries out for fulfillment.

Thus the eschatological dimension of the church brings to the fore some of the essential traits of New Testament salvation and provides an excellent model for understanding it. Salvation involves a waiting for "the Lord who comes," the forgiving God who has begun a good work in us but who will bring it to completion on his return. He is the forgiving and gracing God who comes from "ahead" of us, whom we expect as our future, as our fulfillment which is only in the future.

The gathered and pilgrim church is itself an eschatological community that is like an arrow pointing into the future. It is an eschatological community with the sign of hope written all over it. Remove this sign and it ceases to have genuine form and character. It must look to the future and provide the interpretative direction of the whole of human history. As a sign it can be read by the populace but it cannot be believed without the enabling gifts of the Spirit who groans within the church and makes it yearn for the revelation of the sons of God and the renewal of the universe. For the church indeed points to the completion of a relationship that exists now, its relationship to the Father, to the Son, and to the Spirit, and to the whole of the cosmos. The church points to the ultimate perfection of these relationships, in fact, to the ultimate gathering of the people of God.

The eschatological model of the church ties in with other contemporary views of humanity and its relationship to the future, especially the Teilhardian and the Marxist views. In the Teilhardian view human society is involved in an evolutionary process that is continually directed toward greater complexification and unity. Mankind has already emerged from an evolutionary past of millions of years and is oriented to an indefinite future development. This is not the place to sketch the brilliant vision of the Jesuit paleontologist, but we will find it helpful to glimpse his vision because its eschatological dimension illustrates and affects the mood of theology today and corresponds to the dynamic character of the church.[15] Noteworthy is the goal toward which the whole evolutionary process is directed: the Point Omega. Practically speaking, Christ is the Point Omega, and Christ himself is joined with his

---

[15] It will not be possible here to concern ourselves with some problem areas of his vision, e.g., the place of Christ in the process of evolution, the evaluation of sin in the community, the need for and the effect of grace, the gift character of the final goal.

church. The force behind complexification is love. Love drives men and women to seek ever new and closer bonds of union with other persons in the noosphere, so that ultimately the love process will be consummated in the Point Omega and the whole Christ (the whole church existing eschatologically in the presence of Christ). The victory of love, of course, has already been achieved in Christ and his power is teeming within the dynamic process; but the definitive goal of this victory and its power lie in the future, a future that is assured by the very presence of Christ and his love.

The salvation of men and women depends upon their commitment to love, their desire and effectiveness in promoting the noospheric union of human beings. People can fail in love; they can turn in upon themselves in hate and ill will toward others. But they also have the power in Christ to serve the unification of the world to come. This salvation is achieved both in the present power of Christ and in the drawing force of the Point Omega. Salvation is ultimately eschatological, proceeding from the Point Omega and finding its goal therein.

The Marxist vision also feels the pull of a future in which a classless society will provide the maximum good for the individual. The eschatological paradise, which is analogous to the Christian definitive salvation, is the goal of the present struggle of the classes. The goal is a dynamic pull from the future, a force that governs the orientation of people today. The "salvific," revolutionary struggles of today are designed to bring about the state of peace which is not transcendent but wholly contained within the conditions and boundaries of the world as we perceive it. We need not pursue further the points of comparison between the future-oriented aspects of the Marxist vision and the eschatological dynamics of the church, since the example is cited simply to illustrate the evolutionary and future-oriented dimensions of thought in our world today.

With these illustrations of the eschatological orientation of contemporary thought and theology, especially the theology of the church, we may proceed to our question of the axiom and the ecclesial character of all salvation. We presume the incomplete status of salvation in the present life. It is a salvation that has indeed begun in the redemptive events of Jesus and in the lives of believers but that attains its perfection in the eschatological reality of the end-time.

Salvation, therefore, comes to the person outside the Christian church from the efficacy of the incarnate and exalted Son of God who touches all times and places. Besides being a present reality, it is also a salvation that proceeds from the coming Lord, a salvation that will find its completion in the returning Christ. Salvation, characterized as the definitive life of divine favor in the presence of Christ, comes from "ahead" for the person outside the church, just as it does for the person of the church. It is a final salvation that will be the point of convergence of those who attain to it both within and outside the Church. The eschatological Christ is the meeting place of all who respond to his saving grace, whether they come into direct contact with the pilgrim church or not. All those who are being saved feel the future-oriented dynamism which derives from the Christ who was, who is, and who is coming.

It is true that the ultimate goal of the dynamism is not individualistic; it does not involve isolated relationships with the exalted person of Christ. There is no question about the ecclesial status of the end-time. The New Testament manifests a celestial church, a heavenly assembly, in which the people of God, having come to their definitive relationship to God in Christ, function as a community of worshipers.

Some might argue that the present reality of salvation is always ecclesial because it feels that pull of the future reality which is ecclesial.[16] We cannot deny the future orientation of all grace and salvation present in the world. Nor can we deny that the goal serves as a causal orientation (*causa finalis* in scholastic terminology) of the saving process and that consequently salvation has already an ecclesial impress or character because it is dynamically oriented toward the future ecclesial realization. It seems logical to hold that those being saved outside are related to the eschatological church as to a dynamic ecclesial reality, just as the confessing church is so related. Those outside live a life that finds its ultimate explanation and completion in the eschatological church, the heavenly assembly of those saved in the blood of the lamb. They live in hope, although the final ground of the hope is not clear to them (as analogously it is not clear to those in the church); it is a hope and expectation that remains indistinct in their moral life and belief. The kingdom of God toward which they tend lies hidden in the future and is not the object of an explicit desire. It is the inbreaking of God that will establish the kingdom and gather the "elect" from the world. The kingdom of God comes from "ahead," from "above." (Theo-

---

[16] Cf. Y. de Montecheuil who, while adopting the traditional view of the axiom, at least suggests an explanation in terms of the heavenly church; thus there would be no salvation without entering ultimately into the community of the saints in heaven. *Aspects of the Church* (Chicago: Fides, 1955), p. 153.

logians employ various terms to indicate the unique effectiveness of God in the fulfillment of the kingdom.)

In short, the eschatological character of the church points up the future dimension of grace and salvation and allows an adequate account of those being saved outside the church; it indicates that all grace and salvation is future-oriented. Grace, wherever it is found, points to the future just as the church points to the end-time. The meeting point of the arrows, therefore, is essentially in the future. This is not to deny that the visibility of grace and salvation in the present world already has an orientation to the visible church, as to a pattern of grace, an orientation that need not be detected by the people outside the church but which, given the occasion, can be interpreted by those within the church.

In this chapter we have examined a few models of the church to determine how well or how poorly they clarify the axiom and how they demand or how they do not demand church involvement in the salvation of the unevangelized. We have tried to bring out how the diverse models of the church result in different ways of understanding the axiom and of interpreting the church's involvement in the salvation of those on the outside. Some models demand an involvement on the part of the church. Others do not. The traditional words "medium" or "mediatorship" must be specified in terms of the kinds of relationships that exist between the church and those being saved outside the church. This chapter has, we hope, indicated that the relationships must be understood in a more humble fashion than they were in past scholastic theology where the words "agent causality" were customarily used to describe the activity of the church.

Chapter 5

Development of Doctrine and Outside the Church No Salvation

The previous chapters indicate that a clear development of doctrine has taken place in the understanding of the relationship between the church and the salvation of those outside the church. Though the development continued throughout the history of the church, it has been especially pronounced in the last twenty-five years (1950–1975), at least for Roman Catholics. We call it a development of doctrine as distinct from a development of dogma in the modern technical sense because the precise issue under consideration (the ecclesial character of all salvation) was never the subject of an explicit *de fide* magisterial declaration. It was, however, the more common teaching/doctrine of the church, and as such it entered into many ordinary papal and conciliar statements.

How is this development accounted for? Contemporary theologians find it difficult if not impossible to elaborate one all-embracing theory of doctrinal and dogmatic development. The various instances of development cannot be squeezed into one explanatory mold. Consequently theologians are inclined to invoke a variety of formulas to explain the dimensions of development. In some instances there is a logical development from one statement to another; in others there is a progression from implicit to explicit proposition; in still others there is evidence of a vital and organic growth from old expression to new, from one conceptualization to another, from an unreflexive belief to one that is reflexive and conscious; at times the development appears unexpectedly and spontaneously.

The development of doctrine involves not just a translation from one language to another but a new understanding of the word of God. It results from a new insight into an aspect of the person and

152

message of Christ. The new insight is conceptualized and expressed in a new fashion. Both conceptualization and expression borrow from the historical, philosophical, sociological, and linguistic thought-patterns of the time. Thus the articulation of doctrine or dogma is time-conditioned; it is dependent upon the world view of a particular era.

Dogmatic development does not terminate in an absolutely new divine self-disclosure. It manifests continuity in change. It has its roots in the person and word of Christ. Also, dogmatic formulas are perfectible even though the insights expressed in the formulas are gained for all time. Of course here precisely is the crux of the problem: the development of dogma that authentically unfolds the word of God. It is generally conceded that the mere repetition of ancient dogmatic formulas is not at all effective in proclaiming and safeguarding the Christian message; in fact since the faithful gradually lose sight of the circumstances in which dogmatic statements were made, the continual repetition of them often results in a distorted or even opposite understanding of dogma (cf. the difficulty of employing "person" language in Trinitarian dogma in an age which extols the uniqueness and independence of the person). It would seem that doctrinal development, as distinct from dogmatic development, is allowed a greater measure of freedom. The break between the old expression and the new insight can be greater; in fact the old may be simply abandoned and the new insights assumed. It is our contention that the *extra ecclesiam nulla salus* axiom pertains to the latter type of development, namely, a doctrinal development that can result in the abandonment of the previous formulation and in the acceptance of new insights and their expressions, even though the axiom never received dogmatic authentication.

It is not only possible for the church but incumbent upon it to relinquish the traditional axiom. It cannot be taken literally; it never could, even in its original formulation. Thus linguistic honesty requires its abandonment. Here is a formulation problem that is ripe for the excisive tools of linguistic analysis, at least in its demand for reasoned, logical, and referent language within a particular system of thought. The axiom does not mean what it says; or rather, what it is interpreted to mean is not expressed by the formulation. If it is presupposed as a dogmatic maxim (as was common in theology) a long and strained disquisition is necessary to explain away the literal implications of the formula.

Moreover, the development does not involve a mere verbal or conceptual translation of the axiom. The content of the axiom in its historical genesis was itself unfaithful to the message of Christ.

Consequently its very content and formulation must be retired from the theological scene. What is involved here is more than the reformulation or reconceptualization of a dogmatic statement of the past. It is the abandonment of an adage that in its literalness never was a dogmatic position.

Having verified the fact of doctrinal development in the issue of church and salvation, we turn to the causes of the development. What movements within the church and the world, especially in the last twenty-five years (1950–1975), facilitated and even necessitated a development of this doctrine? One obvious factor is demographic. The church embraces a fraction of the world population and it is clear that the fraction is becoming smaller, not greater. The realization of the minority status of the church, it is true, grew sharply with the worldwide voyages and "discoveries" of the fifteenth and sixteenth centuries. Since then theologians faced more directly the question of the salvation of those outside the boundaries of Christianity. But generally, though not always, they still viewed the church as the locus of salvation, attachment to which in some form or other was required for the saving grace of God.

The demographic factor forced theologians to ponder the ecclesial status of those who do not know Christ and who do not receive his message. If such non-Christians respond to the movements of grace, are they thereby attached to the church? Does the grace come to them by way of the church? Some theologians answered both questions in the affirmative. Others began to question whether it was biblically and theologically proper to include such people within the church — even at a distance or through invisible attachment. These theologians were prepared to claim salvation for them without ecclesial attachment. This stance corresponds better with the demographic facts, with the reflexive consciousness of individuals, and with the distinctiveness of the Church of Christ.

Another factor in this development is the deeper appreciation of the richness and universality of grace. If it is true that the Spirit breathes where he will and that God's grace is present to all peoples, one may expect that the gifts of the Spirit and the movements of divine grace will be expressed in discernible ways. They will not remain entirely invisible but will become manifest in human actions, rituals, and institutions. Concretely, many theologians have come to value the positive features of non-Christian religions. These religions are not given blanket commendation but neither are they condemned outright as works of the devil, as was often done in the past. Many of their features can be ascribed to the movement of the Spirit in the hearts of their founders and disciples. Grace becomes incarnate in diverse ways. The non-Christian religions are the prime examples of such grace; but other movements for peace, justice, and world fellowship may also be expressions of the divine Spirit.

It is the realization of the richness of grace outside the boundaries of the Christian church that led some theologians to doubt whether the church is always the source of this grace, at least by way of medium, because it was not apparent how or in what capacity the church acts as a channel of grace. It seemed better to conclude (once one arrived at a positive appraisal of the non-Christian expressions of grace) that the divine Spirit is operative everywhere, and not exclusively in and through the church. Of course it can be granted that the expression of grace, its incarnation anywhere in this world, is the foundation for a positive relationship between the non-Christian expressions and the visible and distinctive Christian church.

Another factor in the development, one related to the increased appreciation of the richness of grace, is the more positive attitude of the church toward the world, an attitude exemplified in Vatican II's *Pastoral Constitution on the Church in the Modern World*. This does not mean, of course, that the church closes its eyes to the forces of evil in the world, that it pronounces a blessing on everything indiscriminately. But it does mean that the Christian church in general views and positively esteems the wholesomeness of many movements and institutions in the world. It lauds the works of governments and other organizations that exist for the benefit of peoples; it sanctions the international movements of peace, justice, and fellowship. They cannot be regarded as purely secular in the sense that they have no relationship to God or to the sacred, that they have no significance in the realm of grace and salvation. A reevaluation of the world opens up the possibility of seeing in it stirrings of grace and salvation.

The ecumenical movement is not without its influence in this development. There is not only the fact that many Protestant theologians proclaimed a non-ecclesial mode of salvation for those living at a distance from the church, but there is also a mutual recognition of the ecclesial features common to the Roman Catholic, Protestant, and Orthodox Churches. This led certain Catholic theologians both to identify the ecclesial realities of other Christian churches and to value the distinctiveness of the Christian church when compared to other religions and movements of the world. The ecumenical movement drew Christians closer together and set off their distinctive character from other confessions. The distinctiveness, therefore, pointed up the need to account for the salvation of those who exist outside the boundaries of the Church of Christ.

A third factor in the development is the improved concept of divine grace. Theological treatises and popular notions of the recent past left many with the impression that grace, at least "actual grace," is some species of physical force. It "flows" somewhat mechanically when certain conditions are met, e.g., the administration of the sacraments and the proper disposition of the recipient. Physical contact is not always necessary, but normally grace becomes effective in some contactual circumstance. Discussion of the sacraments was the optimal context within which to speak of grace, for the seven sacraments of the church were viewed as the principal sources of grace, in fact, as the sources of diverse kinds of grace. The principle of the necessity of the church appeared all the more compelling because the church was proclaimed as the privileged source of the sacraments. This brief description of the former concepts of grace certainly caricatures the extensive treatises of the past, especially when one leaves out of consideration the understanding of grace as divine indwelling and the gifts of the Holy Spirit. But it seems undeniable that many Roman Catholics lived the Christian life with deficient notions of divine grace.

Today the concept of grace is set more in terms of experience, presence, and personal encounter. Surely the incarnational dimension of divine grace must continue to receive consideration in any treatise on grace, but its description must be less physical, or less tied to specific actions and events. The universality of grace, in fact, implies that it is not confined narrowly to occasional, ecclesial actions. The personal presence of God and his Spirit greatly magnify the events of grace and enable men and women to respond to the needs of others, to reconcile peoples, and to obtain justice and peace for them. Grace is multi-dimensional and manifold; it pervades the whole of human existence because it is, essentially, the presence of God.

These more comprehensive notions of divine grace, therefore, promote development in the area of church and salvation. They explain why it is not always necessary to cite the church as a specific source of grace, for grace is more widespread than the church and is not limited to its ministrations. The more one admits the presence of justifying grace outside the church, the easier one can acknowledge salvation outside the church.

A fourth factor in the development of this doctrine is the reevaluation of the mission of the church in the world. What is the church's stance in regard to the world, in regard to non-believers? How should the church understand its missionary dimension? What are its goals? Recent times, especially the 1960's, witnessed a crisis of mission. At one time it seemed plain to all missioners that they were about the business of bringing the word and sacraments to pagans in order to ensure their salvation. But a deeper appreciation of the universality of grace and of the positive characteristics of non-Christian religions (among other factors) called into question the clear purpose of the missionary effort.

It is still admitted, of course, that the church has a missionary dimension, that it is missionary by essential design. The church is positively turned toward the world of men and women and serves them, though all too haltingly and imperfectly. The church cannot muffle the word that abides within it through the operation of the Lord and his Spirit. It continues to proclaim and announce the word, not only to those who are within its midst as believers, but also to those who would lend a sympathetic ear. It continues to celebrate the sacraments, pointing to the Lord who was among us, who is present, and who is coming. It continues to exist as a perceptible community with patterns of organization and governance. It continues to serve the needs of the world in various capacities of education, health care, etc.

Many questions arise when one attempts to determine the specifics of the above missionary tasks: the reinterpretation of the word for hearers of today; the predispositions necessary for the reception of the word; the manner and frequency of celebrating the sacraments; the type of governance; the specific services offered to people and the way in which they are rendered. Even as reconsideration of all these traditional missionary activities continues, theologians and missioners in general are beginning to outline a more humble role for the church in the world; they are revising the notion of mission. They realize, for instance, that in the realm of service the church cannot be all things to all peoples; that it can only remain sensitive to the needs that continually arise in human communities and assist in whatever way possible, by support, by inspiration.[1] In the realm of word and sacrament it is not now, and in the foreseeable future will not be, effective on a worldwide basis. They see the church in the capacity of a sign and witness, a movement, a pointer indicating the future and the coming Lord.

In this context we may take account of the church's mission to its

---

[1] Cf. J. Theisen, O.S.B., "A Theological Analysis and Critique of the Mission and Responsibility of the Church," in *Metropolis: Christian Presence and Responsibility.* Ed. by Philip D. Morris (Notre Dame, Ind.: Fides, 1970), pp. 173–189.

own constituency. For Christian believers the church functions indeed as a source of consolation and direction. It serves as the locus of the Word of God and his Spirit, the celebration of the sacraments, and the fellowship of mutual love and assistance. The church is truly a source of grace, dependent of course on the saving work of Christ. This mediational task of the church was never in question, and here we need to insist on it. For many people the sacramental and instrumental task of the church is so necessary that their salvation depends on it. They need the strength of the Christian community — its proclamation of the divine word, its service of love, its sign of forgiveness — to maintain their orientation toward God. Without the church the signals of the divine word and of conscience would be too weak (at least for them) to support them in their faith and resolve. Thus this much of the *content* of the axiom could abide in our theological teaching: that for some the church is necessary. But it would be inappropriate to continue to cite the axiom to express this possibility.

Therefore a reconsideration of the missionary task of the church results in reevaluation of the necessity of the church for the salvation of all the saved. Though the church continues to exercise an important missionary role in regard to the world, it is not the exclusive mode of salvation.

A solution to the issue of the ecclesial character of all salvation depends on one's notion of church, more specifically, on one's notion of the boundaries of the church. One who prefers a broad concept of church may wish to include anonymous or latent Christians within its confines. That is, one may wish to include those who are graced and reconciled at a distance from the visible Christian church and to regard them as belonging in some inchoative fashion to the church. Whoever is graced and reconciled, no matter at what distance from the visible church, is "church." Thus all salvation would be ecclesial because all those being saved are in some way church.

On the other hand, one may prefer, as we do, to confine the church to those who expressly profess belief in the lordship of Jesus Christ, who worship God the Father sacramentally in Jesus Christ, and who proclaim the Christian message by word and style of life. Then there is still question whether or not all saving grace is ecclesial for those who receive it at a distance from the visible Christian church. In the last few centuries, because of the prevalent notion of grace and of church, the common teaching was that such grace is still ecclesial because it becomes a reality only through the church. The church is necessary because it communicates grace wherever people are being saved. Thus all grace is ecclesial and the church is necessary for salvation. The axiom *extra ecclesiam nulla salus* comes to mean that the church is necessary for all salvation because it makes possible the presence of grace, and those in the process of salvation are attached to the visible church at least by implicit desire.

Another way in which one could argue for the ecclesial character of all salvation is this: one could hold that everyone being reconciled to God in faith and love, even at a distance from the visible Church of Christ, is nevertheless oriented toward the church as toward the fulness of the expression of grace in word, worship, service, and life. Such grace and salvation at a distance from the church may also be called ecclesial because of its likeness to the saving grace that is found in the church itself; it is a grace that is embodied in the lives of people and finds expression in a way of belief, a type of commitment, and a style of life. According to this position the axiom outside the church no salvation means that all salvation has a relationship to the church. It is not necessary, according to this position, that the visible church communicate directly or indirectly the grace of the word, the presence of the Spirit, the sacramental worship of God, and the pattern of moral living.

Our own position is similar to the one just enunciated. We believe that the Church of Christ must be confined rather narrowly to those who profess Jesus as Lord and Savior, who are committed to his message, who celebrate his sacraments, who pattern their lives on the teachings of the gospel. In this sense the church is necessary, for there must continue a Christian people who are dedicated to his name and memory and who proclaim his message. The continuance of the church is ensured by Jesus himself and his Spirit. For some people, perhaps for many people, the church is necessary as the place where they come to know and receive the word of forgiveness and the Spirit of new life, where they need to remain in order to receive continually the life of God in Jesus Christ. For them there is salvation in the church and outside the church there is no salvation, or at least it is found with difficulty.

Then there are those who do not profess faith in Jesus Christ: the greater part of mankind. We need not doubt that Christ's salvific power reaches them, that his Spirit is present to them, that they receive the inspiration of God in the diverse circumstances of their lives. We need not regard the church as the specific source of these graces in the sense that the word of the church has reached them, that the external sacramental worship of the church has been celebrated in their presence, that the charitable service of the church has touched them directly. We acknowledge, of course, the prayer involvement of the church in all salvation but we need not regard the church as the source of all graces that those outside the church receive. We must admit, however, that the form of salvation found at a distance from the church has an orientation toward the church, that its fulness is manifest in the church.

We understand too that the ultimate goal of the justification of a person at a distance from the church is an ecclesial situation. The terminus of the whole process of salvation is the celestial gathering of the church. However the eschatological condition of justified men and women may be envisioned in particular, its basic feature must be ecclesial. It is the heavenly assembly in and around the person of Jesus. Even now, therefore, there is a certain parallel or analogy between the believers of the church who expressly and confidently anticipate the end-time realities and the people justified at a distance from the church who, all unknowing, are directed to the same goal. Their condition is ecclesial in the sense that the grace of Christ which they already possess is patterned on the eschatological gathering in Christ. Since it is the grace of Christ and his Spirit, it is the already realized justification which acts as a guarantee and pledge of the final assembly.

The Church of Christ is involved in the process of salvation of those living at a distance insofar as it offers up prayers of petition for them and for all peoples. It petitions the Father for the spiritual peace and well-being of all mankind. Of course there arises here the whole question of the efficacy of prayers of petition. How much does God "need" them to effect his designs? Are others really helped by prayers? The mystery of prayer is bound up with the whole mystery of the human relationship to God in Christ. It cannot be reduced to ultimate clarity. But as Christians we have the command to pray, to pray for our fellow Christians and to pray for our enemies. We pursue the practice of prayer as a basic feature of the Christian life, not understanding to our satisfaction its deepest rationale. The prayers of Christians are indeed of value for those who are being saved at a distance from the church. Thus in some minimal way the church enters into the Christic and Spirit process of salvation.

If these conclusions are meager, we must remind ourselves that they nevertheless evince a sizeable development of doctrine, especially since the Holy Office's letter of 1949 to Archbishop Cushing; in that letter the axiom was called infallible dogma. The development results in a drastic reconsideration of the axiom: the suggestion of its elimination from catechetical instruction. The development further results in attempts to understand the axiom in a variety of ways: it should not be used negatively to exclude people from salvation; it points up the Christ-willed character of the Christian church; it means that there is salvation in the church for particular people, no judgment being made about others.

These years have seen a development of doctrine with regard to an understanding of the mediatorship of the church. Traditionally the church was understood as mediating grace and salvation to those outside. It is concluded now that this task of the church must be understood in a more humble fashion. The church is indeed necessary as the gathering of Christ's followers, committed to his message and memory; but it is not designed to channel all graces and means of salvation. It assumes an attitude of prayer for the whole of mankind and so enters into the work of Christ.

It would seem apparent from our study that the concept of mediatorship has been too closely associated with the axiom. As theologians and the magisterium continued to revise their understanding of the axiom — for its literalness was unacceptable — they stressed more and more the mediatorship of the church for the salvation of those outside its visible boundaries. With the stress on the mediatorship of the church they were able to account for the necessity of the church. It is this notion of the mediatorship of the church which we have endeavored to nuance in this study.

We conclude not that the church is without a task in the world but that its task of salvational mediation must be understood in a more modest sense than heretofore. In this regard the church must not be absolutely identified with Christ. The church has an important mission to the world. The facets of this mission, which we cited at random in our study, are the subject of vigorous research today and will constitute the argument of our final chapter.

Chapter 6

Tasks of the Church

In this final chapter we propose to sketch out some tasks of the church, especially tasks of service for the world at large. If up to this point in our study we have ascertained and argued that the church is not always the effective means of salvation, that many if not most people achieve a right relationship to God outside its limits, we do not and cannot imply that therefore the church is without purpose or task in the world. As a reality rooted in the world and in society the Church of Christ undertakes a burden of service. The church is indeed necessary if certain works of witness and service are to be accomplished, if the reality of salvation is to assume divinely inspired and concrete visibility in the world. Important charges accrue to the community that believes in the Lord and Savior Jesus Christ.

The Church of Christ is not an immobile monument to the reconciling person and life of Jesus. That it is a perceptible phenomenon no one can gainsay. But it is not static. It is not a piece of lifeless statuary or solid architecture. If the church is an observable community of believers, it cannot fail to receive the gaze of men and women, but its task is not completed when it draws attention to itself, when it is only an object of admiration or criticism. The Church of Christ cannot be satisfied until it has become purposefully alive for the human community. How does it become alive for others? How does it exercise a salvational office in the world? These are some of the questions that come to mind when we consider the church as servant to the world.

When we speak of the tasks of the church, we do not exclude the work of the Father, the Son, and the Holy Spirit acting through the people of the church. We wish to emphasize, however, that the work of the church is not coextensive with the work of God. The

162

church's charge is limited in scope and cannot presume to be as far-reaching as the power and presence of God. God works where the church is not yet present and perhaps never will be.

Servanthood is incumbent upon the church universal. But the total church is present in a variety of ways. It is present in its leaders, its bishops, priests, teachers, administrators. It is present in its local congregations and in the individuals who form the congregations. Its service is directed to individuals and to institutions. The church is concerned about individuals, about their relationship to God, about their welfare in the world. But it is also concerned about the institutions that effect human lives, e.g., government agencies, business corporations. As we examine the tasks of the church, we mean to include the efforts of the universal and local church in regard to both individuals and institutions.

1. Sign of Salvation

The Church of Christ functions as a sign of salvation. Its very presence in society is a perceptible sacrament of salvation. It is assumed, of course, that the church as sign permits a message to be read in its word and action. The church as sign is not an empty sanctuary or an uncertain movement. It is an articulate sign which is not beyond the comprehension of people in society. The significance of the church is communicated through the many ways the church acts in society: as agent of reconciliation, as servant, as catalyst of change. The sign dimension of the church may be regarded as the broadest description of its task in the world.

The central message that the church signifies is "salvation." When the word "salvation" (surely a traditional word which is becoming more and more unintelligible to people today) is unpacked, it yields an understanding of the love and favor of God toward mankind, the forgiveness of sins, the union of persons in the presence of the divine power, the anticipation and ultimate experience of the kingdom of God. This in outline is salvation, though assuredly its dimensions are many and mysterious but continually explored by those who are themselves the sign.

The church functions as a sign of the deepest realities of a person's relationship to God. Since these realities are ultimately beyond understanding, the church itself does not comprehend the final meaning of its own existence. Its self-understanding continually develops as its existence evolves through the course of history.

As a sign of salvation set up in the world, ideally rooted in each country and culture, the church manifests a message of salvation for *all* people, not just for a select few. The church is the God-designed manner of communicating to the world the ultimate direction of human life and activity.

The sign value of the church enters into all the functions of the church, into all the ways in which the church is significantly manifest to people. We can cite only a few examples in the following sections.

2.   *Herald of the Word of God*

Christians wish to hear the word of God *today*. It is not that they deny the historical Word of the Father in Christ Jesus or the word of the scriptures in the primitive church. They accept Jesus as the way of salvation. They accept the writings of the early church as guides for Christian living. But they also seek an articulation of the word of God in today's language. They want to hear the word of God addressed to today's concerns. It is difficult to make the transition from the historical word to the current word of God in the here and now. The translation is problematic and precarious.

At issue here is the whole question of the authentic and faithful transmission of the word of God. We cannot do more than allude to the controversy about an indefectible church which unfailingly hands on the word of God in Christ Jesus. It is assumed that the person and message of Jesus still retain significance for people today. It is assumed that some kind of translation or reunderstanding of the historical message is required if people are to receive the word intelligibly and fruitfully. It is assumed that the church as a whole will not prove unfaithful to the person and message of Jesus. It is assumed that the church as a whole passes on the message of Jesus. But our question regards the manner in which the message gets articulated authentically and officially, especially in the event of disagreement about the actual sense of the word of Jesus. Roman Catholic theologians look to the college of bishops, including the bishop of Rome, to bring to official expression the meaning of the Christian message. Orthodox look to the bishops in council and to the consensus that develops in and around an issue. Many Protestants stress close conformity to the word of the scriptures.

We cannot pursue this problem further. It is sufficient for us to recognize that the Church of Christ, in some manner or other, functions as the interpreter of the person and message of Jesus. The church receives the word of Christ, expresses it in contemporary terms, unfolds it, celebrates it in worship, lives it in its daily existence. The church as a whole is active in bringing the message of Jesus down to our times in words and expressions that are comprehensible to the people of today. The words of Jesus take on flesh in the message and actions of Christian believers. This message in turn serves the Christian community. Christians help each other to understand the message of Jesus. They aid each other to make the translation from the word of God in the past to the articulation of today.

The church performs this task for its own members. But its word goes out beyond its limits. The church functions as a communicator of the word of God for those who believe in God and for those who do not. The church broadcasts the word to individuals and to institutions, to those who would receive it and to those who would not.

If we are to sketch out various tasks of the church, we cannot fail to count as primary the need to keep the word of God alive in the community of believers and in the larger human society. Without the reinterpretation and rearticulation of the word of God today, the church itself would soon cease to exist as a viable influence in the world.

3. Sign of the Divine

The function of the church is not always bound up with specific action. The church also functions when it simply exists in the world as a sign of the divine. We must remind ourselves of the rich reality of the church: its faith in Jesus Christ, its life of hope and love, its worship of the living and present God. The church is a manifest and visible reality, based solidly in society. Its inner life is beyond the comprehension of men and women, beyond the understanding of the church itself. In short, it is a divine/human reality, displaying a human form and a divine life.

The church exercises its task by being what it is; and by being what it is the church is present in the world as a sign of the divine among peoples. Men and women can look upon the church and come to realize the immanence of God, his presence in the world, his goal for all mankind. The sign value of the church can exist without a great display of words and actions, though these of course contribute to the total sacrament of the church in the world. Its being in the world is already an invitation for people to rethink the understanding of self, of others, and of the universe.

Divine trascendence looms large as the most crucial issue for Christianity today. Is theism necessary for the Church of Jesus Christ? Is it necessary to postulate a transcendent in order to remain within the community of Christian believers? Is it sufficient to look to human beings for an adequate explanation of the universe? Do humans, including the human Jesus, throw the only shaft of

light on the puzzlements of the universe? These questions are put
to the Christian community by those who prefer a secular Christianity, by those who believe that the transcendent or divine dimension is not necessary for a true relationship to the person of
Jesus. They believe that a non-theistic explanation of the evolving
universe is the only one that adequately (not without acknowledged deficiencies) accounts for the observed realities of consciousness and immensity. The "death of God" movement, at least
in some of its forms, advanced this secular version of Christianity.
The life, parables, and actions of Jesus retain their importance as
inspiring guides to human living, so it is argued, but they do not
require the postulate of divine transcendence.

Obviously, therefore, not everyone who claims some relationship
to the person of Jesus would acknowledge the church as a sign of
the transcendent. The vast majority of Christian believers would
maintain, however, that confession of lordship in Jesus Christ pertains to the core of the Christian religion. Once the transcendent
character is removed from the person of Jesus, from the church, and
from the universe at large, an essential feature of the Christian
understanding of the universe is removed and Christianity really
becomes a radically different phenomenon. Non-theistic Christianity can draw much inspiration from the person of Jesus and from
the long history of the church, but it has abandoned the central
article of belief which has been transmitted by the community of
Israel and by the Church of Christ.

It is our contention that theism is an essential characteristic of the
Church of Christ. In whatever way God is viewed, his reality must
be acknowledged as fundamental to Christian believers. Many are
the concepts and expressions of the divine reality: the transcendent, the beyond, the absolute future, the powerfully present.
All definitions of God are inadequate, some more so than others.
But the various descriptions are necessary attempts to concep-
tualize the divine reality in the midst of the church and of the
world. They are needful even when inadequate.

The Church of Christ is the place of articulation. It is here that
believers struggle with the question of God and attempt to communicate a not altogether incredible image of God. It is here that
believers confess the God in Jesus Christ, worship him in word and
sacrament, and look expectantly for a more fulfilled relationship
with him in the future. The church itself, therefore, because of its
acknowledged relationship to God, because of its attempts at enun-
ciation of the divine, functions as a sign of the divine and the sacred
in the midst of the world. Its very existence calls men and women to

ponder the ultimate realities of the universe, to reflect on the mysterious dimension of life, and to consider the possibility of God as the explanation of human existence.

4. *Promoter of Worship*

The liturgical life of the church benefits the whole of mankind. A sound theology of liturgy points up its multi-directional purpose, including intercessions for human needs the world over. It is true that in liturgy the Church of Christ celebrates and pronounces primarily the glory of God who manifested great works in the people of Israel and in the person of Jesus. But the liturgical celebration is also directed to the upbuilding of the community of the church itself. Baptism and ordination, for instance, initiate individuals into the body of the church or into an office of the church. Christian prayer of any type puts persons in relationship with the most significant Other.

Identifying the purpose of worship in a Christian community is easier than discerning the relationship of worship to the people of the world as a whole. The church at prayer, whether in the more official liturgy of the word and the sacraments or in the less formal patterns of groups and individuals, espouses the needs of all mankind:

First of all, then, I urge that supplications, prayers, intercessions, and thanksgivings be made for all men, for kings and all who are in high positions, that we may lead a quiet and peaceable life, godly and respectful in every way. This is good, and it is acceptable in the sight of God our Savior, who desires all men to be saved and to come to the knowledge of the truth (1 Tm 2, 1–4).

No one is excluded from the intercessory benefactions of the church, for no one is outside the pale of God's saving activity. The prayer of the church cannot be more restrictive than the will of God.

Put in terms of this study the church's work is prayer for the whole of mankind. It functions as a praying community whose concern extends to everyone in the world. This does not mean, of course, that men and women reflectively appreciate, understand, or acknowledge that the Christian church includes them in its labor of prayer. Prayers and intercessions are directed to God through Jesus Christ, and in the final analysis it is God who grants their fruit. But if it is God who touches the heart of everybody, what is the point of prayer? Does God really need to be interceded with to approach the lives of people and lead them along paths that will ultimately bring about their reconciliation?

We cannot enter upon an extended disquisition on the value and power of prayer. The issue is complicated indeed. It will be sufficient to recall the incarnational aspect of salvation, namely, that God effects the salvation of people through the earthly reality of word and sacrament, through the community of Israel and the person of Jesus Christ. The mystery of Christian prayer is bound up with the mystery of salvation, incarnated in human and worldly realities. The fact is that prayer remains mysterious. The Christian stance of prayer is not subject to an analysis that would result in a patent understanding of the phenomenon. The individual Christian intuits much of its meaning in his or her personal experience of prayer, but he or she cannot hope to receive adequate insight into its nature, much less to communicate a convincing rationale to others. Perhaps the Christian can find some assurance, not in the perception of the ultimate basis of prayer, but in the command of Jesus and the practice of the primitive church. Jesus not only prayed but he encouraged his disciples to pray to the Father for their daily needs. The Father knows our needs; he realizes the wants of everybody in the world. Yet prayer is demanded. It is demanded not just for the sake of the one who prays, but also for the men and women who are the objects of prayer. Here precisely is the amazing mystery: the Christian is fruitful in prayer when he or she prays to the Father through Jesus Christ; the prayer is heard and it redounds to the good of the whole world. Such is the power and mystery of prayer. Such also is the task of the church.

The church of prayer turns outward to the needs of all people and petitions God on their behalf. At times the church pinpoints the specific needs and the actual persons in need, but more often it cannot name individuals and needs. It must pray in general and trust the discerning beneficence of God.

If what we have stated thus far is true, must we admit that the church is after all necessary for salvation? Does salvation come to the individual (even to the one who lives at a distance from the church) through the mediation of the church, that is, through the intercessory prayer of the church? Does God require prayer on the part of the church, so much so that no favor is granted without it? Here again we are confronted with the question of the concept of "necessity" and "medium." Prayer for all peoples is necessary in the sense that God demands it; it is a necessary dimension of Christian life. Can it be regarded as a "medium" of salvation? Would there be any salvation of the non-Christian without it? This much we can affirm: the praying church cannot name the specific people in the world, nor can it divine their particular needs. Thus its prayer must often be indeterminate with regard to person and need. If this kind of prayer is necessary, it is so only in and through the person of Jesus Christ. The church associates its prayer with his and so it becomes effective; it cannot be regarded as effectively salvational in itself. It becomes so only in union with Jesus whose prayer is sufficient and all-pervasive. The church is prayerfully associated with Jesus. Only in this dependent and limited sense, therefore, can we speak of the necessity of the church for salvation.

We might add here that the church at prayer is one dimension of the visible presence of the church. While it is true that much Christian prayer is, by command of the Lord, secret, it cannot fail to come to the knowledge of some people in the world. The official liturgy especially is apparent and even open to spectators. Thus it shares in the sign value of the church.

5. *Symbol of Community Life and Human Unity*

In this age of space travel and instant communication the peoples of the world find themselves closely bound together. Humankind is living on a shrinking globe. But does easier and more frequent interchange between peoples necessarily tighten the bonds of friendship, peace, and human community? Does the pressure of increased population and communication result in a better understanding of the norms of community life? Without doubt the increased interaction of peoples in this confined space underscores and augments the problems of living. The problems of housing, health care, and education, for example, are massive in congested areas. The juxtaposition of peoples, especially those of diverse backgrounds and cultures, is not a guarantee of community.

The Church of Christ exists as a community in this new world. It is a faith community gathered in and around the person of Christ. It is a visible community of believers united with Christ and with one another by visible bonds: a confession of faith, a sacred word, a lively hope. The church is not a secret society which forever guards its membership rolls and schedule of tenets. It takes its place in society as a fellowship of believers who recognize various credal, liturgical, and ministerial bonds of unity. People in society can appraise these bonds and the Christian community itself.

The community of Christian believers can become a pattern for others in society. The visibility of the church and the explicitness of its confession cannot fail to attract the attention of others. Granted that the intensity of love and unity between Christians leaves much to be desired in every age, it is important to note that the ideal is present and that in some dim fashion it strikes home in the hearts and minds of people.

Christian community can become a pattern of mutual concern. From the beginning the Christian message inculcated concern for the poor and the needy. Saint Paul inspired and procured financial aid for the poor Christians of Jerusalem. Throughout its history the church set aside funds for the poor. The community of believers showed concern for its own needy and for the indigent outside its membership. It may be conceded that other groups and institutions were also engaged in "poverty programs"; but the fact remains that the church's efforts were often present as pattern, instigation, and support. A community of mutual concern becomes a sign of concern for others.

The community of Christian believers can also become a symbol of responsible leadership. The officers of the church are indeed in a position of authority with regard to the direction of the church in its liturgy, its faith formulations, its sundry disciplines and practices. But they are placed in positions of authority for the sake of the community, for the profit and benefit of those over whom they preside. Of course, countless instances of failure in this regard may be cited: churchmen in search of power, domination, and personal ease. But our reflection is about *responsible* governance in the genuine Christian tradition. Insofar as the ideal is realized, it becomes a pattern of action for those who view the church.

The Church of Christ is model of concern for the community, for an understanding of individual needs, for an upholding of freedom and personhood, for humility and simplicity in high office (consider John XXIII), for proper order, for providential planning:

In their own relations to one another Christians and their church should demonstrate what is really meant by respect for human dignity, for equality, and for the free expression of opinion in both speech and writing. The same could be said regarding racial discrimination, to the abolition of which on a world-wide scale the church can contribute with little credibility until it has abolished it entirely within its own community.[1]

The community which Christians build up and experience among themselves can become a drive and inspiration for fellowship activity in the community at large. If they as Christians learn to cultivate the bonds of union in the Christian communion, they can make similar efforts on behalf of the larger community. There are Christian action groups that build up the structures of the civic community, for example, the various urban task forces that are designed to

---

[1] Hans-Heinrich Wolf, "Towards an Ecumenical Consensus," in *Technology and Social Justice*. Ed. by Ronald H. Preston (London: SCM Press, 1971), p. 441.

benefit the cause of education, welfare, city planning. Municipal agencies are also engaged in these needs. But special motivation and character are brought to the task by the Christian assembly, by those who have learned Christian community and who are enabled thereby to bring this power to bear on the work of community building.

The function of the church as symbol of community life extends also to the experimental organizations which it initiates among its members. The church tests styles of leadership, patterns of involvement, methods of communication, types of communitarian association. If they are successful, they can become models for the civic community. The Christian commune, for instance, is in its various manifestations a contemporary experiment in community living.

A study group sponsored by the Department on Studies in Evangelism of the World Council of Churches focused on the missionary structure of the congregation and reviewed the issue of experimental organizations:

In the second place, the decision by the North American Working Group not to study the traditional structures of local congregations but rather to explore the possibilities of new structures geared to specific needs marked an important step. Task forces were set up in different centres which led to the formation of such new structures as the Delta Ministry in Mississippi, the Los Angeles Goals Project, and the Metropolitan Associates of Philadelphia. Here institutions of a new kind were being created in which Christians co-operated with other men of good will in trying to meet the real needs of the community.[2]

Christians should acknowledge, however, that many or even most of their organizational patterns through the centuries have originated outside the church community and that they were appropriated by the church. Here too it is evident that the God of the human community is not working exclusively within the church but is effectively present in the human community at large.

The community of the church also functions as a symbol of re-created and renewed humanity. The church symbolizes the new humanity as it proclaims the New Man, Jesus Christ, and reveals its omnipresent renewal in his Spirit. The symbol is dynamic and future oriented, for the church is in the process of renewal:

Christ wants his Church to foreshadow a renewed human commu-

---

[2] Steven G. Mackie, "Changing Institutions — What Role Can Christians Play?" *Study Encounter* 6 (1970), p. 122.

nity. Therefore, we Christians will manifest our unity in Christ by entering into full fellowship with those of other races, classes, age, religious and political convictions, in the place where we live. Especially we shall seek to overcome racism.[3]

Humanity is in the process of being remodeled on the pattern of Jesus Christ, and the end of the process is expected with the definitive inbreaking of the kingdom of God. It is not suggested that the church is a perfect model for the human community. The lines of sin and failure mark the church deeply and mar its image. But in some imperfect fashion it already mirrors the face of Christ and his pattern of unity.

In some way, finally, the church manifests to the world the basic unity of mankind:

Churches are called, in their preaching and teaching, including theological education, to set forth the biblical view of the God-given oneness of mankind and to point out its concrete implications for the world-wide solidarity of man and the stewardship of the resources of the earth.[4]

The church harbors no illusion about the many ideologies and societal structures that divide men and women, but it understands its task as including within its membership diverse segments of humanity and as providing a doctrine which proclaims the unity of all. It not only manifests a certain unity in itself but it provides a fundamental and theoretical support for the reality of unity among all peoples. For example, the church proclaims the universal call to salvation and reconciliation with God. A study document of the Commission on Faith and Order says:

The Church is a sign that, in all their diversity, men belong together. It must therefore prove itself the Church by its ability to really embrace the diverse forms of human life and to relate them to one another.[5]

The study lists some examples of relationships and classes which need to be held together in the human community: race relations, man-woman relationships, old people, mentally defective and retarded, the uneducated, new classes of peoples such as technicians. A proclamation of the unity of all peoples is not to overlook fruitful

[3] "A Message from the Fourth Assembly of the World Council of Churches," *The Uppsala Report 1968*. Ed. by Norman Goodall (Geneva: World Council of Churches, 1968), p. 5.

[4] "World Economic and Social Development," a report adopted by the World Council of Churches, *ibid.*, p. 51.

[5] "The Unity of the Church and the Unity of Mankind. A Study Document of the Commission on Faith and Order," *Study Encounter* 5 (1969), p. 175.

differences and specific identities, but it is to promote the larger unifying perspective of humankind.

6. *Source of Reconciliation*

The Church of Christ also functions as a reconciler. It cannot, of course, substitute for Jesus who alone reconciles sinful persons and God. The church both announces this reconciliation and effectively promotes it in word and sacrament. According to genuine Christian tradition the church does more than announce the reconciliation. It acts sacramentally as the agent of reconciliation. It forgives sins and grants access to the Father in the name of Christ.

How does the church act as reconciler for those who do not profess Christian belief? Does the church really touch them in the word and sacrament of forgiveness? It cannot be denied that words of divine forgiveness reach non-Christians and lead them to an attitude of gratitude without resulting in their full profession of the Christian faith. The Christian message is certainly abroad in the land and is a source of consolation beyond the circle of professing Christian believers. How many are there who believe in God and who take courage in his forgiving presence because of what they have learned consciously or unconsciously from the community of Christians? Assuredly, many others are reconciled to God without any formal announcement of the church and without its explicit ministrations.

Many are the polarizations of beliefs, ideologies, world views. These often destructively split the people of society. Consider, for instance, the polarization of labor and management. The church may supply not only the more remote rationale for understanding and appreciating the oneness of the human community but also the very agency of reconciliation. The example of Cesar Chavez is appropriate. He operated from a Christian background on behalf of people who were by and large Christian, and he enlisted the aid of the church in the persons of bishops, priests, and ministers. The power of the Catholic bishops in this case was one of the deciding factors that at one point effected a reasonable negotiation and a settlement of the rift between the grape pickers and the grape growers.

Another example of reconciliation is the Cuban missile crisis of October 1962. The two major powers, the United States and Russia, confronted each other when it became apparent that Russia was erecting missile bases in Cuba. The world shuddered as it looked into the abyss of nuclear destruction. John XXIII, the peasant become pope and recognized spokesman for many Christians, pleaded with both sides to ponder the consequences of nuclear conflagration. We are not saying that the pope alone brought about wiser counsels in Washington and Moscow, but he aided the reduction of tension by advocating negotiation.

Most often the church's mediatorship is not so obvious. It is more in terms of narrowing the cleft between divergent ideologies. The Christian message of freedom and responsibility, for instance, serves as a humane force in the world, stemming attempts on the part of certain philosophers, biologists, evolutionists, and politicians to extinguish them. The message of Christ is present in the world to promote the cause of freedom and humanity in the face of unfreedom and inhumanity.

The church can function as a reconciliation between classes and races. The rich and the poor, the haves and the have-nots can find shelter under the one common umbrella of Christian belief. Those not of the Christian faith can learn mutual respect and understanding by the latent or patent message of the church. Unfortunately the church itself has accepted too often and too readily the status quo of societal classes and has been all too willing to build up a community without changing the sociological structure. The institution of slavery is a prime example. Here however one must note that even in acknowledging the institution, the church's message was already working to transform it from within. In this context we may recall Paul's compassionate letter to Philemon and his request for human and brotherly treatment for the slave Onesimus. Much later, Christians, especially Protestant clergymen in this country, were active in the abolition of slavery. In a very forceful manner — with many unfortunate exceptions — the church jarred human consciences and narrowed the ideological distance between the races. The church is still a factor in reconciliation and much work has yet to be done. It must continue to proclaim the message of union and show forth in deed the benefits of association.

The church may also serve to reconcile the tensions that exist between the young and the old. It numbers both groups in its membership — a fact which is apparent to the non-Christian world. It teaches a respect for the wisdom and tradition of the elders and also a willing ear for the suggestions and inspirations of youth. The church itself must continually live with this tension, and through its various programs it can offer an example of reconciliation. Its promotion of peace among nations, for example, can serve as a rallying point for the young and the old. Its concern for the sacredness of life, for the artistic and beautiful, can bring together the two ages of life or at least serve as a pattern of their reconciliation.

7. Prophet to the World

The Church of Christ serves the world as prophet. It functions in a way not unlike the prophets of scripture, especially *the* prophet, Jesus Christ. It acknowledges, of course, the unique prophetic mission of Israel and the centrality of the prophetic activity of Jesus. The prophets of old had their distinctive roles in the work of salvation, and their activities cannot be repeated. But their prophetic message is still normative for the church today. The church does not strike their words out of its living tradition; it assimilates them, procures ever new insights from them, interprets them, and proclaims them to the people of today.

Prophets still exist in the church, prophets of extraordinary dedication, vigor, and insight. The whole church, in fact, is prophetic, and this means that each person in the church is at least to some extent a prophet. The prophetic profile of the church, generally low in individual Christians, has a cumulative effect. The aggregate of the whole church results in a large pattern of prophecy. The single voice is small but the chorus of voices becomes a shout. We do not wish to imply that the individual members of the church speak with one mind and one voice. This ideal of the past — insofar as it was an ideal — cannot serve as a norm today. The ideal never was realized and it cannot be placed before the church today as a standard of prophecy. Different cultural mindsets, different linguistic expressions, different insights, and different interpretations of the original prophetic message ensure a continuing variety of prophetic proclamation.

Since the church numbers only a fraction of the world population (though it is present in most lands), there is some question about the perceptibility of its prophetic voice. Do all peoples hear the prophetic church? Is it large enough and loud enough to be heard? Must we assume that its message has reached the ears of every person? It seems that it has not. This is true not only of countries such as China where Christianity is repressed, but also of so-called Christian countries where the voice of the church is often muted and muffled in such a way that the message is received garbled if at all. The larger metropolitan areas are no exception to this silence, in spite of the fact that church structures are still visible on the skyline of the city. Thus for many people the church does not function as a prophetic community.

But for many it does manifest itself as a prophet. In what ways does it act as prophet? The prophet voice of the church is, first of all, one of consolation, one which relieves the guilt anxieties of people with the divine word of forgiveness. Its voice proclaims that God's attitude is one of favor and forgiveness, that men and women need not despair in their sins, that their humble approach to God is acceptable. The church is a bearer of this good news: "Get you up to a high mountain, O Zion, herald of good tidings; lift up your voice with strength, O Jerusalem, herald of good tidings, lift it up, fear not; say to the cities of Judah, 'Behold your God'!" (Is 40, 9). The voice of comfort and consolation is the voice of God himself resounding through the cries of the church. The human burden of sin is eased through the prophetic word of the church.

The prophetic word of the church thus becomes a center of consciousness of the divine word and revelation. This ecclesial center does not imply, of course, that the word of God is present only within the visible confines of the Church of Christ. It is acknowledged that the experience of God and of his self-communication can be actualized within the lives and religions of non-Christians. But the self-communication of God reaches its apex in the person of Jesus Christ and in the ecclesial community that continues his tradition. The church is the point of concentration and the center of the prophetic word. Christians are committed to the proposition that the divine word, the personal word of God, dwells within their midst in a way that it is not found elsewhere. It is not pride that leads to this affirmation but confident faith in the person of Jesus. Christ, the word and the prophet, is present within his church, and the ecclesial community is the prophetic spokesman of his message.

Although we are speaking of the prophetic dimension of the church as a whole, we may single out as the center of centers the See of Rome. Admittedly Roman messages are at times stilted and out-dated, mistimed and out of focus. Nevertheless Rome is a point of focus for the Christian message. Its pronouncements on behalf of peace and justice, on behalf of life and freedom, on behalf of the poor and the needy are words which make a wide appeal. What is significant for our purposes is that these words are spoken by a center of Christian unity. For those who receive the proclamations it is not easy to bypass their Christian import and motivation.

A joint message of the bishops of a country commands at least a modicum of attention. The same may be said for a statement issued by local pastors, a statement of position, for instance, about living conditions in sections of a city — crumbling buildings, high rent, poor sanitation facilities, inadequate fire and police protection. The Christian pastors become a center of consciousness for the word of justice and humanity. The statement need not be markedly Christian in decoration and ring, but it will be obvious enough that it derives from Christian concern. It is a prophetic word which gathers up the word of God and casts it upon the city.

As prophetic, the church is at the service of the world in the realm of divine truth. It has an understanding of human beings, a word which it receives from the self-communication of God, a word instructive of life. It is a word that concerns the lives of people — their well being, their peace, their mutual respect. It is a good word whether it points out a way of peace and consolation or whether it brands a festering evil.

This leads us to another aspect of the prophetic role of the church: the condemnation of the demonic in the world. The prophetic word of the church judges the demonic in society. It exposes the evil even as it corrects with salutary admonition. For example, in the matter of poverty housing the demonic can take the form of greed on the part of landlords, of neglect on the part of city officials.

The demonic can assume many forms. It can be an ideology such as Nazism which exalts blood and soil. It can be a form of power such as war and military strength. It can be domination such as the endeavor of some labor unions to keep their numbers small by practices of discrimination. The prophetic word of the church continually judges, not only the members of the church but also the sins and injustices of society. The prophetic word reminds society and governments of their provisional and finite character. It condemns idol worship that continually lurks on the borders of society. It can expect criticism for its efforts. It can even expect persecution, a mark of the church in many ages.

Other ideologies may be not so much demonic as incorrect or inadequate. Many forms of humanism and agnosticism could be so classified. The prophetic word of the church may point up their deficiencies and deviations, proclaiming the word of God as the way of truth.

The prophetic word of the church can also function as a critique of non-Christian religions. It is not a matter of outright condemnation of such religions, as if they were the products of the devil. It is rather a matter of the correction and purification of their official doctrines, e.g., those concerning the value of the body and human life, the dignity of the person, the worship of non-divine realities. The presence of the prophetic word of the church can supply the needed corrective and perspective.

We conclude, therefore, that the church functions as a prophet in the world. It has a crucial task and a necessary mission in the world. But it is an effort which does not touch everyone. It is not present in such a way that everyone can perceive its message and direction.

The church indeed has a prophetic purpose, but many people adhere to the way of salvation without this dimension of the church.

8. *Catalyst of Change*

The church also functions as a catalyst of change. It cannot be otherwise. Insofar as the Christian conviction captures the minds and hearts of people, it is bound to redirect their goals and strivings. Men and women cannot become enthralled with the person and message of Jesus without having this attachment enter into their lives and actions. A Christian dimension, at least in motivation, will impress itself upon all they do and say. We do not imply that every action on behalf of the human community will clearly manifest a Christian purpose. It is obvious that humanitarian actions often appear no different from those pursued by Christians, even though the actions themselves may derive from the all-pervading Spirit and grace of God. But actions undertaken by Christians for the welfare of people often bear the imprint of Christian conviction; even when the imprint is not obvious, the matter of motivation cannot be left out of consideration. The same outward action may result from diverse motivations, one of which can be Christian conviction. It seems that motivation and world view must be pondered when determining the character of an action, and that thus the background, thinking, and motivation of the Christian who acts on behalf of fellow human beings enter of necessity into the analysis of the action. We repeat that the external action need not appear outwardly any different to the casual observer. But we may presume that it often does, for one's thoughts and convictions are not purely spiritual phenomena; they assume flesh and take shape in the world; they become realized and externalized in action. It is questionable that one's inner views can forever remain in the realm of the spirit and never manifest themselves in an outward and visible form.

If it is true that the actions of the Christian community or of individual Christians in the community are at least in a minimum way marked by a Christian character, it must be acknowledged that the Church of Christ is indeed a catalyst of change in the world. No one can deny that the course of European and Western civilization has been profoundly influenced by Christian believers. This influence is a matter of history and need not be documented here. It must be admitted, of course, that the influence of Christians has not always been salutary, that it often led to the repression and sufferings of peoples (cf. the Jewish community of the European middle ages). But it must be granted too that a genuine Christian message led to beneficial changes in society. It aided the liberation of people from various forms of idol worship, e.g., the worship of nature or of self. It offered a wider perspective on the position of men and women in the world. Its official message was one of concern for the welfare of persons — for their well-being, health, education, government. Obviously we cannot bypass the many failures of Christians in the past, their tendencies to dominate peoples, their repressions of freedom, their pursuit of personal glory. But neither can we neglect their many achievements. Pursuits such as care of the sick, the uneducated, the imprisoned had a definite Christian motivation and direction. Our contention is that Christianity has been a catalyst of change in society and that it is still an agent of change today.

It would be impossible here to list all the ways in which the Christian community can act as an agent of change. The ways are as varied as there are genuine needs of peoples. It will be sufficient to name a few representative examples.

The church is still involved in education, even in the arts and the sciences. While more and more education is provided by civil government, a place is still ensured for educational efforts of the Church of Christ. Its involvement includes, but is not limited to, explicit studies of Christian doctrine. Such schools (professional, graduate, or liberal arts) are necessary if the length and breadth of Christian studies (scripture, history of the church and of doctrine, present-day perspectives) are to be pursued. Under the present arrangement of state schools in the United States of America, for instance, it is generally not possible to offer the total curriculum of Christian studies. But beyond the explicit offering of Christian studies there is the Christian perspective that is offered in the pursuit of the sciences and humanities. They are studied with all scientific seriousness and method, but they are viewed within the broader perspective of the Christian view of the cosmos. Such a view is not designed to prejudge the results of the scientific method, but it prevents the presumption that the method of science is the only way of pursuing knowledge and that scientific knowledge is the only genuine type of knowledge. Such a view can be presented not only at a church-related school but also by Christian teachers and researchers wherever they pursue their work.

Another example of church agency is or can be the task of representing the needs of the poorly housed. Usually such people are not in a position to make their voices heard or to apply the appropriate pressure for effecting change. In this case the church can become their spokesman. Individual Christians may see the need and put forth their efforts; or officeholders of the church may back the cause of the poor. The church can make others aware of the needs by publicizing the plight of the underprivileged and it can represent them to the people and to the authorities that are in a position to bring about change. Church leaders can bring pressure to bear on city officials to ameliorate and govern the housing conditions of the poor (e.g., rent control, inspection, repair, police and fire protection). Of course other agencies not explicitly Christian can and do take up the cause of the poor. But sometimes they do not. Then especially the church must act. The church can be an agent of change, however imperfect it may be or however timidly it may pursue its cause.

Another example is the financial pressure which the church can bring to bear on economic structures in society. It can refuse to retain stock in and to do business with those corporations that discriminate against classes of workers or peoples. The World Council of Churches applied this pressure when it withdrew its monies from the corporations doing business with the Union of South Africa; it requested its member churches to do the same. Its goal was to change the apartheid policies built into the governance of the country.

These are three examples of the church as a catalyst of change in society. Individual Christians, operating from their view of the world, have a vast field open before them if they have eyes to see and courage to act according to the convictions of their faith. It is not our contention, however, that every single person who is being saved has come into direct contact with the church as catalyst. We presume that many people achieve salvation without experiencing the church as an agent of change.

9. *Promoter of the Future*

The Church of Christ promotes the future because it believes in the future. The eyes of the church are not so fixed on the events of the past, not even on the historical advent of Jesus, that they cannot look courageously into the future. The church does not pine after the so-called ages of faith (which were in fact blended with much unbelief) and move into the future only with reluctance and sadness. It looks into the future with the eyes of hope and expectation.

The Church of Christ does not distribute a timetable of future events. The book of Revelation provides no exact schedule of happenings that will come upon the universe. Believers in Jesus, together with all peoples in the world, receive the unexpected and the surprising from the future. It is true that to some extent individuals can extrapolate the shape of the immediate future from present and past events. But the accuracy of such extrapolation diminishes with the lengthening of the time period. The Church of Christ shares the inaccuracy of any prediction.

The Christian believer acknowledges the darkness surrounding the future but also lives in hope and expectation with regard to it. He accepts the word of Jesus about the impending reign of God. He regards Jesus as the initial embodiment of the reign, an embodiment which sketches out real features of the kingdom such as forgiveness of sins and union with God, and which promises a fulfillment in a time to come. The believer accepts the future reality of the completed reign of God.

But does the Church of Christ believe in a future for this world, this universe, this human community? Will the future kingdom of God destroy the only universe that people know? Is the reign of God a happy outcome for this universe and this human community? What shape will the future reign of God take? Christian believers disagree among themselves about its general shape. Some surmise that the universe itself will be destroyed and that humans will either share the life of God or not, depending upon the merit of their lives. Others prefer to hold that the universe itself will not be destroyed but enhanced by the advent of the final reign of God. According to this doctrine people will not be removed from their accustomed universe but will enjoy the living God in a universe struck by the definitive advent of God. Mental pictures of this transformed universe fail in precision and detail. But some attempt at articulation is made in such terms as the redemption of the universe, the transformation of the universe, the glorification of the universe. The imagery and symbols of sacred scripture do not allow greater precision.

In any event, the Church of Christ promotes an ultimate future. It is committed to a fulfillment of the present state of the universe, to an outcome to the developments of the universe. In the midst of a maze of conflicting ideologies, some advocating a terrestial utopia, others resigned to the mere chance and meaninglessness of the whole of reality, the Church of Christ continues to proclaim a confidence in the ultimate direction of the universe. The church indeed is committed to the future and promotes the future. It is committed to an ultimate future of this universe.

But does the Church of Christ promote the immediate or short-range future? Is it really interested in the future that will be experienced by the human community 100 or 1000 years from now? To answer this question one only needs to turn to the way in which the church understands its task in the world today. As catalyst of change, as agent of unity, the church involves itself in the affairs of people and wishes to be of profit to them. Its gaze is not only toward the realities of the ultimate future but also to the needs of the immediate future of the world. It holds in tension a concern for the "now" and an expectation of the "not yet."

Bibliography

Introduction

Alfaro, J., S.J. "Christus, Sacramentum Dei Patris: Ecclesia, Sacramentum Christi Gloriosi." *Acta Congressus Internationalis De Theologia Concilii Vaticani II.* Rome: Typis Polyglottis Vaticanis, 1968, pp. 4–9.

Beinert, W. *Um das dritte Kirchenattribut; die Katholizität der Kirche im Verständnis der evangelisch-lutherischen und römisch-katholischen Theologie der Gegenwart.* 2 vols. Essen: Ludgerus-Verlag, 1964.

Beumer, J., S.J. "Die Heilsnotwendigkeit der Kirche nach den akten des Vatikanischen Konzils." *Theologie und Glaube* 37–38 (1947/48), pp. 76–86.

———. "Extra ecclesiam nulla salus." *Lexikon für Theologie und Kirche.* 2nd ed. Vol. 3. Freiburg: Herder, 1959, cols. 1320f.

A Catechism of Christian Doctrine. Revised edition of the Baltimore Catechism. Paterson, N.J.: St. Anthony Guild Press, 1949.

Denzinger, H., and Schönmetzer, A., S.J. (eds.). *Enchiridion Symbolorum Definitionum et Declarationum de Rebus Fidei et Morum.* 33rd ed. Barcelona: Herder, 1965.

Dulles, A., S.J. "The Church, the Churches, and the Catholic Church." *Theological Studies* 33 (1972), pp. 199–234.

Eminyan, M., S.J. *The Mystery of Salvation.* Valletta: Malta University Press, 1973.

Feiner, J. "Decree on Ecumenism. Commentary on the Decree." *Commentary on the Documents of Vatican II.* Edited by H. Vorgrimler. Vol. 2. New York: Herder and Herder, 1968, pp. 57–164.

Fenton, J. "The Necessity of the Church and the Efficacy of Prayer." *The American Ecclesiastical Review* 132 (1955), pp. 336–349.

———. *The Catholic Church and Salvation in the Light of Recent Pronouncements by the Holy See.* Westminster, Maryland: The Newman Press, 1958.

Hamer, J., O.P., "Les ministères protestants dans le cadre de l'ecclésiologie du II concile du Vatican." *Revue Thomiste* 71 (1971), pp. 509–519.

Lubac, H. de, S.J. *Catholicisme: Les aspects sociaux du dogma.* Paris: Éditions du Cerf, 1938.

McBrien, R. P. *Do We Need the Church?* New York: Harper and Row, 1969.

Schillebeeckx, E., O.P. "The Church and Mankind." *The Church and Mankind.* Concilium, Vol. 1. New York: Paulist Press, 1965, pp. 69–101.

Semmelroth, O. *The Church and Christian Belief.* Glen Rock, N.J.: Paulist Press, 1966.

Stolz, A., O.S.B. "Extra Ecclesiam nulla salus." *Der Katholische Gedanke* 10 (1937), pp. 101–112.

Chapter 1

Althaus, P. *The Theology of Martin Luther.* Transl. by R. C. Schultz. Philadelphia: Fortress Press, 1966.

Augustine. *Sermon to the People of the Church of Caesarea*. CSEL 53.
———. *On Baptism*. CSEL 51.
———. *Letters*. CSEL 34 and 41.
———. *Commentary on the Gospel of John*. PL 35.
———. *Questions in the Heptateuch*. CSEL 28.
———. *Against the Letter of Parmenian*. CSEL 51.
———. *Against Faustus*. CSEL 25.
———. *Sermons*. PL 38.
———. *On the Correction of the Donatists*, or *Letter 185*. CSEL 57.
Barnard, L. W. *Justin Martyr. His Life and Thought*. Cambridge: Cambridge University Press, 1967.
Barth, K. *Church Dogmatics*. Vol. IV. *The Doctrine of Reconciliation*. Part One. Transl. by G. W. Bromiley. Edinburgh: T. & T. Clark, 1956.
Bellarmine, R., S.J. *De Controversiis Christianis Fidei Adversus hujus Temporis Haereticos*. *Opera Omnia*. Tom. II. Milan: Natale Battezzati, 1858.
Boase, T. S. R. *Boniface VIII*. London: Constable & Co., 1933.
Brown, P. *Augustine of Hippo*. Berkeley: University of California Press, 1967.
Brown, R. E., S.S. "One Baptism for the Remission of Sins — New Testament Roots." *Lutherans and Catholics in Dialogue II. One Baptism for the Remission of Sins*. Ed. by P. C. Empie and W. W. Baum. Washington, D.C.: NCWC, 1967, pp. 9–21.
Butler, B. C., O.S.B. "St. Cyprian and the Church." *The Downside Review* 71 (1953), pp. 1–13; 119–134; 258–272.
———. *The Idea of the Church*. Baltimore: Helicon, 1963.
Calvin, J. *Institutes of the Christian Religion*. Vol. 2. Transl. by H. Beveridge. Grand Rapids, Mich.: Wm. B. Eerdmans, 1966.
Catechismus ex decreto Ss. Concilii Tridentini ad Parochos. Pii V. Pont. Max. jussu editus. Typis Seminarii Patavini Gregoriana Edidit, 1930.
Chenu, M. D., O.P. "Unam Sanctam." *Lexikon für Theologie und Kirche*. Vol. 10. Freiburg: Herder, 1965, col. 462.
———. "Dogme et Théologie dans la bulle *Unam Sanctam*." *La Parole de Dieu*. Vol. I. *La Foi dans l'Intelligence*. Paris: Éditions du Cerf, 1964, pp. 361–369.
Clement of Alexandria. *The Tutor*. PG 8.
Corwin, V. *St. Ignatius and Christianity in Antioch*. New Haven: Yale University Press, 1960.
Crowe, M. B. "St. Thomas and the Greeks: Reflections on an Argument in Hans Küng's *Infallible?*" *The Irish Theological Quarterly* 39 (1972), pp. 253–275.
Cyprian. *Letters*. CSEL 3.
———. *The Unity of the Catholic Church*. CC 3.
———. *The Lapsed. The Unity of the Catholic Church*. Transl. and annotated by M. Bévenot, S.J. *Ancient Christian Writers*. Vol. 25. Westminster, Maryland: The Newman Press, 1957.
Daly, C. B. "Absolution and Satisfaction in St. Cyprian's Theology of Penance." *Studia Patristica*. Vol. 2. Berlin: Akademie Verlag, 1957, pp. 202–207.
Escobar, A. de, O.S.B. *Tractatus Polemico-Theologicus de Graecis Errantibus*. Ed. by E. Candal, S.J. Rome: Pontificium Institutum Orientalium Studiorum, 1952.
Friedberg, E. *Corpus Iuris Canonici*. Vol. 1. Leipzig: Ex officina Bernhardi Tauchnitz, 1879.
Fulgentius of Ruspe. *On Faith, to Peter*. PL 65.
Gilby, T. *Principality and Polity. Aquinas and the Rise of State Theory in the West*. London: Longmans, Green and Co., 1958.

Giles of Rome. *De Ecclesiastica Potestate*. Ed. by R. Scholz. Weimar: H. Böhlaus, 1929. Reprint: Scientia Aalen, 1961.

Glorieux, P. "Autour du *Contra errores Graecorum*. Suggestions chronologiques." *Autour d'Aristote. Recueil d'études de philosophie ancienne et médiévale offert à Monseigneur Mansion*. Louvain: Publications Universitaires de Louvain, 1955, pp. 497–512.

Grabowski, S. *The Church. An Introduction to the Theology of St. Augustine*. St. Louis: Herder, 1957.

Greenwood, R. P. "*Extra Ecclesiam nulla salus*: Its Treatment in Recent Catholic Theology." *Theology* 76 (1973), pp. 416–425.

Gregory I. *Moralium Libri sive Expositio in Librum B. Job*. PL 76.

Hertling, L., S.J. *Communio. Church and Papacy in Early Christianity*. Transl. with an introduction by J. Wicks, S.J. Chicago: Loyola University Press, 1972.

Hippolytus. *Philosophumena*, or *The Refutation of All Heresies*. Transl. by F. Legge. London: SPCK, 1921.

Hoare, F. R. *The Papacy and the Modern State. An Essay on Political History of the Catholic Church*. London: Burns, Oates & Washbourne, 1940.

Hofmann, G., S.J. (ed.) *Epistolae Pontificiae ad Concilium Florentinum Spectantes*. Rome: Pontificium Institutum Orientalium Studiorum, 1946.

Hus, J. *The Church*. H. A. Oberman, *Forerunners of the Reformation. The Shape of Late Medieval Thought Illustrated by Key Documents*. Translations by P. L. Nyhus. New York: Holt, Rinehart and Winston, 1966, pp. 218–237.

Ignatius of Antioch. *Letter to the Philadelphians. Early Christian Writings. The Apostolic Fathers*. Transl. by M. Staniforth. Baltimore: Penguin Books, 1968.

Irenaeus. *Adversus Haereses*. PG 7.

Jerome. *Letter 15*, PL 22.

Justin Martyr. *Apology I. Apology II. Writings of Saint Justin Martyr*. Transl. by T. B. Falls. New York: Christian Heritage, Inc., 1948.

Kelly, T. A., C.S.C. *Sancti Ambrosii Liber de Consolatione Valentiniani*. A Text with a translation, introduction and commentary. Washington, D.C.: The Catholic University of America Press, 1940.

King, J. J., O.M.I. *The Necessity of the Church for Salvation in Selected Theological Writings of the Past Century*. Washington, D.C.: The Catholic University of America Press, 1960.

Korbacher, J. *Ausserhalb der Kirche kein Heil? Eine Dogmengeschichtliche Untersuchung über Kirche und Kirchenzugehörigkeit bei Johannes Chrysostomus*. Munich: M. Hueber, 1963.

Küng, H. *The Church*. New York: Sheed and Ward, 1967.

Lawlor, F. X., S.J. "The Mediation of the Church in Some Pontifical Documents." *Theological Studies* 12 (1951), pp. 481–504.

Leith, John H. (ed.) *Creeds of the Churches*. Garden City, N.Y.: Doubleday & Co., 1963.

Luther, M. *Kirchenpostille* (1522). *D. Martin Luthers Werke. Kritische Gesamtausgabe*. Weimar, 1883ff. Vol. 10, 1, 1.

———. *Eine kurze Form der zehn Gebote, eine kurze Form des Glaubens, eine kurze Form de Vaterunsers* (1520). WA Vol. 7.

———. *The Large Catechism* (1529). *The Book of Concord*. Transl. and ed. by T. G. Tappert. Philadelphia: Fortress Press, 1959.

———. *Vom Abendmahl Christi. Bekenntnis* (1528). WA Vol. 26.

Mansi, I. *Sacrorum Conciliorum nova et amplissima collectio*. Florence (later Paris and Leipzig), 1759ff.

Migne, J. *Patrologiae cursus completus*. Series Graeca. Paris, 1857ff.

——. *Patrologiae cursus completus*. Series Latina. Paris, 1844ff.

Newman, J. H. "A Letter Addressed to His Grace the Duke of Norfolk on occasion of Mr. Gladstone's Recent Expostulation." *Certain Difficulties Felt by Anglicans in Catholic Teaching*. Vol. II. London: Longmans, Green and Co., 1896, pp. 171–347.

Origen. *Homilies on Jeremiah*. PG 13.

——. *On First Principles*. Transl. by G. W. Butterworth. New York: Harper and Row, 1966.

——. *Homily 2 on Psalm 36*. PG 12.

——. *Homilies on Joshua*. PG 12.

Pelikan, J. *The Christian Tradition*. Vol. I. *The Emergence of the Catholic Tradition (100–600)*. Chicago: The University of Chicago Press, 1971.

Spinka, M. *John Hus' Concept of the Church*. Princeton: Princeton University Press, 1966.

——. (ed.) *Advocates of Reform: From Wyclif to Erasmus*. Philadelphia: Westminster Press, 1953.

Tertullian. *Apology. De Spectaculis*. With an English translation by T. R. Glover. Cambridge, Mass.: Harvard University Press, 1966.

——. *Homily on Baptism. Tertullian's Homily on Baptism*. The Text edited with an Introduction, Translation and Commentary by Ernest Evans. London: SPCK, 1964.

Thomas Aquinas. *De Veritate. S. Thomae Aquinatis Opera Omnia*. Vol. 9. Parma: Peter Fiaccadori, 1859.

——. *Contra Errores Graecorum*. Ed. by Raymond A. Verardo, O.P. *Opuscula Theologica*. Vol. 1. Turin: Marietti, 1954.

——. *Expositio Primae Decretalis ad Archidiaconum Tudertinum*. *Opuscula Theologica*. Ed. by Raymond A. Verardo, O.P. Vol. 1. Turin: Marietti, 1954.

——. *Summa Theologiae*. 3 Vols. Turin: Marietti, 1952f.

——. *In Symbolum Apostolorum, scilicet "credo in Deum" Expositio. Opuscula Theologica*.Vol. 2. Ed. by Raymond M. Spiazzi, O.P. Turin: Marietti, 1954.

Tierney, Brian. *Foundations of the Conciliar Theory. The Contribution of the Medieval Canonists from Gratian to the Great Schism*. Cambridge: Cambridge University Press, 1955.

Torrance, Thomas F. *The Doctrine of Grace in the Apostolic Fathers*. Edinburgh: Oliver and Boyd, 1948.

Tosti, Louis. *History of Pope Boniface VIII and His Times*. Transl. by E. J. Donnelly. New York: Samuel R. Leland, Inc., 1910.

Vallaresso, Fantinus. *Libellus de ordine generalium conciliorum et unione Florentina*. Ad fidem manuscriptorum edidit introductione-notis-indicibus ornavit Bernardus Schultze, S.I. Rome: Pontificium Institutum Orientalium Studiorum, 1944.

Vatican I. *Schema constitutionis dogmaticae de Ecclesia Christi Patrum examini propositum. Acta et decreta sacrorum conciliorum recentiorum*. Collectio Lacensis. Vol. 7. Freiburg: Herder, 1890.

Chapter 2

Schema Constitutionis Dogmaticae De Ecclesia (1962). *Acta Synodalia Sacrosancti Concilii Oecumenici Vaticani Secundi*. Volumen I: Periodus Prima. Pars IV. Congregationes Generales XXXI-XXXVI. Typis Polyglottis Vaticanis, 1971, pp. 12–91.

Schema Constitutionis Dogmaticae De Ecclesia (1963). *Acta Synodalia Sacrosancti Concilii Oecumenici Vaticani Secundi.* Volumen II: Periodus Secunda. Pars I. Sessio Publica II. Congregationes Generales XXXVII-XXXIX. Typis Polyglottis Vaticanis, 1971, pp. 215–281.

Schema Constitutionis De Ecclesia (1964). *Acta Synodalia Sacrosancti Concilii Oecumenici Vaticani Secundi.* Volumen III: Periodus Tertia. Pars I. Sessio Publica IV. Congregationes Generales LXXX-LXXXII. Typis Polyglottis Vaticanis, 1973, pp. 158–375.

Constitutio Dogmatica De Ecclesia. Caput VII De Indole Eschatologica Ecclesiae Peregrinantis Eiusque Unione Cum Ecclesia Caelesti (1964). *Acta Synodalia Sacrosancti Concilii Oecumenici Vaticani Secundi.* Volumen III: Periodus Tertia. Pars V. Congregationes Generales CIII-CXI. Typis Polyglottis Vaticanis, 1975, pp. 49–57.

Schema Decreti De Oecumenismo (1963). *Acta Synodalia Sacrosancti Concilii Oecumenici Vaticani Secundi.* Volumen II: Periodus Secunda. Pars V. Congregationes Generales LXV-LXXIII. Typis Polyglottis Vaticanis, 1973, pp. 412–441.

Schema Decreti De Oecumenismo (1964). *Acta Synodalia Sacrosancti Concilii Oecumenici Vaticani Secundi.* Volumen III: Periodus Tertia. Pars II. Congregationes Generales LXXXIII-LXXXIX. Typis Polyglottis Vaticanis, 1974, pp. 296–329.

Abbott, W., S.J., and Gallagher, J. (eds.). *The Documents of Vatican II.* New York: America Press, 1966.

Alfaro, J., S.J. "Christus, Sacramentum Dei Patris: Ecclesia, Sacramentum Christi Gloriosi." *Acta Congressus Internationalis De Theologia Concilii Vaticani II.* Rome: Typis Polyglottis Vaticanis, 1968, pp. 4–9.

Baum, Gregory, O.S.A. "The Magisterium in a Changing Church." *Man as Man and Believer. Concilium,* Vol. 21. New York: Paulist Press, 1967, pp. 67–83.

Beckel, A., Reiring, H., Roegele, O. (eds.) *Zweites Vatikanisches Konzil. 2. Sitzungsperiode. Dokumente. Texte. Kommentare.* Osnabrück: Verlag A. Fromm, 1964.

Becker, W. "Decree on Ecumenism. History of the Decree." *Commentary on the Documents of Vatican II.* Ed. by H. Vorgrimler. Vol. 2. New York: Herder and Herder, 1968, pp. 1–56.

Berard, A., S.J. (transl.) *Preparatory Reports. Second Vatican Council.* Philadelphia: The Westminster Press, 1965.

Berkouwer, G. C. *The Second Vatican Council and the New Catholicism.* Grand Rapids, Mich.: Wm. B. Eerdmans Pub. Co., 1965.

Bernards, M. "Zur Lehre von der Kirche als Sakrament. Beobachtungen aus der Theologie des 19. und 20. Jahrhunderts." *Münchener Theologische Zeitschrift* 20 (1969), pp. 29–34.

Brechter, S., O.S.B. "Dekret über die Missionstätigkeit der Kirche, Einleitung und Kommentar." *Lexikon für Theologie und Kirche. Das Zweite Vatikanische Konzil.* Vol. III. Freiburg: Herder, 1968.

Doepfner, J. "Die Reform der Kirche." *Zweites Vatikanisches Konzil. 3. Sitzungsperiode. Dokumente. Texte. Kommentare.* Ed. by A. Beckel, H. Reiring, and O. Roegele. Osnabrück: Verlag A. Fromm, 1965, pp. 15–32.

Fischer, E. *Kirche und Kirchen nach dem Vatikanum II. Die Lehre des Konzils über die Kirchenzugehörigkeit aus ökumenischer Sicht.* Munich: C. Kaiser, 1967.

Flannery, A., O.P. (ed.) *Vatican II. The Church Constitution.* Chicago: Priory Press, 1966.

Hamer, J., O.P. "Les ministères protestants dans le cadre de l'écclésiologie du II concile du Vatican." *Revue Thomiste* 71 (1971), pp. 509–519.

Kodell, J., O.S.B. "Vatican II and 'Outside the Church No Salvation'." *The American Benedictine Review* 23 (1972), pp. 314–324.

Küng, H., Congar, Y., O.P., and O'Hanlon, D., S.J. (eds.) *Council Speeches of Vatican II*. Glen Rock, N.J.: Paulist Press, 1964.

Leahy, W.K., and Massimini, A. T. (eds.) *Third Session. Council Speeches of Vatican II*. Glen Rock, N.J.: Paulist Press, 1966.

Lindbeck, G. A. *The Future of Roman Catholic Theology. Vatican II — Catalyst for Change*. Philadelphia: Fortress Press, 1970.

Loffeld, E., C.S.Sp. "De functione salvifica religionum praechristianarum in contactu praeparando pleno cum Christo eiusque Ecclesia." *Acta Congressus Internationalis De Theologia Concilii Vaticani II*. Rome: Typis Polyglottis Vaticanis, 1968, pp. 383–388.

McNamara, K. (ed.) *Vatican II: The Constitution on the Church. A Theological and Pastoral Commentary*. Chicago: Franciscan Herald Press, 1968.

Miller, John H., C.S.C. (ed.) *Vatican II. An Interfaith Appraisal*. Notre Dame, Ind.: University of Notre Dame Press, 1966.

Papali, Cirillo B., O.C.D. "Oeconomia Salutis et Religiones Non-Christianae." *Acta Congressus Internationalis De Theologia Concilii Vaticani II*. Rome: Typis Polyglottis Vaticanis, 1968, pp. 425–431.

Peters, E. H., C.S.P. (ed.). *De Ecclesia. The Constitution on the Church of Vatican Council II*. Foreword by Basil C. Butler. Commentary by G. Baum, O.S.A. Glen Rock, N.J.: Paulist Press, 1965.

Quanbeck, Warren A. (ed.). *Challenge . . . and Response. A Protestant Perspective of the Vatican Council*. Minneapolis: Augsburg Pub. House, 1966.

Ricken, Friedo, S.J., "Ecclesia . . . universale salutis sacramentum. Theologische Erwägungen zur Lehre der Dogmatischen Konstitution 'De Ecclesia' über die Kirchenzugehörigkeit." *Scholastik* 40 (1965), pp. 352–388.

Schillebeeckx, Edward, O.P. "De Ecclesia ut sacramentum mundi." *Acta Congressus Internationalis De Theologia Concilii Vaticani II*. Rome: Typis Polyglottis Vaticanis, 1968, pp. 48–53.

———. *Christ the Sacrament of the Encounter with God*. New York: Sheed and Ward, 1963.

Semmelroth, Otto, S.J. *Church and Sacrament*. Notre Dame, Ind.: Fides Pub., 1965.

Vagaggini, Cyprian, O.S.B. *The Theological Dimensions of the Liturgy*. Collegeville, Minn.: The Liturgical Press, 1959.

Vorgrimler, Herbert (ed.) *Commentary on the Documents of Vatican II*. Vol. I. New York: Herder and Herder, 1967.

Wenger, Antoine. *Vatican II*. Vol. I. *The First Session*. Westminster, Md.: The Newman Press, 1966.

Chapter 3

Baum, Gregory, O.S.A. *That They May Be One. A Study of Papal Doctrine (Leo XIII — Pius XII)*. Westminster, Md.: The Newman Press, 1958.

———. *Progress and Perspectives. The Catholic Quest for Christian Unity*. New York: Sheed and Ward, 1962.

———. "Who Belongs to the Church?" *The Ecumenist* 1 (1963), pp. 49–51.

———. "Theological Reflections on the Second Vatican Council." *Ecumenical Dialogue at Harvard. The Roman Catholic-Protestant Colloquium*. Ed. by Samuel H. Miller and G. Ernest Wright. Cambridge, Mass.: The Belknap Press of Harvard University Press, 1964, pp. 71–90.

———. "Constitution on the Church." *Journal of Ecumenical Studies* 2 (1965), pp. 1–30. Reprinted as *De Ecclesia. The Constitution on the Church of Vatican Council II.* Ed. by H. Peters, C.S.P. Foreword by B. C. Butler, O.S.B. Commentary by G. Baum, O.S.A. Glen Rock, N.J.: Paulist Press, 1965.

———. "The Mystery of Salvation is Celebrated in the Church." *National Catholic Reporter* 3 (January 25, 1967), p. 6.

———. "The Magisterium in a Changing Church." *Man as Man and Believer. Concilium*, Vol. 21. New York: Paulist Press, 1967, pp. 67–83.

———. *The Credibility of the Church Today. A Reply to Charles Davis.* New York: Herder and Herder, 1968.

———. *Faith and Doctrine. A Contemporary View.* Paramus, N.J.: The Newman Press, 1969.

———. "The New Ecclesiology."*Commonweal* 91 (October 31, 1969), pp. 123–128.

———. and Ruether, Rosemary. "Who was Jesus? What is the Church?" *National Catholic Reporter* 6 (March 18, 1970), pp. 1, 6–7.

———. *Man Becoming: God in Secular Experience.* New York: Herder and Herder, 1970.

———. "The Presence of the Church in Society." *The Catholic Mind* 68 (1970), pp. 35–41.

———. "Toward a New Catholic Theism." *The Ecumenist* 8 (1970), pp. 53–61.

———. "Truth in the Church — Küng, Rahner, and Beyond." *The Ecumenist* 9 (1971), pp. 33–48.

Congar, Yves, O.P. *Chrétiens désunis, principes d'un 'oecuménisme' catholique.* Paris: Les Éditions du Cerf, 1937. English transl.: *Divided Christendom; a Catholic Study of the Problem of Reunion.* London: The Centenary Press, 1939.

———. "Je Crois en la Sante Église . . . " *Revue des Jeunes* (January 1938), pp. 85–92. Reprinted in *Sainte Église; études et approches ecclésiologique.* Paris: Les Éditions du Cerf, 1964.

———. "Apostolicité." *Catholicisme, hier, aujourd'hui, demain.* Ed. by G. Jacquemet, Vol. I. Paris: Letouzey et Ané, 1947. Cols. 728–730.

———. "Hors de l'Église pas de salut." *Ecclesia. Lectures Chrétiennes*, No. 26 (May 1951), pp. 34–35.

———. "Position de l'Église. Dualité et Unité." *Forma Gregis* 4 (1952). Reprinted in *Sainte Église*, pp. 45–67.

———. "Ecclesia ab Abel." *Abhandlungen über Theologie und Kirche.* Festschrift für Karl Adam. Ed. by Marcel Reding, H. Elfers, and F. Hofmann. Düsseldorf: Patmos-Verlag, 1952, pp. 79–108.

———. "Le Saint-Esprit et le Corps Apostolique, realisateurs de l'oeuvre du Christ." *Revue des Sciences Philosophiques et Théologiques* 36 (1952), pp. 613–625; 37 (1953), pp. 24–48. Reprinted in *Esquisses du mystère de l'Église.* 2d ed. Paris: Les Éditions du Cerf, 1953, pp. 129–179.

———. "Salvation and the Non-Catholic." *Blackfriars* 38 (1957), pp. 290–300. Reprinted in *Sainte Église*, pp. 433–444.

———. "Hors de l'Église, pas de Salut." An article written in 1956 and published in *Sainte Église*, pp. 417–432.

———. "Hors de l'Église, pas de salut?" *Ecclesia. Lectures Chrétiennes*, No. 129 (December 1959), pp. 146–151.

———. *The Mystery of the Church.* Baltimore: Helicon, 1960.

———. *Vaste Monde ma Paroisse; verité et dimensions du salut.* Paris: Temoignage Chrétien, 1959. English transl.: *The Wide World My Parish. Salvation and its Problems.* Baltimore: Helicon Press, 1961.

———. "Le Concile, l'Église et 'les Autres'," *Lumière et Vie* 45 (1960)

pp. 69–92. English transl.: "The Council, the Church, and the Others."
Cross Currents 11 (1961), pp. 241–254.

———. "Hors de l'Église, pas de salut." *Catholicisme, hier, aujourd'hui, demaine.*
Ed. by G. Jacquemet. Vol. 5. Paris: Letouzey et Ané, 1963. Cols. 948–956.

———. *Sainte Église; études et approches ecclésiologiques.* Paris: Les Éditions du
Cerf, 1963.

———. *Le Concile au Jour le Jour. Deuxième Session.* Paris: Les Éditions du Cerf,
1964.

———. *Chrétiens en Dialogue. Contributions catholiques à l'oecuménisme.* Paris:
Les Éditions du Cerf, 1964. English transl.: *Dialogue Between Christians:
Catholic Contributions to Ecumenism.* London: G. Chapman, 1966.

———. *Le Concile au Jour le Jour. Troisième Session.* Paris: Les Éditions du Cerf,
1965.

———. "The Church: The People of God." *The Church and Mankind. Concilium,*
Vol. 1 New York: Paulist Press, 1965, pp. 11–37.

———. "L'Église, sacrement universel du salut." *Église Vivante* 17 (1965), pp. 339–
355.

———. "The Church. Seed of Unity and Hope for the Human Race." *Chicago
Studies* 5 (1966), pp. 25–39.

———. "The People of God." *Vatican II. An Interfaith Appraisal.* Ed. by J. H.
Miller, C.S.C. Notre Dame, Ind.: University of Notre Dame Press, 1966, pp.
197–207.

———. "La Signification du salut et l'activité missionnaire." *Parole et Mission* 10
(1967), pp. 67–83.

———. and M. Peuchmaurd, O.P. (eds.) *L'Église dans le monde de ce Temps. Constitution pastorale Gaudium et Spes.* 3 vols. Paris: Les Éditions du Cerf, 1967.

———. *Cette Église que j'aime.* Paris Les Éditions du Cerf, 1968. English transl.:
This Church That I Love. Denville, N.J.: Dimension Books, 1969.

———. Voillaume, R., and Loew, J. *À Temps et à contretemps; retrouver dans
l'Église le visage de Jesus-Christ.* Paris: Les Éditions du Cerf, 1969.

———. *Au Milieu des Orages; l'Église affronte aujourd'hui son Avenir.* Paris: Les
Éditions du Cerf, 1969.

———. *L'Église de Saint Augustin à l'époque moderne.* Paris: Éditions du Cerf,
1970.

———. "La personne 'Église'." *Revue Thomiste* 71 (1971), pp. 613–640.

———. "Renewed Actuality of the Holy Spirit." *Lumen Vitae* 28 (1973), pp. 13–30.

———. *Blessed Is the Peace of My Church.* Denville, N.J.: Dimension Books, 1973.

Jossua, J.-P., O.P. *Yves Congar. Theology in the Service of God's People.* Chicago:
Priory Press, 1968.

Küng, Hans. *Rechtfertigung. Die Lehre Barths und Eine Katholische Besinnung.*
Einsiedeln: Johannes Verlag, 1957. English transl.: *Justification: the Doctrine
of Karl Barth and a Catholic Reflection.* New York: Nelson, 1964.

———. *That the World May Believe.* New York: Sheed and Ward, 1963.

———. *Structures of the Church.* New York: Nelson, 1964.

———. "The World Religions in God's Plan of Salvation." *Christian Revelation and
World Religions.* Ed. by J. Neuner, S.J. London: Burns and Oates, 1967, pp.
25–66.

———. "Anmerkungen zum Axiom 'Extra Ecclesiam nulla salus'." *Ex Auditu
Verbi.* Festschrift für G. C. Berkouwer. Ed. by R. Schippers, G. C. Meuleman, J.
T. Bakker, H. M. Kuitert. Kampen: Uitgeversmaatschappij J. H. Kok N. V., 1965,
pp. 80–88.

————. "God's Free Spirit in the Church." *Freedom and Man*. Ed. by John Courtney Murray, S.J. New York: P. J. Kenedy & Sons, 1965, pp. 17–30.

————. *The Church*. New York: Sheed and Ward, 1967.

————. *Truthfulness: the Future of the Church*. New York: Sheed and Ward, 1968.

————. *Infallibility? An Inquiry*. Garden City, N.Y.: Doubleday, 1971.

Rahner, Karl, S.J. "The Meaning of Frequent Confession of Devotion." *Theological Investigations*. Vol. 3. Baltimore: Helicon, 1967, pp. 177–189.

————. *Encounters with Silence*. Westminster, Md.: The Newman Press, 1960.

————. *Spirit in the World*. New York: Herder and Herder, 1968.

————. *Hearers of the Word*. New York: Herder and Herder, 1969.

————. "Priestly Existence." *Theological Investigations*. Vol. 3. Baltimore: Helicon, 1967, pp. 239–262.

————. "Membership of the Church according to the Teaching of Pius XII's Encyclical *Mystici Corporis Christi*." *Theological Investigations*. Vol. 2. Baltimore: Helicon, 1963, pp. 1–88.

————. "The Church of Sinners." *Theological Investigations*. Vol. 6. Baltimore: Helicon, 1969, pp. 253–269.

————. "Personal and Sacramental Piety." *Theological Investigations*. Vol. 2. Baltimore: Helicon, 1963, pp. 109–133.

————. "Forgotten Truths Concerning the Sacrament of Penance." *Theological Investigations*. Vol 2. Baltimore: Helicon, 1963, pp. 135–174.

————. "On Conversions to the Church." *Theological Investigations*. Vol. 3. Baltimore: Helicon, 1967, pp. 373–384.

————. "The Christian among Unbelieving Relations." *Theological Investigations*. Vol. 3. Baltimore: Helicon, 1967, pp. 355–372.

————. *The Church and the Sacraments*. New York: Herder and Herder, 1964.

————. "The Church of Saints." *Theological Investigations*. Vol. 3. Baltimore: Helicon, 1967, pp. 91–104.

————. "Die Kirche als Ort der Geistsendung." *Geist und Leben* 29 (1956), pp. 94–98.

————. *The Dynamic Element in the Church*. New York: Herder and Herder, 1964.

————. *Nature and Grace. Dilemmas in the Modern Church*. New York: Sheed and Ward, 1964.

————. "Nature and Grace." *Theological Investigations*. Vol. 4. Baltimore: Helicon, 1966, pp. 165–188.

————. *The Christian Commitment. Essays in Pastoral Theology*. New York: Sheed and Ward, 1963.

————. "The Spirit That is Over all Life." *Theological Investigations*. Vol. 7. New York: Herder and Herder, 1971, pp. 193–201.

————. "The Sacramental Basis for the Role of the Layman in the Church." *Theological Investigations*. Vol. 8. New York: Herder and Herder, 1971, pp. 51–74.

————. "Some Implications of the Scholastic Concept of Uncreated Grace." *Theological Investigations*. Vol. 1. Baltimore: Helicon, 1961, pp. 319–346.

————. "Christianity and Non-Christian Religions." *Theological Investigations*. Vol. 5. Baltimore: Helicon, 1966, pp. 115–134.

————. *On the Theology of Death*. New York: Herder and Herder, 1965.

————. "Dogmatic Notes on 'Ecclesiological Piety'." *Theological Investigations*. Vol. 5. Baltimore: Helicon, 1966, pp. 336–365.

———. "Some Theses on Prayer 'In the Name of the Church'." *Theological Investigations.* Vol. 5. Baltimore: Helicon, 1966, pp. 419–438.

———. "Kirchengliedschaft II." *Lexikon für Theologie und Kirche.* 2d ed. Vol. 6. Freiburg im Breisgau: Herder, 1961, cols. 223–225.

———. "The Theology of the Restoration of the Diaconate." *Theological Investigations.* Vol. 5. Baltimore: Helicon, 1966, pp. 268–314.

———. "Latin as a Church Language." *Theological Investigations.* Vol. 5. Baltimore: Helicon, 1966, pp. 366–416.

———. "Remarks on the Theology of Indulgences." *Theological Investigations.* Vol. 2. Baltimore: Helicon, 1963, pp. 175–201.

———. "Anonymous Christians." *Theological Investigations.* Vol. 6. Baltimore: Helicon, 1969, pp. 390–398.

———. *Theology of Pastoral Action.* New York: Herder and Herder, 1968.

———. "Church, Churches, and Religions." *Theological Investigations.* Vol. 10. New York: Herder and Herder, 1973, pp. 30–49.

———. Greinacher, N., Schuster, H., and Dreher, B. *La Salvezza nella Chiesa. Strutture fondamentali della mediazione salvifica.* Rome: Herder, 1968.

———. "Dogmatic Constitution on the Church. Chapter III, Articles 18–27." *Commentary on the Documents of Vatican II.* Ed. by Herbert Vorgrimler. Vol. 1. New York: Herder and Herder, 1967, pp. 186–218.

———. *The Church After the Council.* New York: Herder and Herder, 1966.

———. *The Christian of the Future.* New York: Herder and Herder, 1967.

———. "The Apostolate of Prayer." *Theological Investigations.* Vol. 3. Baltimore: Helicon, 1967, pp. 209–219.

———. *Die eine Mittler und die Vielfalt der Vermittlungen.* Wiesbaden: Steiner, 1967.

———. "Church. IV. Universality of the Church." *Sacramentum Mundi.* Vol 1. New York: Herder and Herder, 1968, pp. 330–332.

———. "Church and World." *Sacramentum Mundi.* Vol. 1. New York: Herder and Herder, 1968, pp. 346–357.

———. "Missions. II. Salvation of the Non-Evangelized." *Sacramentum Mundi.* Vol. 4. New York: Herder and Herder, 1969, pp. 79–81.

———. "The Church and the Parousia of Christ." *Theological Investigations.* Vol. 6. Baltimore: Helicon, 1969, pp. 295–312.

———. "Anonymous Christianity and the Missionary Task of the Church." New York: IDOC-North America, April 1970, pp. 70–96.

———. *Do You Believe in God?* New York: Paulist Press, 1969.

———. "Secular Life and the Sacraments." *The Tablet* 225 (March 6, 1971), pp. 236–238; 225 (March 13, 1971), pp. 267–268.

———. "Anonymer und expliziter Glaube." *Stimmen der Zeit* 99 (1974), pp. 147–152.

Schlette, H. *Towards a Theology of Religions.* New York: Herder and Herder, 1966.

Chapters 4 and 5

Bea, A., S. J. *The Church and Mankind.* Chicago: Franciscan Herald Press, 1967.

Beinert, W. *Um das dritte Kirchenattribut; die Katholizität der Kirche im Verständnis der evangelisch-lutherischen und römisch-katholischen Theologie der Gegenwart.* 2 vols. Essen: Ludgerus-Verlag, 1964.

Bernards, M. "Zur Lehre von der Kirche als Sakrament. Beobachtungen aus der Theologie des 19. und 20. Jahrhunderts." *Münchener Theologische Zeitschrift* 20 (1969), pp. 29–54.

Black, M. *Models and Metaphors. Studies in Language and Philosophy*. Ithaca, New York: Cornell University Press, 1962.

Brooke, O., O.S.B. "The Church: Sacrament of Mankind in Christ." *The American Benedictine Review* 21 (1970), pp. 79–87.

Congar, Y., O.P. "The Church: The People of God." *The Church and Mankind. Concilium*. Vol. 1. New York: Paulist Press, 1965, pp. 11–37.

Dulles, A., S.J. *Models of the Church*. Garden City, New York: Doubleday & Co., 1974.

Feiner, J. "Kirche und Heilsgeschichte." *Gott in Welt*. Ed. by J. B. Metz, et al. Vol. 2. Freiburg: Herder, 1964, pp. 317–345.

Holböck, F. "Das Mysterium der Kirche in dogmatischer Sicht." *Mysterium Kirche in der Sicht der theologischen Disziplinen*. Ed. by F. Holböck and T. Sartory, O.S.B. Vol. 1. Salzburg: Otto Müller Verlag, 1962, pp. 201–346.

Jáki, S., O.S.B. *Les tendances nouvelles de l'écclésiologie*. Rome: Herder, 1957.

Journet, C. *The Church of the Word Incarnate*. Vol. 1. *The Apostolic Hierarchy*. London: Sheed and Ward, 1955.

Kühn, U. "Christentum ausserhalb der Kirche?" *Erneuerung der einen Kirche. Arbeiten aus Kirchengeschichte und Konfessionskunde*. Ed. by J. Lell. Göttingen: Vandenhoeck and Ruprecht, 1966, pp. 275–305.

Lawlor, F. X., S.J. "The Mediation of the Church in some Pontifical Documents." *Theological Studies* 12 (1951), pp. 481–504.

Lindbeck, George. *The Future of Roman Catholic Theology. Vatican II — Catalyst for Change*. Philadelphia: Fortress Press, 1970.

McBrien, Richard P. *Do We Need the Church?* New York: Harper and Row, 1969.

Metz, J. B. "Kirche für die ungläubigen." *Umkehr und Erneuerung; Kirche nach dem Konzil*. Ed. by T. Filthaut. Mainz: Mattias-Grünewald-Verlag, 1966, pp. 312–329.

Miller, J. H. (ed.). *Vatican II: An Interfaith Appraisal*. Notre Dame: University of Notre Dame Press, 1966.

Montcheuil, Yves de, S.J. *Aspects of the Church*. Chicago: Fides Pub., 1955.

Montini, Giovanni B. *The Church*. Baltimore: Helicon, 1964.

Mueller, Alois. *Obedience in the Church*. Westminster, Md.: The Newman Press, 1966.

Röper, Anita. *The Anonymous Christian*. New York: Sheed and Ward, 1966.

Rosa, Peter de. *God our Savior. A Study of the Atonement*. Milwaukee: Bruce Pub. Co., 1967.

Schillebeeckx, Edward, O.P. *God the Future of Man*. New York: Sheed and Ward, 1968.

———. "The Church and Mankind." *The Church and Mankind. Concilium*, Vol. 1. New York: Paulist Press, 1965, pp. 69–101.

Schoonenberg, Piet, S.J. *God's World in the Making*. Pittsburgh: Duquesne University Press, 1964.

Semmelroth, Otto, S.J. *Church and Sacrament*. Notre Dame, Ind.: Fides Pub., 1965.

Shea, F. S. "The Principles of Extra-Sacramental Justification in Relation to 'Extra Ecclesiam Nulla Salus'." *Proceedings of the Catholic Theological Society of America* 10 (1955), pp. 125–151.

Chapter 6

"The Unity of the Church and the Handicapped in Society." *Study Encounter* 7 (1971), pp. 2–4.

"Theological Reflections on the Missionary Task of the Church." *Bulletin*. Division of Studies. World Council of Churches 7 (1961), pp. 3–17.

"The Church for Others." *Study Encounter* 5 (1969), pp. 26–36.

"The Unity of the Church and the Unity of Mankind. A Study Document of the Commission on Faith and Order." *Study Encounter* 5 (1969), pp. 163–181.

Aagaard, Johannes. "Some Main Trends in the Renewal of Roman Catholic Missiology." *Challenge . . . and Response. A Protestant Perspective of the Vatican Council*. Ed. by Warren A. Quanbeck in consultation with Friedrich Kantzenbach and Vilmos Vajta. Minneapolis: Augsburg Pub. House, 1966, pp. 116–144.

Anderson, Gerald H. (ed.). *Christian Mission in Theological Perspective. An Inquiry by Methodists*. Nashville: Abingdon Press, 1967.

Bennett, John C. (ed.) *Christian Social Ethics in a Changing World*. New York: Association Press, 1966.

Bergen, William J., S.J. "The Institutional Church's Role in the World." *The American Ecclesiastical Review* 166 (1962), pp. 446–456.

Bianchi, Eugene C. *Reconciliation: The Function of the Church*. New York: Sheed and Ward, 1969.

Davis, Charles. *God's Grace in History*. New York: Sheed and Ward, 1967.

Delcuve, George, S.J. "Should We Still Proclaim the Gospel? Some Thoughts on the Constitution *Lumen Gentium* (16 and 17)." *Lumen Vitae* 20 (1965), pp. 651–663.

Frazier, William B., M.M. "Guidelines for a New Theology of Mission." *World Mission* 18 (1967–1968), pp. 16–24.

Gardner, Edward C. *The Church as a Prophetic Community*. Philadelphia: Westminster Press, 1967.

Goodall, Norman (ed.). *The Uppsala Report 1968*. Official Report of the Fourth Assembly of the World Council of Churches. Uppsala July 4–20, 1968. Geneva: World Council of Churches, 1968.

Guillou, Marie-Joseph de, O.P. "Mission as an Ecclesiological Theme." *Re-Thinking the Church's Mission. Concilium*, Vol. 13. New York: Paulist Press, 1966, pp. 81–130.

Hahn, Ferdinand. *Mission in the New Testament*. London: SCM Press, 1965.

Hillman, Eugene, C.S.Sp. "'Anonymous Christianity' and the Missions." *Downside Review* 84 (1966), pp. 361–379.

———. "The Main Task of the Mission." *Re-Thinking the Church's Mission. Concilium*, Vol. 13. New York: Paulist Press, 1966, pp. 3–10.

———. *The Church As Mission*. New York: Herder and Herder, 1965.

Hollenweger, W. J. "Christus extra muros ecclesiae." *Planning for Mission. Working Papers on the New Quest for Missionary Communities*. Ed. by Thomas Wieser. New York: U. S. Conference for the World Council of Churches, 1966, pp. 56–61.

Mackie, Steven G. "Changing Institutions — What Role Can Christians Play?" *Study Encounter* 6 (1970), pp. 117–128.

Neuner, Joseph, S.J. *Christian Revelation and World Religions*. London: Burns and Oates, 1967.

Noyce, Gaylord B. *The Church Is Not Expendable*. Philadelphia: Westminster Press, 1969.

Richardson, William J., M.M. (ed.). *Revolution in Missionary Thinking. A Symposium*. Maryknoll, N.Y.: Maryknoll Pub., 1966.

Riga, Peter. *The Church and Revolution; Some Reflections on the Relationship of the Church to the Modern World*. Milwaukee: Bruce Pub. Co., 1967.

Saliers, Don E. "A Servant Church Today." *Worship* 46 (1972), pp. 473–481.

Theisen, Jerome P., O.S.B. "A Theological Analysis and Critique of the Mission and Responsibility of the Church." *Metropolis. Christian Presence and Responsiblity*. Ed. by Philip D. Morris. Notre Dame, Ind.: Fides Pub., 1970, pp. 173–189.

Uthe, Edward W. (ed.). *Significant Issues for the 1970's*. Philadelphia: Fortress Press, 1968.

Vaughan, Benjamin N. Y. *Structures for Renewal: A Search for the Renewal of the Church's Mission to the World*. London: Mowbray, 1967.

Whitley, Oliver Read. *The Church: Mirror or Window? Images of the Church in American Society*. St. Louis: Bethany Press, 1969.

Willie, Charles Vert. *Church Action in the World; Studies in Sociology and Religion*. New York: Morehouse-Barlow, 1969.

Wolf, Hans-Heinrich. "Towards an Ecumenical Consensus." *Technology and Social Justice*. Ed. by Ronald H. Preston. London: SCM Press, 1971, pp. 425–445.

Index